MORE
Taste
THAN
Time

Abby Mandel

Illustrations by Lauren Jarrett

SIMON AND SCHUSTER

New York · London
Toronto · Sydney · Tokyo

Simon and Schuster
Simon & Schuster Building
Rockefeller Center
1230 Avenue of the Americas
New York, New York 10020

Designed by: H. L. Granger/Levavi & Levavi
Illustrations by: Lauren Jarrett
Manufactured in the United States of America

10 9 8 7 6 5 4 3 2 1

Library of Congress Cataloging in Publication Data

Mandel, Abby.
   More taste than time.

   Includes index.
   1. Quick and easy cookery.   I. Title.
TX833.5.M36   1988   641.5'55   88-26421
ISBN 0-671-66207-4

Dedication

This book is dedicated to my mother, Frances Evarts, who, at ninety-four, still sparkles at the prospect of a good home-cooked meal; and to my husband, John Friend, whose interest and support in my work mean the world to me.

Acknowledgment

My deepest and fondest appreciation to my good friend and associate, Patricia Dailey, with whom I am in perfect rapport, for making the work on this book a happy experience.

Contents

Introduction

My continuing love of home cooking and all the joys inherent in it have inspired this book. I believe that cooking is one of life's great pleasures, and that it can fit comfortably into the lifestyle of everyone, even that of the busiest people. The worlds of home cooking and active work lives need not be mutually exclusive. The prevailing attitude that allows cooking and meals at home to fall by the wayside, dismissing them as mere chores, strikes me as a sad symptom of a world that moves too fast. These rituals of cooking and eating together at home enrich our lives; they transform a house into a home, providing unique opportunities for communication and fulfillment, both for the cook and those who enjoy the food.

I feel the strength of these values in my personal life. When I was a child, those occasions that found friends and extended family at the same dinner table were heaven to me, an eagerly awaited pleasure. Though I may not then have had the words to express it, nor the capacity to fully understand the meaning, it was as clear as day to me that these were as much social interactions as they were good meals. And now, quite apart from my profession as a cook and food writer, I love to cook at home, to gather my family and friends around the table to enjoy my cooking amid lively conversation. The cooking need not be serious or great—rather, it can simply be good food that's fresh, personal and home cooked with an element of care and love. For all of us, such meals are definitely among our finest moments, welcome respites from the pressured, impersonal world we live in. The potential for pleasure is enormous, in all respects.

These feelings are the essence of *More Taste Than Time,* a cookbook that has been nurturing within me for a long time. It is specifically designed for those who, in spite of their busy lives, share these same values and want to experience the joys and satisfactions of cooking. The recipes are for food that tastes wonderful, is lively and appealing to make, yet involves minimal hands-on effort. They are adaptable to many different cooking needs, from everyday meals through entertaining. Although the recipes are mindful of health, as I am, they are not preoccupied with it. Each recipe focuses on delivering more taste, flavor and style than its preparation time indicates. I have tested each repeatedly until it has become as time-effective and easy to make as possible. It is my hope that the recipes will be so pleasing that they will be made again and again. To me, that represents success.

Over the last fifteen years, home cooking has undergone dramatic changes. Even a decade ago, there was an inclination to prepare complicated and rich dishes. Now, only the memory of such cooking is with us. Our food tastes have evolved to new levels. We prefer simpler, more direct foods that reflect freshness and vitality. This doesn't mean we demand less from the foods we cook or that we're willing to sacrifice style. To the contrary. Travels, restaurant dining, and more extensive media coverage of food have all created a high level of expectation about food. Good-tasting food, presented with style and a personal touch, is an absolute requisite.

With the increase in two-career families, it is no longer a given that all meals will be cooked at home as they once were. The fact is, there are countless ways to avoid cooking. Restaurants proliferate, carry-out shops offer dinner all packed up and ready to go, and the supermarket freezer case holds a staggering number of frozen entrees. Enjoyable or essential as these options may be at times, they leave a sense of personal style and taste unfulfilled, a creativity unexpressed. There is also less control over the amount of fat, sugar, salt and artificial ingredients in these prepared foods, a serious consideration in these health-conscious times.

As time has become more precious and fractured, high-tech kitchen equipment has edged into the cook's world. The food processor and microwave oven, now prominent in American kitchens, have had an enormous time-saving impact on cooking. When cooking time is short and at a premium, I am dedicated to the belief that it is far preferable to take shortcuts by using such equipment than to resort to commercially prepared foods. Intelligent use of the food processor and microwave oven is a boon to my cooking, and does not compromise my standards as either a cook or a discriminating diner.

In *More Taste Than Time,* the bottom line is wonderful-tasting food, based on fresh ingredients, and a practical, commonsense approach to preparing it. I suggest timesaving equipment options when the results are comparable to conventional methods of preparation and cooking. Loving good food as I do, I will never compromise the final outcome of a recipe merely for the sake of making it more quickly in a microwave oven or with the help of a food processor.

Some recipes here are so simple that the food processor or microwave oven is not even a factor. When they are effective options, it becomes a matter of choice. These options are intended to accommodate the cook, not to confuse. In my own cooking, I often vary my preparation and cooking rhythm according to the particulars at hand and the pressures of the moment. Basically, I relish cooking the old-fashioned, conventional way. But when I am in a rush, I am eternally grateful for these technological shortcuts which allow me to cook good, fresh food easily and quickly.

Busy people need to know if a recipe is manageable timewise, before they start to cook. With this in mind, the preparation and cooking times are included with each recipe. They are intended as guidelines, not as a strict minute-to-minute countdown. Working at a reasonable pace, most preparation times run under 20 minutes. Timing starts once the ingredients are on the counter, ready to be measured, then peeled, chopped, sliced or mixed. The preparation of a recipe does not reflect the use of a processor, except where it is the only equipment used, as in yeast breads, mayonnaise and pastries. So, when you use a processor in any of the other recipes, you can expect the preparation time to be shorter. Occasionally, cooking or baking time is long, but it goes on without much attention from the cook. I have not included the time it takes to boil water for pastas or vegetables, so keep that in mind in those recipes. Before beginning to cook, you will save time and aggravation if you read through the recipe so you have some familiarity with the sequence, a definite sense of direction.

Whenever possible, I include do-ahead steps, eliminating last-minute pressures. Many recipes can be refrigerated up to several days, or kept frozen much longer. This is an enormous convenience for weekday dinners as well as for entertaining.

The creative ritual of cooking fresh, full-flavored foods and the enhancing dimension of sharing meals with friends and family provide unique pleasures. *More Taste Than Time* is a collection of many of my favorite recipes, designed to make these pleasures possible for you. Cooking is fun and satisfying, and it is my hope that this message is conveyed on each page.

Stocking Up

A well-stocked kitchen is essential to efficient and enjoyable cooking, even if you only cook a few times a week. What constitutes basic ingredients varies from person to person and often, from season to season. Even with well-stocked shelves, you will still have to do some marketing to complete most meals, mainly to pick up fresh ingredients and satisfy whims. The following are items I try to have on hand all the time. You will want to tailor this list to fit your own taste and particular needs.

OILS: safflower oil, extra virgin olive oil, light-tasting olive oil, Oriental sesame oil

VINEGARS: distilled white, cider, red wine, white wine or Champagne, balsamic, sherry, raspberry, rice wine and sushi

CONDIMENTS: Dijon mustard plus 1 or 2 other varieties according to taste, Tabasco sauce, Worcestershire sauce, prepared horseradish, catsup, anchovy paste, soy sauce

PASTA AND RICE: spaghetti, fettuccine, quick-cooking couscous, long-grain white rice

FLOURS AND MEALS: unbleached all-purpose flour, whole-wheat flour, yellow cornmeal, polenta or grits, rolled oats

SWEETENERS: granulated sugar, light-brown sugar, dark-brown sugar, honey, molasses, maple syrup, confectioners' sugar

DRIED FOODS: sun-dried tomatoes, domestic or imported mushrooms, raisins, prunes, currants, apricots

CANNED GOODS: beef broth, chicken broth, tomato paste, tomato sauce, plum tomatoes, Italian-style tuna in oil, anchovies, green and black olives, anchovies, raspberry jam, apricot preserves

DRIED HERBS AND SPICES: salt, whole black and white peppercorns, whole nutmeg, cinnamon, cayenne pepper, curry powder, dill, basil, oregano, tarragon, chili powder, whole and ground cumin, ground cloves, sage, bay leaves, allspice, ground ginger, seasoned salt, salt

NUTS (stored in the freezer so they stay fresh): pecans, walnuts, pine nuts, almonds

BAKING GOODS: unsweetened cocoa powder, unsweetened chocolate, bittersweet or semisweet chocolate, sweet cooking chocolate, baking powder, baking soda, active dry yeast, pure vanilla extract

THE FREEZER: phyllo dough, puff pastry, bread, bread crumbs, unsalted butter, tiny peas, minced or shredded imported Parmesan cheese, beef and chicken stock, chicken paillards (see Food Storage, below, on how to wrap foods for the freezer)

THE REFRIGERATOR: milk, whipping cream, sour cream, plain yogurt, large eggs

PRODUCE: parsley, cilantro, hot peppers, onions, garlic, shallots, carrots, potatoes, celery, ginger, green onions

HOMEMADE BASICS (from the Basics, Vegetables and Pasta chapters): Pesto Sauce, Italian Tomato Sauce, Tomato Marmalade, Red Pepper Marmalade, Lemon Grass Butter, Garlic Oil

Food Storage

How foods are stored is very important to their quality. The little bit of extra attention it takes to wrap something properly pays off handsomely when it comes time to use it.

Oils should always be kept in a cool, dry spot away from light. I keep certain oils that I'm not likely to use up quickly, such as hazelnut and walnut, in the freezer so they don't become rancid. Instead of freezing the whole bottle, I pour the oil into several smaller bottles so I can use them as needed without thawing the whole amount.

Once opened, condiments should be refrigerated. Always wipe off the top of the bottle and the cap after using.

Flours and meals should be stored in airtight containers so they stay dry. This also discourages mites, which occasionally infest grains. Whole-grain products like wheat germ should be refrigerated so their natural oils don't become rancid.

Keep dried foods such as apricots and raisins tightly wrapped so they stay moist. If they dry out, they can be softened in hot liquid before using—either water, fruit juice or a liquor if desired.

Dried herbs and spices will lose their strength over time. As a rule, they will begin to deteriorate after about 6 months. Taste before using and adjust the amount as necessary. For best results, keep them in a cool, dry spot away from direct light. Buy them in small quantities.

The freezer is ideal for long-term storage of many foods. Some people are reluctant to freeze foods lest they take on off-flavors or become freezer-burned. These concerns are completely unwarranted *if* certain precautions are taken. Make sure your freezer is kept at a steady temperature as recommended by the manufacturer. Foods must be wrapped properly. Occasionally, I find myself taking a shortcut and freezing something carelessly. I always regret this and pay the price by having to throw the food away. In an amazingly short time, improperly wrapped foods will become covered with crystals and pick up an unpleasant freezer taste.

The best method for wrapping food for the freezer is double-bagging. Place the food in a plastic bag, squeeze out all the air and twist the top of the bag into a tight coil. Fold the coiled part over itself and seal tightly with a twist tie. Label the bag with the contents and date. Repeat the bagging a second time. Meat, poultry, fish and other foods that have been wrapped in butcher's paper should also be handled this way, replacing their original wrapping with the plastic bags.

A Kitchen Equipped for Efficiency

Having the right tool to do a job ensures that the task is done correctly, efficiently and with pleasure. This is as true in the kitchen as anywhere else. Certain pieces of kitchen equipment are standard. Imagine not having a toaster or a coffee maker! Beyond such basics, the lines become more hazy as to what is essential and what is superfluous. Each cook has his own *batterie de cuisine,* a collection of personal favorites that are right for his cooking style.

As important as I consider the right equipment to be, I do not see it as a pair of miracle hands that takes the place of good common sense. A food processor does not ensure success—it simply makes reaching it easier. The same can be said for most equipment, whether it be copper pots or a French mandoline. Nothing replaces the need for care and thoughtfulness in cooking.

Stocking a kitchen can be quite expensive. Fortunately, most times it is done over the course of years. The expense of a good knife or pan is not so great as it may seem initially. Properly cared for, these items will last longer than the cook who made the purchase. As with all other purchases, it makes sense to buy quality goods up front and have them forever, instead of replacing poorly made ones after several years' use. Consider it from another view. It costs less to buy a good skillet than it does to have dinner for two in a fine restaurant. Looked at from that perspective, it strikes me as an extraordinary bargain with lasting value. Not all equipment is expensive. My cast-iron skillets cost under $10 each, have 20 years of use behind them and will last at least that long again.

There is usually a correlation between how much cooking one does and how his kitchen is equipped. An occasional cook will not, most likely, have the same gear as the person who cooks every day. Another important consideration is how much space you have for storing equipment. A compact kitchen should, in a marriage of practicality and necessity, be sparsely yet sensibly outfitted.

Knives, pots and pans and small appliances are the three main categories of equipment in the kitchen. Beyond that is a world of gadgets, some very worthwhile, others just plain silly. When stocking your kitchen, be realistic about what kind of cooking you do and then determine what you need to proceed with efficiency.

Basic Equipment

1. 10-inch cast-iron skillet
2. 1-quart covered saucepan
3. 10-inch covered skillet
4. 5-quart sauté pan
5. 8-inch nonstick skillet
6. 6- to 8-quart pot
7. 2½- to 3-quart saucepan
8. 4- to 6-quart casserole
9. Glass or metal baking pan, 13 by 9 by 2 inches
10. Teakettle
11. Coffee maker
12. Food processor
13. Microwave oven
14. Electric hand mixer
15. Toaster
16. Paring knife
17. Serrated bread knife with a blade at least 10 inches long
18. Chef's knife with an 8-to-10-inch blade
19. Zip-Zap or sharpening steel
20. Swivel-bladed vegetable peeler
21. Kitchen shears
22. Large colander
23. Grater
24. Pepper mill
25. Nutmeg grater
26. Citrus zester
27. Fine mesh strainers, small and medium-sized
28. Flour sifter
29. Timer
30. Oven thermometer
31. Bottle opener
32. Wine opener
33. Can opener
34. At least 1 set graduated measuring spoons

35. At least 1 set graduated liquid measuring cups
36. At least 1 set graduated dry measuring cups
37. At least 1 set mixing bowls
38. Rolling pin
39. Polypropylene cutting board
40. Tongs, preferably spring tongs
41. At least 2 rubber spatulas
42. Metal spatula
43. At least 2 wooden spoons
44. Balloon whisk
45. Long 2-pronged fork
46. Heavy metal spoon
47. Heavy metal slotted spoon
48. Pastry brush
49. 8- or 9-inch square baking pan
50. Muffin tins
51. Baking sheet
52. Ladle
53. Melon baller
54. Ice cream scoop
55. Instant reading thermometer
56. Juicer

Additional Equipment

57. Tart pan with removable bottom
58. Springform pan
59. Griddle
60. 8-inch and/or 9-inch round layer cake pans
61. Bundt pan
62. Tube pan
63. 2-quart soufflé dish
64. Small custard cups or soufflé dishes
65. Pizza pan
66. Meat pounder
67. Standard loaf pan with 8-cup capacity
68. Gravy strainer
69. Jelly roll pan
70. Salad spinner
71. Barbecue grill
72. Pressure cooker
73. Electric knife
74. Wok

The Selection and Care of Knives

Many people overlook the importance of good knives in the kitchen. Perhaps part of the resistance stems from the fact that a well-made knife is expensive, while there are many inexpensive ones on the market. Further, knives require regular maintenance, without which they'll quickly become little more useful than a butter knife. Nevertheless, good-quality, well-maintained knives are a pleasure to use and an absolute must for efficiency. They allow for faster, more precise results when slicing anything from bread to celery root to ripe tomatoes to roast beef.

The qualities that make a good knife are, to some degree, a personal matter. I prefer high-carbon stainless steel knives, versus all-stainless steel or carbon steel. The high-carbon stainless combines the best qualities of the other two, while minimizing either of their shortcomings. Carbon steel sharpens well and holds the best edge. On the downside, they stain, react with acidic foods, and will rust if not dried quickly and properly, or even if they are stored in damp areas. Stainless steel is very hard, and so doesn't sharpen as well or hold its edge. A high-carbon stainless steel is the top choice, for its ability to hold an edge, to resist staining, rusting, and reacting with food.

A knife should have a full tang handle, meaning that the metal part in the center of the handle runs the full length. This lessens the chance of the handle breaking and also balances the knife. I generally prefer hardened plastic handles to wooden ones, though I use some of each. The plastic is more sanitary than wood; but wood absorbs fat so the handle doesn't slip around in your grasp as much. A big consideration is how the knife feels in your hand. It should feel weighty and solid, with a comfortable grip.

There are many different knives, each designed for a specific purpose, though they all fall into three general categories: chopping, butchering and slicing/cutting. Many feel that a kitchen can function perfectly well with a chef's knife and a paring knife. I would add a serrated slicer to that list. A chef's knife, also known as a cook's knife, is generally about 12 to 14 inches long overall, with the blade itself ranging from 7 to 10 inches. The blade is wide at the handle end and tapers gradually to a point. It is a chopping knife, though it can also be used for other chores in the absence of a selection of knives.

Paring knives are the smallest knives in most kitchens, about 8 inches overall. They look like a chef's knife in miniature, though the curve of the blade is not as defined. They are used for peeling and paring vegetables as well as cutting and slicing small items.

Knives should be sharpened before each use. This may seem

like a lot of bother, but actually it takes only seconds. Once a knife loses its edge, it is very difficult to revive it. You're more likely to cut yourself with a dull knife than a sharp one since cutting with a dull knife requires more force. To sharpen a knife, you need something that is harder than the knife. Sharpening steels are the most common sharpeners, but I prefer and heartily recommend a Zip-Zap. Zip-Zaps are made of ceramic (and hence are breakable, so be careful), which is harder than any sharpening steel. The Zip-Zap is very small, less than 6 inches, and costs only several dollars. I don't recommend the use of electric knife sharpeners, which grind off more of the blade than is necessary.

To sharpen knives, hold the sharpener at a 20-degree angle to the knife. If you use a Zip-Zap, it moves while the knife is held still. The process is usually reversed when using a steel; the knife is drawn across it.

Pots and Pans

So much is written about pots and pans that it is hard to sort fact from fiction. Nevertheless, since pots and pans lie at the heart of cooking and are the foundation of your *batterie de cuisine,* it is important to understand the properties of the various metals and alloys of which they are made. Among the most common choices are aluminum, stainless steel, copper, cast iron and enamel-coated cast iron. There is no one single material that suits all cooking needs. Most cooks will find it useful to have different pots and pans for their varied cooking needs. Understanding their various properties will make selecting them much easier.

A well-seasoned cast-iron skillet is apt to be passed down from one generation of cook to the next. These skillets are a true joy to cook with. Cast iron is extremely heavy and allows for slow, even heating. Once hot, it retains that temperature throughout cooking. This makes it ideal for frying and searing. Its negatives are that it is reactive with certain foods, rusts and pits easily, absorbs flavors and must be seasoned before it is used the first time. I have a set of three cast-iron skillets, inherited through marriage, that I simply wouldn't part with. One is enough for most kitchens, with 9 or 10 inches being the most versatile size. They should never be washed in water, rather wiped out with a paper towel or rubbed with salt if something has burned. Always dry them well since they rust very easily. Also available are porcelain enamel-coated cast-iron pans. These are exceptionally good-looking and very versatile, but, like uncoated cast iron, are heavy. They are not good for browning or sautéeing, but are useful for many other cooking operations. Unlike uncoated cast iron, they don't rust or react with foods. They will chip, however, and must be handled carefully. Many of them are stove-to-oven candidates, unless they have a wood handle.

Stainless steel has a list of good points that would make it seem to be the ideal alloy for cooking. It is light, nonreactive, stays shiny and doesn't dent or buckle easily. Since it is not a good heat conductor, it is rarely used by itself in the construction of pots and pans. It must be used in combination with other metals; most often this is done by sandwiching and cladding another metal, usually aluminum or copper, in between layers of stainless steel. There are many excellent pots constructed this way, though they do have several drawbacks. The cladding is only on the bottom, while the sides are stainless; hence the heat conductivity will be different on the sides. Also, the bottom holds its heat, making it a poor choice for delicate cooking. These disadvantages aside, they are often a good choice.

Aluminum conducts heat very well and is lightweight yet tough and sturdy. It reacts with certain foods, especially those that are highly acidic, giving them a dark color and off-taste. The pan will also darken when in contact with alkalis. Calphalon pans were introduced a number of years ago and sidestep the inherent problems of cooking with aluminum. A grey satin finish is electro-chemically applied to aluminum pans in such a manner that it doesn't scrape off. This finish is impervious to pitting, discoloration and flavor reactions that a plain aluminum pan will fall prey to. It is also said that such pans have a release finish, meaning that foods won't stick. While I don't find that particular aspect to be their strong point, they are very good, all-purpose pans. Their handles, made of metal, allow for stove-to-oven cooking, but they do get very hot.

Copper pans, lined with tin, silver or stainless steel, would be the first choice of many were it not for their high price tags. Copper is an excellent heat conductor and loses its heat quickly, making it a good choice for delicate procedures. And—of no small consequence—it is beautiful to look at, though admittedly at the cost of high maintenance. Copper, as we know it in pans, is really a copper alloy, a well-planned effort to mitigate some of its drawbacks. Unlined copper rusts easily, distorts and reacts with food.

Also worth mentioning are those pans coated with non-stick finishes such as Silverstone, Supra and Teflon. These pans deserve consideration in any kitchen. Enormous strides have been made since they were first introduced, improving both their durability and non-stick properties. A nylon plastic finish coats a pan, usually and most usefully a skillet, that is made of aluminum, stainless steel or even cast iron. They are absolutely wonderful for cooking with little or no fat, an appealing aspect for many cooks. Most manufacturers of these pans caution against the use of metal utensils and abrasive cleansers. Become familiar with these specifics when you purchase the pan and you will be rewarded with a versatile pan that will last for many years. A word of caution in their use: never place an empty non-stick pan over heat for any length of time and never use them under the broiler, since they will release a potentially harmful gas.

How you stock your kitchen with bakeware is even more heavily weighted by the type of cooking you do. If you don't bake, there's simply no reason to have an array of cake and pie tins. On the other hand, those who do bake enjoy having a wide array of them. If storage space is not a problem, the choices are endless and easily affordable. Oven heat is not as direct as stove top heat so the properties that you look for in a saucepan do not necessarily carry over to the oven. Nor do wide generalities always apply. As a rule, a sturdy, well-built pan is the top choice for baking. However, I do like lightweight tart pans and have one fairly light aluminum cookie sheet that heats and cools quickly, an asset when baking fragile cookies. Heat-tempered glass, such as Corning, is a good choice for pie plates and soufflé dishes. As for bread pans, the heavier the better. Some people feel strongly about baking bread in a black surfaced pan, which absorbs the heat (rather than reflecting it). Except for pizzas, where I fully agree that they are essential, I am less rigid on that point and find that a dull satin metal or Pyrex pan is fine. In quick breads I prefer a dull satin finish, but the difference is not that noticeable for yeast breads. Aluminum layer cake pans and square baking pans are ideal and multi-purpose. There are so many manufacturers that it is nearly impossible to make suggestions; so buy good-quality wares with the expectation that they will perform well.

Electric Appliances

Electric appliances are part of every kitchen. Coffee makers, toasters and mixers are so basic that they are practically taken for granted. My enthusiasm for food processors and microwave ovens is no secret; those two appliances are covered in more detail in the sections that follow (pages 23-30). Beyond these, my kitchen is not overly mechanized. I use an electric juicer and recommend one if you like freshly squeezed juice in the morning. But a hand reamer is satisfactory unless you use really large quantities of fresh juice. I long ago put my electric can opener in the basement, opting instead for a well-designed hand model which is more than adequate for the small number of cans that are opened in my kitchen. I occasionally pull out the electric carving knife, a relic from meatier days that I am glad to have, though probably won't replace should it break down. I feel the same way about my blender. It has largely been replaced by the food processor, though it is terrific for making drinks, shakes and very smooth sauces. As for my standing mixer, it isn't used all that often, but I love it dearly and wouldn't trade it for the world. A small hand mixer is also handy to have. That is the extent of my electronic gadgetry. You may find a particular piece of equipment suits your own cooking style, but remember, these appliances take up space.

Using Your Food Processor: Basic Techniques

Though food processors are relative newcomers to the kitchen, they are now considered basic equipment. Frankly I can't imagine a kitchen without one. True, many of us survived life in the kitchen without a food processor. And while there isn't a single job a processor does that can't be done some other way, a processor often offers the fastest, most efficient means of getting the work done. And that element of time is an important consideration in many kitchens. The fact is that the processor allows us to accomplish many preparations that we simply would not undertake routinely otherwise.

In most of the new cookbooks and articles on food, certain recipes are prepared only with a processor. Pastries, mayonnaise and purees are routinely made in the processor. This points not only to the processor's effectiveness in making these recipes, but also to its timesaving function. It is safe to say across the board that food processors are here to stay. In time, knowing their best functions, and using them accordingly, will be as instinctive and natural as using a mixer.

To bridge the gap for people who are still uncertain about how to use food processors, I have written many of the recipes with easy-to-follow options, using the processor or not. When it is a time-effective alternative, I list the preparation using the food processor first.

In many instances, due to time or esthetic reasons, I recommend doing a job by hand. If, for instance, the only thing the food processor is used for in a recipe is slicing a zucchini, I then recommend slicing it by hand. Factor in the time it takes to clean the processor, and you're ahead when you slice it by hand. At times I prefer the look of something cut with a knife and will say so. Marvelous machine that it is, the processor doesn't dice, cut wedges or 2-inch pieces.

Above all, develop your own pace and tempo in the kitchen so you feel at ease as well as efficient. Occasionally I find the rhythmic movement of mincing parsley by hand to be comforting. Other times, I marvel at how quickly I can mince a whole bowl of it in the processor. And while I, personally, knead bread dough only in the food processor, others swear they prefer the tactile sensation of doing this by hand.

There are many different sizes of food processors. When I refer to a food processor, it means a standard-size processor, such as a Cuisinart DLC-10, Basic, or one of the other original models: a Kitchen-Aid, Sunbeam or Robot-Coupe. Some makers, specifically Cuisinart, sell processors that are larger than the standard size. These, of course, can also be used. The recipes have not been designed for the mini-processors, such as the Seb or Cuisinart Mini-Mate, nor for the small processors like the Sunbeam Oskar or Cuisinart Little Pro. Occasionally, I mention a mini-processor or small processor for a specific mini-task, one that is too small for a standard-sized processor. Small processors are interchangeable with standard-sized processors for many tasks, though not all. The distinction is particularly important with batters, doughs and other mixtures where a large quantity of food is combined in the bowl for chopping, mixing, kneading or puréeing.

Throughout the book, I have assumed a certain working knowledge of food processors, at least as much as you garner from reading the instruction booklet that comes with the machine. Following is a list of basic techniques and tips for using the processor with maximum efficiency.

Metal blade: The metal blade, also called the chopping knife or steel blade, is what you're likely to use most often. It is used for all "bottom of the bowl" functions, including mincing, chopping, pureeing, mixing and kneading.

To mince small things like garlic, shallots, ginger and hot peppers, put the metal blade in a dry work bowl. Turn the machine on and drop the ingredients through the feed tube while the machine is running. They will bounce off the metal blade and around the work bowl. Stop the machine when all the little pieces are stuck to the side of the bowl.

When chopping or mincing larger foods, it is important not to overload the work bowl. As a general rule, up to 2 cups of food can be chopped in a standard-size processor. If you have a larger machine, consult the instruction book for its capacity. · The ingredients should be cut into pieces that are roughly 1 inch square. · If you want to control the chopping, pulse the machine on and off instead of using continuous processing. Many machines have a separate pulse/off lever that runs the machine only as long as the lever is held down. If yours doesn't have that feature, you can achieve the same effect by quickly turning the machine on and off as many times as it takes to chop the ingredients. One pulse or on/off motion should last about ½ second. Pause for a second between each pulse to let the food fall back to the bottom of the bowl. · Check the ingredients by looking through the top of the work bowl. It usually isn't necessary to remove the cover. · For fine chopping, such as for *mirepoix* vegetables, minced chocolate, cheese and citrus zest with sugar, continuous processing can be used.

To purée, the food must be very soft. · Fruits must be ripe. · Vegetables must be cooked until they are quite soft, almost to the point of falling apart. · Drain cooked foods very well so the purée is not watery, unless they are to be puréed for a soup. · If the food has been cooked in a liquid, drain before puréeing, then purée only the solids. · Prolonged processing will give the best results. Let the machine continue to run even after the mixture looks smooth. Up to 2 minutes of processing will give the best results. · Straining is usually not necessary unless there are seeds or skin to remove.

Mixing with the metal blade uses the processor like a spoon, whisk or electric mixer for a variety of tasks, from making salad dressing to cake. Because such mixtures involve liquids, it is important to know the capacity of your processor and not add too much liquid. If too much liquid is added, it will leak out under the metal blade or between the rim and cover when the machine is running. Especially when mixing batters, there is apt to be some spatter onto the sides and even the cover of the work bowl. Stop the machine as necessary and scrape any spatters back into the work bowl with a rubber spatula. While there is no rule that applies to all situations here, it is safe to say that once all the ingredients look mixed to the eye, they usually are.

Kneading is done with either the metal blade or the plastic dough blade. All the dry ingredients plus any eggs and shortening are placed in the bowl. The processor is then turned on and the proofed yeast mixture plus any additional liquids are added through the feed tube while the machine is running. For best results, have the liquids in a spouted measuring cup and pour them through the feed tube only as quickly as they are absorbed by the flour. If you add them too quickly, they will slosh around the bottom of the bowl. Once all the liquids have been added and absorbed into the flour, you must decide if the dough is the right consistency—in other words, whether the flour/liquid balance is right. When it is, the dough will clean itself from the sides of the work bowl as it is being processed. If you stop the machine and feel the dough, it should be slightly tacky and feel like it will almost stick to your fingers. If it is too dry, the texture of the baked bread will be heavy. If it is so moist that the dough sticks to your hands, it will be too difficult to handle. If you're not satisfied that the consistency is right, add more liquid if it is too dry or more flour if it is too moist. Add them in small amounts while the processor is running, then process well before adding more. When the dough is the right consistency, process it until it is soft, supple and stretchy, with no hard knots. This kneading usually takes about 40 seconds, though sometimes longer, particularly if there is a high proportion of whole-grain flours.

When emptying liquids from the work bowl, hold the metal blade in place from the bottom of the bowl with your finger. Once the blade can easily be removed from the bowl, do so.

To clean sticky batters from the metal blade, clean out as much batter from the work bowl as you can, holding the metal blade in place as described above. Then place the bowl on the base, reinsert the metal blade and run the machine for a second. The batter will spin from the metal blade onto the sides of the bowl for easy removal.

Very often, you can do several chopping and mincing steps simultaneously. Consider an herbed salad dressing: You can mince the herbs and set them aside; you can do the same with a shallot. As a third step, you could put the vinegar, oil, mustard and seasonings into the processor and blend them. And finally, the minced herbs and shallot could be returned to the oil and vinegar. Or, far more efficiently, put them all in the work bowl together and process until the shallots and parsley are minced. I have tried to indicate this logical time-saving sequence whenever possible.

In addition to the metal blade, all food processors come with a shredder and an all-purpose slicer, which is usually 4mm thick. These two discs are used for the "top of the bowl" functions of slicing, double-slicing and shredding.

Some manufacturers also sell a range of accessory slicers and shredders. Accessory slicers include the following: extra-thin (1mm), thin (2mm), medium (3mm), thick (6mm) and ultra-thick (8mm). Accessory shredders are finer than the one that comes with the processor. Julienne discs are also sold. These are similar to shredders except that they cut square sides rather than two flat surfaces.

Depending on the type of cooking you do, you may find it

useful to own some of these accessories. You will find that I call for accessory discs in some recipes. They are, however, only an option, and the slicing can be done by hand as well.

With slicing and shredding, the question of expanded feed-tube design versus standard design arises. Cuisinart food processors have been sold with expanded feed tubes for many years, while original Cuisinart machines and those of other manufacturers have the standard one. A standard feed tube measures approximately 3 inches wide, 1¾ inches deep and 4 inches high. An expanded feed tube, which allows you to slice or shred more food at once, or larger pieces, is about 4¼ inches wide, 2½ inches deep and 3 inches high. An expanded feed tube also has a smaller, round center feed tube for slicing small foods. If an expanded feed tube seems clumsy to you, get familiar with it by using it. These tubes aren't nearly as complicated as they may appear to be, and they do allow for much faster slicing and the slicing of larger foods.

In both slicing and shredding, the foods can be placed in the feed tube either horizontally or vertically. This placement will then determine the size of the slice or shred. Picture a carrot, for example. If you lay it down in the feed tube, you will get slices or shreds that are as long as the piece of carrot. Stand it up and they will be the crosswise width or diameter of the carrot.

Since many foods don't grow to perfect feed-tube size, some trimming is often necessary. For best results trim the piece (or pieces) just enough to fit the feed tube. If you frequently use your processor for slicing and shredding, you'll probably find yourself selecting food processor-perfect specimens—onions, apples and zucchini that are just the right size.

Hard cheeses like Parmesan and Romano must be at room temperature before they are shredded. Trim off the hard, dried rind before shredding. As with all cheeses, always shred them with a very light touch on the pusher. Never force the cheese through the shredder by using too much pressure on the pusher. Softer cheeses like mozzarella, Cheddar, Monterey Jack and Swiss must be chilled so they are firm when shredded. And again, use light pressure. If the cheese sticks, don't be tempted to force it through, which could break the processor; instead, guide it through very gently by lightly pressing the pusher. Shredded cheese can be double-wrapped in plastic bags and frozen for several months. Only minimal thawing is required before using. This is the best method for lengthy storage.

Slicing is easy and often an enormous timesaver when done in the food processor, especially when you're slicing a lot of fruits or vegetables. Here are some tips:

—Cut a flat bottom on rounded foods like oranges, lemons and onions so they don't roll over.

—If the food is to be sliced standing up in the feed tube, fill the feed tube enough so the food stands upright without tipping over.

—Use pressure to guide the food through the feed tube that correlates to the texture and consistency of the food. For instance, use firm, but not forceful, pressure on hard foods like raw potatoes, onions and apples; use medium pressure on medium-textured foods like leeks, celery and zucchini; and light pressure on soft foods like tomatoes, mushrooms and strawberries.

All parts of the food processor except the base are dishwasher safe, so cleaning these is easy.

The Microwave Oven

In some ways, I'm surprised to find myself writing about microwave ovens with genuine enthusiasm. Like so many food professionals, I regarded them with skepticism when they first appeared on the market. Over time, when it was proved beyond a doubt that they were safe, I accepted them in a somewhat limited realm. They were great for warming up a cup of coffee, softening butter and reheating leftovers, but not for real cooking.

I have come to reconsider microwave ovens. An understanding of them has led to a new respect and an enthusiastic acknowledgment of what they do well. The microwave oven now features prominently in my cooking style, and its use strikes me as completely natural. I've always looked for shortcuts to good cooking, —never those that compromise quality, just those that make a job quicker, easier and more enjoyable. How, then, could I continue to overlook some of the more notable applications of microwave ovens? They are remarkable, not just for cooking frozen dinners and making popcorn, but, more importantly, for their ability to cook some "real" foods and do it well. Some, not all, recipes are adaptable to the microwave oven, adding a timesaving element to my cooking that is always welcome. Many of the recipes in this book include instructions for using the microwave oven as well as conventional stove or oven cooking. However, this is not a microwave cookbook; it is rather a collection of recipes designed to fit a certain lifestyle. I want people to be able to make a choice, based on time and efficiency, as to how to make a dish.

In developing these options, my priority was to make them meet certain criteria of style, taste and ease. It was not essential to me that each and every recipe be cooked in the microwave oven.

The criteria for using the microwave oven were whether there would be a saving in time, effort and/or cleanup, without altering the taste and style of the dish. You may come across a recipe that appears to be a likely candidate for the microwave oven but that doesn't include instructions for using it. Each recipe was carefully considered from the microwave point of view and often tested side by side with the same recipe cooked conventionally. If it didn't meet the basic criteria, I didn't include microwave instructions. When conventional cooking methods are quicker and easier, that is the preferred method.

I've tested the recipes in full-sized microwave ovens with 650 to 700 watts of power. This is what the cooking times in the book are based on. Many microwave ovens, especially the compact ones, have power ranging only from 400 to 500 watts. If you are using one of these ovens, the cooking time will be longer. In that case, you may wish to follow conventional cooking instructions. Manufacturers claim that most microwave owners do not know the wattage of their oven. Before you attempt any of these recipes in your microwave oven, please find out the wattage.

Many variables affect cooking time in the microwave oven. I think the same is true in conventional cooking, but because we're more experienced with stovetop and oven cooking, we anticipate these variables and instinctively know how to correct them. Also, since microwave cooking is faster, the margin of error is smaller.

Consider that quantity, density, temperature and configuration of the food and the shape of the cooking vessel all play a part in cooking time. Add to that the other variables, such as altitude and what is plugged into the same circuit as your microwave oven, and you get an idea as to why there often is a spread on cooking time. For these reasons, it is important that instructions be closely heeded. If a 2-quart dish is called for, the cooking time is based on that and will quite possibly be different if you use a smaller or larger dish. Thus, always cook for the shortest time given, then cook longer, if necessary.

You'll probably find that your own cupboards contain some dishes suitable for cooking in the microwave oven. Quite an array of special microwave cookware is available as well. Never use metal containers or even dishes that are trimmed with metallic elements. Ovenproof glass, porcelain and ceramic dishes may be appropriate to use. To determine if a dish is microwave-safe, fill a 1-cup glass measuring cup with water. Place it in the microwave, on or beside the dish to be tested. Cook on high power (100%) for 1 minute. If the dish gets hot instead of the water it is not suitable for use in the microwave oven.

In some recipes I suggest covering the dish during cooking. Most often I use a microwave-strength plastic wrap. Please be aware that when a dish is covered, especially with plastic wrap, a large amount of steam builds up during cooking. To prevent the possibility of burning yourself when the cover is removed, pierce the plastic once with the tip of a sharp knife. This can be done either before cooking or afterward—I prefer the latter. If you pierce the plastic after, let the dish rest for a minute with the cover still on. In either case, always remove the plastic away from you because the steam is very hot. Also, remember that dishes themselves will often get hot in the oven as the food transfers heat to the dish. Use pot holders when removing dishes from the microwave oven.

Part of the appeal of the microwave oven is the easy cleanup that goes along with cooking in it. I like to exploit this as much as possible to my advantage, and have stocked my kitchen with a good supply of paper goods for cooking in the microwave oven. I keep several sizes of paper plates on hand as well as small paper bowls, waxed paper and plastic wrap. They are perfectly acceptable for cooking many foods in the microwave oven. Their big advantage is clear—they are disposable, so there is no dish to wash. There is some concern about using recycled paper products in the microwave oven. Tiny bits of metal in these recycled products can cause a fire in the microwave oven, so, to be safe, do not use them.

1 · For Memorable Mornings

Five mornings a week, most people find that breakfast is a hurried affair, most likely combined with reading the newspaper, mapping out a strategy for the rest of the day or squeezing in some other activity before dashing out the door. Weekends are another story altogether. That's the time when people feel free to relax, unwind and indulge themselves. If leisurely morning meals are out of the question Monday through Friday, they come into their own on Saturday and Sunday. Then, it's okay to sleep late, read the papers at a slower pace and stroll out into the kitchen without paying any real attention to the clock.

Weekend breakfasts are often called brunch, a word I'm not especially fond of. It seems contrived. I do, however, like what we take it to mean—the first meal of the day on weekends, starting later than breakfast typically does and progressing at a leisurely, carefree beat. It takes the place of two meals, breakfast and lunch, so it's heartier than usual and has a diverse array of wonderful foods, culled from both breakfast and lunch. Whatever it's called, it is the first meal of the day, and I therefore prefer the emphasis on breakfast foods like eggs, fresh fruit, pancakes and muffins, accompanied with a bright-tasting salad or vegetable. When the occasion goes beyond breakfast and is more festive, a lightly spiked drink may be in order.

The recipes for Memorable Mornings are just as they sound, a collection of some of my favorite morning foods. Tradition takes a strong stance in this chapter, putting eggs, pancakes and breakfast breads in the forefront. Each recipe was picked for its adaptability, both to when and how it is served and prepared. Since so many people look to the weekends as a time for R and R, the recipes are appropriately easy. It seems to be at cross-purposes to plan a big, elaborate meal that takes up all the extra time and energy a weekend offers. These recipes are easy and relaxed, in hopes that weekends will be the same.

Do-ahead steps are important to me at every meal, and breakfast is no exception. Knowing that breakfast has already been started, either by having muffins in the freezer, pancake batter mixed and ready to cook, or a fruit compote just waiting to be served, allows me to sleep a little later or even take in one of morning's pleasures, a walk perhaps or a tennis game to rustle up an appetite.

Sliced oranges are a light and simple way to bring fresh fruit to the breakfast table. Here, they're set awash in a refreshing sauce of tangerine juice.

Frozen juice concentrate is a year-round alternative to fresh tangerines. By all means, use the juice of fresh tangerines when they're in season. Grenadine syrup intensifies the orange hue of the juice, adding a cheerful, rosy glow. It can be omitted if you prefer.

Sliced Oranges in Tangerine Sauce

Preparation time: 15 minutes
Yield: 4 to 6 servings

1. Remove 1 teaspoon zest, the colored part only, from 1 orange with a zester or grater and set it aside. Cut away the ends to leave a flat top and bottom on all the oranges. Stand them on a board and cut off all the peel and white pith with a paring knife. Slice the oranges crosswise into ¼-inch slices and place them in a large serving dish.

2. Mix the zest, tangerine juice, sugar, grenadine and vanilla and pour over the oranges. Serve immediately or cover tightly and refrigerate overnight. Serve well chilled.

Note: ½ cup frozen tangerine juice concentrate and ½ cup water can be used in place of the fresh tangerine juice.

6 *navel oranges*
1 *cup tangerine juice*
1½ *tablespoons sugar*
2 *teaspoons grenadine syrup*
2 *teaspoons pure vanilla extract*

This is an elegant way to serve mixed fresh fruit, shimmering in a light syrup, and topped, if you wish, with a deliciously rich sauce. The syrup has a warm, spiced citrus flavor that enhances just about any fruit without overpowering even the most delicately flavored ones. A perfect all-seasons medley follows, just one of countless possibilities for the changing seasons. The syrup is sufficient for 6 to 7 cups of fruit. Use any mixture that the season calls to mind.

Four Seasons Fruit Compote

Preparation time: 15 minutes
Cooking time: 5 minutes (Microwave: 5 minutes)
Chilling time: At least 1 hour
Yield: 6 servings

SYRUP:
1 cup water
⅓ cup sugar (2⅓ ounces)
 Juice of 1 orange
 (about ⅓ cup)
 Zest of 1 lemon,
 removed with a zester
 or grater
1 cinnamon stick
2 whole allspice berries
1 tablespoon pure vanilla
 extract
1 tablespoon Grand
 Marnier, optional

FRUIT:
½ of a ripe pineapple (use
 about 1¾ pounds)
2 kiwifruits
 (6 to 7 ounces)
1 large banana
 (8 ounces)
1½ cups grapes, preferably
 a mix of green and red
 seedless

GARNISH:
 Sweet Vanilla Cream,
 optional (see page 317)
 Fresh mint leaves,
 optional

1. For the syrup, combine the water, sugar, orange juice, lemon zest, cinnamon stick and allspice berries in a 3-quart non-aluminum pan. Bring to a boil over high heat, then simmer for 5 minutes.

2. Strain into a large bowl, add the vanilla and the Grand Marnier, if using, and refrigerate until chilled, about 1 hour. The syrup can be made up to 2 weeks in advance and refrigerated.

3. Peel and core the pineapple and cut it into ¾-inch cubes. Peel the kiwis and the banana and cut them into ¼-inch slices.

4. Add the pineapple, kiwis, banana and grapes to the chilled syrup. Serve immediately or refrigerate up to 6 hours before serving. Bring the compote to room temperature before serving.

5. To serve, spoon the fruit and syrup into bowls, top with a dollop of Sweet Vanilla Cream, if using, and garnish with fresh mint, if desired.

MICROWAVE: Combine the water, sugar, orange juice, lemon zest, cinnamon stick and allspice berries in a 4-quart microwave dish. Cook, uncovered, on high power (100%) for 5 minutes, stirring once halfway through. Continue with steps 2 through 5.

Note: Although microwave cooking time for the syrup is the same as conventional cooking, it is included since the syrup can be cooked and stored in the same container, making cleanup easier.

The combination of orange and Marsala wine imparts a light fragrance to the best berries of springtime. Raspberries are a dazzling addition, tossed in at serving time.

Strawberries Marsala

Preparation time: 10 minutes
Marinating time: 2 to 4 hours
Yield: 6 servings

1. Wash the berries and pat dry, then remove the hulls. Place in a large plastic bag.
2. Add the zest, Marsala, orange juice and sugar and toss together lightly. Seal the bag with a twist tie placed close to the berries. Refrigerate 2 to 4 hours before serving, turning the bag over several times.
3. At serving time, transfer the berries to a large bowl or to individual dishes.

2   pints small strawberries
    Zest of 1 orange
¼   cup Marsala wine
¼   cup orange juice
2   to 4 tablespoons sugar, depending on sweetness of berries

◆

A meal-in-a-glass is an invigorating way to start the day, especially when time is short. Fresh fruit, frozen so it whips up to a frothy texture, is bolstered by protein from two low-fat sources, yogurt and egg white. The basic formula is open to many variations, depending on what fruit is available. I always like to use the banana, since it adds natural sweetness and body. Peaches, papaya, mango, pineapple and raspberries are all delicious.

Sunshine Smoothie

Preparation time: 5 minutes
Freezing time: At least 1 hour or up to 3 months
Yield: 3½ cups, 3 to 4 servings

1. Hull the fresh strawberries and cut them in half. If you're using frozen strawberries, keep them in the freezer until you blend the smoothie. Peel the bananas and cut them into 1-inch slices. Arrange the fruit on a baking sheet lined with waxed paper and freeze until solid. Once frozen, the fruit can be used right away or wrapped in plastic bags and kept frozen for up to 3 months.
2. Just before serving, combine the frozen strawberries and bananas with the yogurt, orange juice, egg whites, sugar or honey

2   cups fresh or loose-pack frozen strawberries
2   small bananas (12 to 14 ounces total)
¾   cup plain low-fat yogurt
⅔   cup orange juice
2   large egg whites
1   tablespoon sugar or honey
1   teaspoon pure vanilla extract

and vanilla in a blender. Blend until smooth and frothy. Serve immediately.

◆

The sheer simplicity of this recipe makes it practical for the morning hours. It's just the kind of thing you can make without any preamble or marketing since the basic ingredients are most likely on hand. Eggs are cracked into a little splash of cream, seasoned with minced onion, topped with cheese and baked. A bit of diced tomato and some fresh tarragon in place of the dried are perfect summer additions; julienned sorrel leaves in the spring.

_____Shirred Eggs in Tarragon Cream_____

Preparation time: 5 minutes
Baking time: 12 to 15 minutes
Yield: 4 servings

2 tablespoons whipping cream
4 large eggs
½ teaspoon dried tarragon
¼ small onion (use ¼ ounce), peeled
1½ tablespoons minced Parmesan cheese, preferably imported
Salt, if desired
Freshly ground pepper
2 teaspoons minced fresh chives or minced parsley

1. 15 minutes before baking, place the rack in the center of the oven and preheat oven to 350 degrees. Butter 4 1-cup custard cups or soufflé dishes.
2. Put 1½ teaspoons cream into each dish and crack an egg in, being careful not to break the yolk. Sprinkle with tarragon.
3. Cut the onion into fine dice. Sprinkle it over the eggs, then add the cheese, a pinch of salt, if desired, and pepper.
4. Bake until the white is set, 12 to 15 minutes. Sprinkle with chives or parsley and serve immediately.

◆

Frittatas are the Italian counterpart of omelets, and happily they demand much less skill and dexterity to make. No rolling, turning or careful coddling—just simple stove-top cooking, followed by a run under the broiler for a golden-brown finish. Another point in their favor—frittatas aren't necessarily last-minute as omelets are. They are just as good served at room temperature as when served hot. This frittata is full of vegetables, sausage and oozy bits of melted cheese.

Sausage, Cheese and Vegetable Frittata

Preparation time: 15 minutes
Cooking time: 20 minutes (Microwave: 14 minutes plus 8 minutes standing time)
Yield: 4 to 6 servings

1. Crumble the sausage and brown it in a 6-cup stove-to-oven gratin or an ovenproof skillet. Drain off the fat.

2. Cut the mushrooms and zucchini into ¼-inch slices and the red or green pepper into ¼-inch dice. Cut the cheese into ¼-inch dice.

3. Add the zucchini, mushrooms, red or green pepper, basil, pepper flakes and salt to the sausage. Cook, stirring often, until the vegetables are soft, about 7 minutes. Set aside, off the heat.

4. Whisk the eggs in a large bowl and add the vegetable mixture and the cheese.

5. Heat the oil in the same pan. When it is hot, add the egg mixture and cook over medium heat until the bottom and sides are set, about 6 minutes. The eggs will still be loose in the center.

6. Transfer to a preheated broiler and broil 6 inches from the heat until the frittata is golden and just set in the center, about 3 minutes. Serve hot or at room temperature.

4 ounces bulk hot or sweet breakfast sausage
6 small mushrooms (2 ounces total)
1 small zucchini (3 ounces), washed
½ of a small red or green bell pepper (use 2 ounces)
4 ounces mozzarella cheese
1¼ teaspoons dried basil
¼ teaspoon crushed red pepper flakes
¼ teaspoon salt
5 large eggs
1 tablespoon light-tasting olive oil

MICROWAVE: Crumble the sausage in a shallow, 10-inch round microwave dish. Cook, uncovered, on high power (100%) until brown, about 2 minutes. Drain the fat and then follow step 2 above. Add the oil, mushrooms, zucchini, red or green pepper, basil, pepper flakes and salt to the sausage. Cook, uncovered, on high power for 1 minute. Stir, then push the vegetables around the edge of the dish, leaving the center empty. Cook 2 minutes longer. Whisk the eggs together and add the cheese. Add the egg and cheese mixture to the sausage and vegetables and stir gently. Cook, uncovered, on medium-high power (70 to 75%) for 5 minutes. Push the cooked portion from the edge of the dish to the center, allowing the uncooked part to run to the sides. Cook until almost set, about 4 minutes longer. The center will be slightly loose. Remove the frittata from the microwave oven and let it stand until set, about 8 minutes. Serve hot or at room temperature.

Note: With the standing time, cooking the frittata in the microwave oven takes slightly more time, but it needs less constant attention and the pan is much easier to clean.

This is a simple and logical morning evolution of one of my favorite easy meals. I often make taco "sandwiches" when I need a quick lunch. Here, they are part of breakfast, fitting in very well when a casual meal is in order. Like traditional tacos, the add-ons are endless and strictly up to your own taste. I like hot peppers and a handful of cilantro. Others swear by black olives or chorizo sausage. Salsa is always a must!

Breakfast Tacos

Preparation time: 10 minutes
Cooking time: 10 minutes
Yield: 6 tacos; 4 to 6 servings

6 *flour tortillas*
1 *small, ripe avocado*
   (6 ounces)
8 *large eggs*
1 *tablespoon water*
   Dash Tabasco sauce
3 *ounces shredded Monterey*
   Jack or Muenster cheese
1 *tablespoon unsalted butter*
   Salsa Cruda or Green
   Salsa (see page 332)
   Sour cream, optional

1. Warm the tortillas. This can be done one of three ways. Stack them together, wrap in foil and place in a preheated 400-degree oven for 8 to 10 minutes. Or, stack them between 2 dampened paper towels. Cook on high (100%) power in a microwave oven for 30 to 35 seconds. Or, place them, 1 at a time, over an open flame and cook, turning once with tongs, until warm and browned around the edges (take care—they can burn quickly). When you have the time, this is the best way to warm them, since it adds a slightly smoky taste, but the other ways require less attention. Wrap in a cloth towel to keep the tortillas warm while you prepare the eggs.

2. Cut the avocado into ⅜-inch dice.

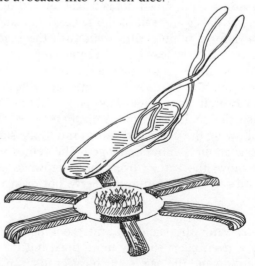

3. Whisk the eggs with the water and Tabasco sauce. Fold in the cheese.

4. Melt the butter in a large skillet. When it is hot, add the eggs and scramble as desired. Remove the pan from the heat and fold in the avocado.

5. To serve, fill the tortillas with eggs and roll up. Place on plates, seam side down. Serve with salsa of your choice and sour cream, if desired.

◆

I'm always so impressed when I take a Dutch Baby from the oven, all golden brown and puffy. Fortunately, it tastes every bit as good as it looks and is very easy to make. Plus, the batter can be mixed the day before so all that needs to be done in the morning is the baking. The pancake, a close relative of popovers and Yorkshire pudding, is really a showpiece when it is filled with fruit, but this must be added as soon as the pancake comes from the oven so the pancake is still high when it gets to the table. Traditionally, Dutch Baby is served with confectioners' sugar and lemon wedges, without the fruit.

Dutch Baby Pancake

Preparation time: 15 minutes
Baking time: 30 minutes
Yield: 2 to 3 servings

¾ cup milk
½ cup unbleached all-purpose flour (2½ ounces)
2 large eggs
1½ tablespoons sugar
½ teaspoon pure vanilla extract
3 tablespoons unsalted butter
1 tablespoon confectioners' sugar
1½ cups thinly sliced peaches, nectarines or strawberries and/or raspberries and blueberries, optional, or lemon, cut in wedges

1. 15 minutes before baking, place the rack in the center of the oven and preheat oven to 450 degrees. Have a 10-inch glass pie plate or cast iron skillet ready.

2. Mix the milk, flour, eggs, sugar and vanilla until smooth, in a food processor, blender or with a whisk. The batter can be made a day in advance and refrigerated.

3. Put the butter in the pie plate or skillet and place in the hot oven until the butter is melted. Brush the butter up the sides and onto the rim of the pan so the entire inside surface is well coated.

4. Slowly pour the batter into the pie plate or skillet and bake for 20 minutes. Reduce the oven to 350 degrees and continue baking until the pancake is well browned and cooked in the center, 8 to 10 minutes longer. Remove from the oven and sift confectioners' sugar over the top. Serve immediately, with fruit spooned into the center or with lemon wedges.

◆

These puffy, golden-hued pancakes just beg to be served in a pool of pure maple syrup. Canned pumpkin is a terrific ingredient, and is in no way a compromise with quality as a substitute for baking a fresh pumpkin and extracting the purée. In fact, it's more reliable since it's less watery than fresh purée, and certainly it's a lot easier.

_____Pumpkin Yogurt Hotcakes _____

Preparation time: 10 minutes
Cooking time: 15 minutes
Yield: 12 4-inch hotcakes

1 cup cake flour (4 ounces)
2 teaspoons baking powder
¼ teaspoon baking soda
⅛ teaspoon freshly grated nutmeg
⅛ teaspoon salt
2 large eggs
3 tablespoons unsalted butter, melted

1. Sift the flour, baking powder, baking soda, nutmeg and salt and set aside.

2. Whisk the eggs, butter and sugar until light. Mix in the pumpkin, lemon juice and vanilla. Spoon the dry ingredients onto the batter, then the yogurt. Fold in very gently with a rubber spatula. Don't overmix or the batter will be too loose. The batter can be made up to 2 days in advance, covered tightly and refrigerated. Do not stir before using.

3. Butter a griddle and heat until it is very hot. Using a scant ¼ cup batter for each cake, spoon neat rounds onto griddle. Cook until very bubbly on top. Turn over and cook the other side. Keep the cooked hotcakes warm in a 200-degree oven while you cook the others.

2 tablespoons sugar
1 cup canned solid-pack
   pumpkin
2 teaspoons fresh lemon
   juice
2 teaspoons pure vanilla
   extract
½ cup plain yogurt
   Unsalted butter, for
   cooking the hotcakes

◆

Canadian bacon is not true bacon, but it is an appealing alternative to bacon and sausage since it is leaner and hence lower in calories. Here, a light mustard glaze glosses over it, giving a sweet edge to its slightly smoky taste.

Mustard-Glazed Canadian Bacon

Preparation time: 5 minutes
Cooking time: 10 minutes
Yield: 6 to 8 servings

1. Combine the sugar, mustard, vinegar and allspice in a small dish.

2. Remove the rind and fat from the bacon. Cut bacon into ⅜-inch slices. Brush both sides of each slice with the glaze.

3. Melt the butter on a griddle or 10-inch skillet. When it is hot, add the bacon in batches, so the pan isn't crowded, and cook over high heat, turning once, until lightly browned, about 5 minutes. Cook the remaining bacon. Keep the cooked bacon warm in a 200-degree oven while you finish the remaining batches. Serve hot or at room temperature.

⅓ cup firmly packed light
   brown sugar (2⅔
   ounces)
1½ tablespoons Dijon
   mustard
¾ teaspoon cider vinegar
1/16 teaspoon ground allspice
12 ounces Canadian bacon
   in 1 piece
1½ tablespoons unsalted
   butter

This is the toast of the breakfast table, richly flavored with sugar and spice. The quality of bread makes a big difference, so use best-quality cinnamon raisin bread—homemade, if you're so inclined, otherwise store-bought. Panettone, brioche and challah are also delicious. I've given freezing and baking instructions for the toast, a good, energy-saving option when you're making breakfast for a crowd.

Cinnamon Raisin French Toast

Preparation time: 10 minutes
Cooking time: 5 minutes on stove top or 15 minutes in the oven
Yield: 6 servings

3 large eggs
1½ cups half-and-half
¼ cup sugar
1½ teaspoons pure vanilla extract
1 teaspoon cinnamon
½ teaspoon freshly grated nutmeg
Pinch of salt
12 thick slices cinnamon raisin bread, stale
Butter, for cooking

1. Whisk the eggs, half-and-half, sugar, vanilla, cinnamon, nutmeg and salt together. Transfer to a shallow dish—a pie plate is ideal.

2. Dip the bread in the egg mixture, turning it once so both sides are saturated. Lift with tongs, letting the excess egg drip off. The bread can be cooked or baked now, or frozen for later use.

3. To cook, heat a thin film of butter on a griddle until it is very hot. Fry bread, turning once, until golden. To bake, divide 3 tablespoons butter between 2 jelly-roll pans. Place pans in a pre-heated 400-degree oven to melt the butter. Tilt the pans so they are completely buttered. Arrange the bread on the pans and bake, turning after 10 minutes, until golden, about 15 minutes. Serve immediately with maple syrup or jelly.

4. To freeze, arrange in a single layer on a baking sheet lined with plastic wrap and place in freezer until frozen. When the bread is frozen, stack slices between sheets of plastic wrap, place in an airtight plastic bag and return to the freezer. To cook, follow the instructions above for the cooking method of your choice. The bread does not have to be defrosted. Cook or bake directly from the freezer, adding several minutes to the cooking time given in step 3.

The adage that you can't tell a book by its cover certainly applies to some old shoe neighborhood diners. I happened into one recently and was served a sensational breakfast sandwich. This is my rendition—simple food, homey and thoroughly, delightfully irresistible.

Breakfast Between Bread

Preparation time: 10 minutes
Cooking time: 10 minutes
Yield: 2 sandwiches

1. Open the muffins and spread each cut side with ½ tablespoon mayonnaise. Cook the 4 halves, cut side down, on a heated griddle or skillet until browned.

2. In this order, divide half the ham, onion, tomato and cheese on cut side of 2 muffin halves. Top with the remaining 2 muffin halves and press together.

3. Melt the butter on the griddle. When it is hot, cook the sandwiches over medium-high heat until the bottoms are golden. Turn over and press top of each sandwich with a spatula to compress it. Cook until other side of each muffin is golden and cheese is melted. Serve immediately.

2 *English muffins*
2 *tablespoons mayonnaise (see page 327 or store-bought)*
2 *ounces smoked ham, sliced paper-thin*
2 *tablespoons minced onion*
2 *tablespoons diced tomato*
3 *ounces brick cheese, thinly sliced*
1 *tablespoon unsalted butter*

Fiber-rich bran muffins, loaded with raisins, are a popular break-fast option, one that combines a good dose of nutritive value with an appealing taste. Of all the recipes, this one, given to me by a student, is my favorite. The batter lasts in the refrigerator for several weeks, so you can bake muffins as needed. They also freeze very well, and I find it easier to bake them all at once and keep them on hand in the freezer.

——Marty's Best Bran Muffins————

Preparation time: 15 minutes
Baking time: 22 to 24 minutes
Yield: 12 muffins

4 tablespoons unsalted butter, cut into 4 pieces
½ cup boiling water
1¼ cups bran cereal—not flakes (3½ ounces)
¾ cup unbleached all-purpose flour (3¾ ounces)
½ cup whole-wheat flour (2½ ounces)
⅔ cup raisins (4 ounces)
⅔ cup sugar (4⅔ ounces)
1¼ teaspoons baking soda
¼ teaspoon salt
1 cup buttermilk
1 large egg
2 tablespoons molasses
Additional cereal for the top of muffins

1. 15 minutes before baking, place the rack in center of oven and preheat oven to 400 degrees. Line 12 muffin cups with paper liners or grease the cups.

2. Put the butter in a food processor or a large mixing bowl. Add the boiling water and mix until the butter melts. Add the cereal and pulse 2 or 3 times in the food processor, or stir, until moistened.

3. Add both flours, the raisins, sugar, baking soda, salt, but-termilk, egg and molasses. If you're using a processor, pulse the machine on and off twice, then run a spatula around the sides of the work bowl. Pulse 1 or 2 more times, just enough to lightly mix ingredients. By hand, stir until batter is mixed. With either method, it is important not to overmix.

4. Spoon the batter into 12 muffin cups and sprinkle each one with ½ teaspoon cereal. Bake until a toothpick inserted in the center comes out clean, 22 to 24 minutes. Remove from pans and serve warm.

5. The batter can be refrigerated for up to 3 weeks and baked as needed. Baked, the muffins can be wrapped so they are airtight and frozen. Reheat in a preheated 300-degree oven or microwave oven on medium-high power (70 to 75%). It is not necessary to thaw them before reheating.

I love the light, cakey texture and puckery lemon flavor of these muffins. Sweet and fragrant, they're delicious at the breakfast table slathered with tangy orange marmalade or apricot preserves, and just as tempting at lunch or supper, lavished with sweet butter or honey. Spread them with lemon curd for a tea-time snack.

Lemon Buttermilk Muffins

Preparation time: 10 minutes
Baking time: 20 minutes
Yield: 12 muffins

1. 15 minutes before baking, place the rack in the center of the oven and preheat to 375 degrees. Line 12 muffin cups with paper liners, or grease the cups.

2. To make in a food processor, process the lemon zest with the sugar until the zest is as fine as the sugar. Add the butter, egg, buttermilk, flour, baking soda, cloves and salt and process for 3 seconds. Run a spatula around the sides of the work bowl, then pulse the machine on and off 2 or 3 times, just until combined.

3. To make by hand, mince the zest and sugar in a blender. Transfer it to a mixing bowl and mix with the melted butter and egg. Stir in the buttermilk, then the flour, baking soda, cloves and salt. Do not overmix.

4. Spoon the batter into the muffin cups. Bake until a toothpick inserted in the center comes out clean, about 20 minutes. Let cool in the pan for 5 minutes.

5. Make the glaze while the muffins are baking. Stir the lemon juice and sugar together. Dip the tops of the baked muffins into the glaze while they are still relatively hot. Let rest at least 30 minutes before serving. Serve at room temperature or reheated in a 300-degree oven or a microwave oven on medium-high power (75%) until heated. They can be frozen for several months. They do not need to be thawed before reheating.

Zest of 2 lemons, removed with a vegetable peeler
1 *cup sugar (7 ounces)*
1 *stick unsalted butter, melted*
1 *large egg*
1 *cup buttermilk*
2 *cups unbleached all-purpose flour (10 ounces)*
1 *teaspoon baking soda*
⅛ *teaspoon ground cloves*
⅛ *teaspoon salt*

GLAZE
¼ *cup fresh lemon juice*
2 *tablespoons sugar*

Oatmeal adds a rustic, wholesome quality to scones that is especially welcome at the breakfast table. I find that using margarine instead of butter makes these scones a bit more tender and that they stay fresh longer, with no compromise to flavor, but by all means use butter if you prefer. As to what to slather on them, sweet butter is always my first choice.

Cinnamon Oat Scones

Preparation time: 15 minutes
Baking time: 16 minutes
Yield: 8 4-inch scones

SCONES:

1½ cups unbleached all-purpose flour (7½ ounces)
½ cup rolled oats (1½ ounces)
½ cup raisins (3 ounces)
⅓ cup sugar (2⅓ ounces)
⅓ cup milk
5½ tablespoons unsalted margarine, melted
1 large egg
1 tablespoon baking powder
½ teaspoon salt

TOPPING:

1½ tablespoons unsalted margarine, melted
2 tablespoons sugar
1 teaspoon cinnamon

1. 15 minutes before baking, place the rack in the center of oven and preheat oven to 375 degrees. Butter a baking sheet.

2. For the scones, mix the flour, oats, raisins, sugar, milk, margarine, egg, baking powder and salt just until combined—do not overmix. You can do this in a food processor or with a wooden spoon. The dough will be very moist.

3. Transfer the dough to a large plastic bag and press it into a circle ½ inch thick. Tear the bag open and cut the dough into 3-inch rounds with a cookie cutter or a clean, small tuna fish can. Transfer to the prepared baking sheet with a metal spatula.

4. For the topping, mix the margarine, sugar and cinnamon and brush over top of the scones.

5. Bake until golden, about 16 minutes. Serve warm. The scones can be made a day in advance and reheated in an oven.

I adore the earliest blueberries of the season, when they are plump, firm and tart. The first basket is always reserved for the simple pleasure of eating them plain. As they become more abundant, some are most certainly destined for this moist, luscious breakfast cake.

Blueberry Streusel Cake

Preparation time: 20 minutes
Baking time: 45 minutes
Yield: 1 8-inch cake

1. 15 minutes before baking, place the rack in the center of the oven and preheat oven to 350 degrees. Butter an 8-inch springform pan.

2. For the streusel, cut the chilled butter into 8 pieces. Work it into the sugar, flour, cinnamon and salt until it is the size of small peas, using a food processor or pastry blender. Refrigerate while you make the cake.

3. To make the cake in a processor, process the eggs, sugar and butter in the same work bowl (it is not necessary to wash it between steps) until fluffy, 1 minute, stopping once to scrape down the sides of the work bowl. With the machine running, add the cream through the feed tube and mix for 5 seconds. In this order, add the flour, baking soda, cinnamon, salt and blueberries and quickly pulse the machine on and off just until combined, 3 to 4 times.

4. To make with a mixer, cream the sugar and butter on high speed until fluffy. Add eggs and mix well. Mix in the cream on low speed, then the flour, baking soda, cinnamon and salt. Gently fold in the berries by hand.

5. Transfer batter to prepared pan and place on a baking sheet. Bake 20 minutes. Sprinkle streusel evenly over the top and return to the oven. Bake until a toothpick inserted in the center comes out clean, about 25 minutes longer, for a total of 45 minutes. Serve warm.

STREUSEL:
1   stick unsalted butter, chilled
¼   cup sugar (1¾ ounces)
¼   cup unbleached all-purpose flour (1¼ ounces)
½   teaspoon cinnamon
    Pinch of salt

CAKE:
2   large eggs
1   cup sugar (7 ounces)
1   stick unsalted butter, softened
½   cup whipping cream
1¼ cups unbleached all-purpose flour (6¼ ounces)
½   teaspoon baking soda
½   teaspoon cinnamon
¼   teaspoon salt
1   cup blueberries

Ask your family or guests to name the mystery ingredient in this quick bread and you're apt to hear things like pumpkin, carrots, zucchini—almost anything but beer. But beer it is, a most unlikely addition that makes for a deeply colored, moist, rich and well-flavored sweet bread.

—————The King of Coffee Cakes—————————

Preparation time: 15 minutes
Baking time: 1 hour
Yield: 1 12-inch Bundt cake

2 cups firmly packed dark brown sugar (1 pound)
2 large eggs
2 sticks unsalted butter, softened
2 cups light or dark beer
3 cups unbleached all-purpose flour (15 ounces)
1½ cups chopped pecans (6 ounces)
1 cup raisins (6 ounces)
1 tablespoon cinnamon
2 teaspoons baking soda
¾ teaspoon ground cloves
½ teaspoon salt
Confectioners' sugar

1. 15 minutes before baking, place the rack in the center of the oven and preheat oven to 350 degrees. Butter a 12-cup Bundt pan and dust the inside with flour.

2. To make in a food processor, process the sugar and eggs until smooth, 1 minute, stopping once to scrape down sides of work bowl. Add the butter and process another minute. With the machine running, pour the beer through the feed tube and process for 10 seconds. Transfer to a large mixing bowl. Add the flour, pecans, raisins, cinnamon, baking soda, cloves and salt and stir just until combined.

3. To make with a mixer, cream the sugar and butter on high speed until light, about 3 minutes. Add eggs and mix well, then mix in beer on low speed. Fold in the flour, pecans, raisins, cinnamon, baking soda, cloves and salt.

4. Transfer to prepared pan. Bake until a toothpick inserted in the center comes out clean, about 1 hour. Cool in pan for 5 minutes, then invert onto a rack and cool completely. Sift confectioners' sugar over the top just before serving.

2·Nibbles

The modes and styles of entertaining have changed so much that no one format is rigorously adhered to anymore. Instead, there's an array of possibilities to match moods with personalities and whims. Personal elements are much more important, and the casual approach is operative more often and more comfortably than in the past.

If at one time it was practically unheard of to throw a kitchen party, now they're as common as they are fun. Add to that the potlucks and picnics, tailgates, cocktail parties and Sunday night suppers and you'll see that such parties are everything they're cracked up to be—and more!

The food at these get-togethers is as free-spirited and serendipitous as the occasion. It is a colorful and lively bazaar of dishes gathered from other categories as well as those traditionally thought of as appetizers. Formal, multi-course meals are saved for another time. In their place is food that can best be described as fun, casual and easygoing. This chapter includes the "little somethings" that are so often a part of these parties. Think of them as finger foods, hors d'oeuvres, appetizers, preludes or nibbles. Or rethink the whole structure of the meal. A hand-picked selection of nibbles could be a party unto itself.

All the nibbles are easy to prepare. Many of them can also be made ahead of time. For large gatherings, I think it is especially important to have as much ready as possible. Then, for smaller groups, I've included a few recipes that require some last-minute cooking. Consider these for kitchen parties where guests join in and lend a hand.

This is a variation on a basic formula, the one I turn to time and again for glazed cocktail nuts. They're crisp, not too sweet and very munchable. I especially like this version, which has only the slightest suggestion of cumin. Other possibilities are endless: Leave them plain; add a bit of bourbon, cayenne, cinnamon or curry; maple syrup in place of the corn syrup is sensational. Whatever you do, keep these nuts on hand in the freezer. They're the perfect choice when you want to serve just a little something with drinks, and a pretty jarful makes a welcome gift.

Spiced Pecans

Preparation time: 5 minutes
Baking time: 1 hour
Yield: 1 pound

1. 15 minutes before baking, place the rack in the center of the oven and preheat oven to 250 degrees. Line a jelly roll pan with aluminum foil.

2. Combine the butter, corn syrup, water, cumin and salt in a 2½-quart pan and bring to a boil. Remove the pan from the heat and add the nuts. Toss gently to coat them with the syrup.

3. Spread the nuts in a single layer on the prepared pan. Bake until they are crisp and dry, about 1 hour, stirring them every 15 minutes with a wooden spoon.

4. Remove the nuts from the oven and immediately transfer them to a clean piece of foil. Spread them in a single layer, breaking apart any nuts that are stuck together. Cool completely. They can be held at room temperature in an airtight container for up to a week, or frozen for 6 months. If they are not crisp and fresh-tasting after storing them, spread the nuts on a baking sheet and bake in a 250-degree oven for 20 minutes.

MICROWAVE: Follow step 1. Combine the butter, corn syrup, water, cumin and salt in a 2½-quart microwave-safe casserole. Cook on high power (100%) until hot, 1½ minutes. Stir in the pecans and toss gently to coat them with the syrup. As in step 3, spread the nuts in a single layer on the prepared pan and bake in a conventional oven until they are crisp and dry, about 1 hour. Finish as in step 4.

4 tablespoons unsalted butter
¼ cup light corn syrup
2 tablespoons water
1 teaspoon ground cumin
1 teaspoon salt
1 pound pecan halves

A delicious, savory dip for raw vegetables. Using reduced-calorie mayonnaise and plain low-fat yogurt keeps the calorie count in line with anyone's diet.

Green Goddess Dip

2 medium garlic cloves, peeled
1 cup parsley leaves
¼ cup fresh chives
4 anchovies, rinsed and dried
1 cup mayonnaise (I use reduced-calorie mayonnaise)
½ cup plain yogurt
Dash Worcestershire sauce

Preparation time: 10 minutes
Yield: About 1½ cups

Mince the garlic, parsley, chives and anchovies in a food processor or blender. Combine with the mayonnaise, yogurt and Worcestershire sauce. The dip can be made up to 2 days in advance and refrigerated. Adjust the seasoning before serving, if necessary.

◆

This is just the kind of dip that gets noticed in a crowd! Its sassy taste never fails to win raves, even amidst protests about how spicy hot it is. It's good with raw vegetables as well as tortilla chips.

Red-hot Jalapeño Dip

1 to 2 jalapeño peppers, seeded, if desired
4 medium green onions (2 ounces total)
8 ounces cream cheese, softened
¼ cup jalapeño jelly
1 to 2 tablespoons milk, if necessary

Preparation time: 10 minutes
Yield: 1⅓ cups

Mince the peppers and green onions in a food processor or blender. Add the cream cheese and jelly and mix until smooth. Thin with milk, if necessary. The dip can be made in advance and refrigerated up to 4 days.

Note: Jalapeño jelly is a sweetened jelly made from hot peppers. Many large supermarkets and specialty food stores carry it.

I usually regard a dip this low in calories with suspicion, since I rarely find one that tastes like something I want to eat. This recipe changes all that. There are no secret ingredients, just a ridiculously simple combination that happens to taste good and have very few calories. So get your carrot sticks ready and indulge.

Skinny Dip

Preparation time: 10 minutes
Yield: 1⅓ cups

1. Mince the ginger in a food processor or by hand.
2. Drain any liquid from the yogurt and transfer yogurt to a small bowl. Stir in the ginger, mustard, dill, sugar and salt to taste. Serve immediately or refrigerate up to 2 days.

1 small piece fresh ginger (⅜-inch cube), peeled
1¼ cups plain low-fat yogurt
5 teaspoons Dijon mustard
2½ teaspoons dried dill
2½ teaspoons light brown sugar
Salt

◆

This mousse is rich and mild-tasting with a nice mustardy tang and a subtle smoky note. The easiest way to serve it is in a crock with an assortment of crackers. Other options—on slices of cucumber or tart apple or piped into spears of Belgian endive.

Many fish stores sell smoked trout. I prefer it to smoked mackerel or sable, which tend to be more oily.

Smoked Trout Mousse

Preparation time: 15 minutes
Yield: 1⅔ cups

1. Carefully separate the flesh from the skin of the fish and remove any bones. Crumble into coarse flakes.
2. Mix the fish, butter, cream, mustard, vinegar and sugar in a food processor or blender until it is completely smooth, 2 to 3 minutes, stopping several times to scrape down the sides of the container.
3. Refrigerate at least 1 hour or up to 5 days before serving. Soften slightly at room temperature before serving.

2 cups flaked smoked trout, about 1 pound total weight with bones
6 tablespoons unsalted butter, softened, cut in thirds
¼ cup whipping cream
2 tablespoons grainy mustard
1 tablespoon white wine vinegar
1 tablespoon light brown sugar

Sweet red pepper contrasts with eggplant in this creamy, smooth spread. It's low in calories, something you'd never guess from its taste and texture. Indulge with abandon—this spread has less than 10 calories per tablespoon. It's delicious on raw vegetables or thinly sliced French bread that has been toasted and brushed with olive oil.

Eggplant and Red Pepper Spread

Preparation time: 10 minutes
Baking time: 50 minutes (Microwave: 10 to 12 minutes)
Draining time: 30 minutes
Yield: 1¾ cups

1 medium eggplant (1¼ pounds)
1 large red bell pepper (8 ounces)
1 medium garlic clove, peeled
2 tablespoons sour cream
½ teaspoon ground coriander
½ teaspoon salt
Freshly ground black pepper

1. 15 minutes before baking, place the rack in the center of the oven and preheat oven to 350 degrees. Line a baking sheet with aluminum foil.

2. Pierce the skin of the eggplant in several places. Place the eggplant and red pepper on the baking sheet and bake until both are completely soft, about 50 minutes.

3. Cut the vegetables in half, transfer to a colander and let drain for at least 30 minutes. Remove the skin and seeds from the red pepper and cut the flesh into quarters.

4. Scrape the pulp from the eggplant into a food processor or blender. Discard the skin. Add the red pepper, garlic, sour cream, coriander, salt and pepper and purée until it is as smooth as possible, about 2 minutes. Serve immediately or refrigerate for up to 1 week. Stir well and adjust the seasoning before serving.

MICROWAVE: Skip steps 1 and 2. Pierce the skin of the eggplant in several places. Place the eggplant and red pepper on a paper plate. Cook on high power (100%) until both are completely soft, 10 to 12 minutes. Finish as in steps 3 and 4.

Potted meats go way back in culinary history, most likely origi-
nating in the kitchen of a thrifty-minded cook faced with leftover
meat. This recipe, a smooth spread, is a tasty solution for a similar
dilemma in your own kitchen. It uses up all the little scraps of
meat that are too small for sandwiches, so nothing is wasted.
Though I use turkey in the recipe, cooked beef, duck or chicken
are good substitutes.

Potted Turkey Pâté

Preparation time: 10 minutes
Yield: 2 cups

Mince the garlic and onion in a food processor or blender.
Add the turkey, anchovies, butter, brandy, thyme, nutmeg and
pepper, in 2 batches if in the blender, or all together in the processor. Mix until completely smooth, about 3 minutes, stopping
several times to scrape down the sides of the container. Cover
tightly and refrigerate at least 1 hour before serving or up to a
week. Let soften to a spreadable consistency before serving.

1 *large garlic clove, peeled*
1 *small onion (2 ounces), peeled*
2 *cups cooked, diced turkey meat*
1 *can (2 ounces) flat anchovies, rinsed and patted dry*
5 *tablespoons unsalted butter, softened*
1 *tablespoon brandy*
¼ *teaspoon ground thyme*
 Freshly grated nutmeg
 Freshly ground white pepper

The Italian tradition of deep frying artichokes commingles with Japanese influences in this most delicious exchange. Tempura batter, used here to coat wedges of artichokes, is very light, delicate and wonderfully crisp. Besides artichokes, the batter can also be used on mushrooms, zucchini, sweet potatoes, onions and parsley (yes, parsley!).

Artichokes Tempura

Preparation time: 20 minutes
Cooking time: 15 minutes
Yield: 2 to 4 servings

⅓ cup cake flour (1⅓ ounces)
⅓ cup ice water
2 tablespoons fresh bread crumbs
1 tablespoon cornstarch
1 tablespoon light-tasting olive oil
1 large egg white
1 teaspoon baking powder
¼ teaspoon salt
2 large artichokes (12 to 14 ounces each)
   Peanut or other vegetable oil, for frying
   Lemon wedges

1. Mix the flour, water, bread crumbs, cornstarch, oil, egg white, baking powder and salt until smooth. The batter will be very thin, almost like milk or light cream in consistency.

2. Cut about 1½ inches from the top of each artichoke. Pare them down to the tender yellow leaves, then cut in half lengthwise. Remove the fuzzy choke with a small knife or a grapefruit spoon. Cut each half into 6 wedges.

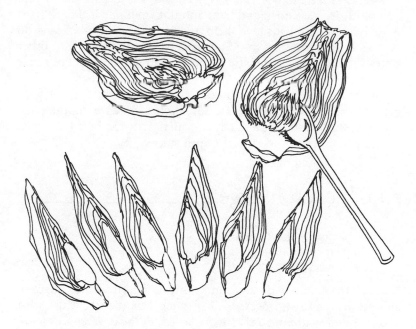

3. Pour the oil into a medium-size frying pan to a depth of 3 inches and heat to 350 degrees.

4. Dip the artichokes in the batter, then fry in the hot oil until nicely golden, about 3 minutes per batch. Drain on paper toweling. Remove each batch of drained artichokes to a jelly roll pan lined with paper toweling and keep warm in a 250-degree oven while you cook the rest. Serve hot with lemon wedges.

These bite-sized nibbles, Cajun-spiced with garlic, cayenne, thyme and basil, are very crisp and light and not at all oily if they're fried quickly in hot oil. Kids love them, they're ideal for picnics, and do well as hors d'oeuvres, too. Sometimes I serve them plain, other times I'll add a sauce, maybe a horseradish-spiked cocktail sauce or a mustard mayonnaise.

The seasoned bread crumbs can also be used on fried vegetables, added to meatloaf or salmon patties or as a topping for casseroles. Almost anything, in fact, that calls for bread crumbs, would benefit from the kick of Cajun spices.

Cajun-Spiced Chicken Nuggets

Preparation time: 15 minutes
Cooking time: 10 minutes
Yield: 4 servings

BREADING:
- 3 *slices good-quality fresh white bread (3 ounces total)*
- 1 *large egg white*
- 1 *small garlic clove, peeled*
- 1 *tablespoon fresh parsley leaves*
- ¾ *teaspoon Hungarian sweet paprika*
- ½ *teaspoon cayenne pepper*
- ¼ *teaspoon ground thyme*
- ¼ *teaspoon dried basil*
- ¼ *teaspoon salt*

CHICKEN:
- 2 *whole boneless chicken breasts, split (about 1¾ pounds total)*
- 2 *tablespoons water*
- 1½ *tablespoons Dijon mustard*
  Vegetable oil, for frying

1. To make the bread crumbs, break the bread into quarters and put it in a food processor or blender. Mix the egg white with a fork and measure out 2 teaspoons to use in the crumbs. (Reserve the rest for another use or discard.) Add the 2 teaspoons egg white, garlic, parsley, paprika, cayenne pepper, thyme, basil and salt to the bread and run the machine until the bread is finely crumbed. The crumbs can be used right away or refrigerated in an airtight plastic bag for several days.

2. Remove the skin and fat from the chicken. Cut crosswise into ¾-inch strips.

3. Put the water and mustard in a pie plate or shallow dish and the bread crumbs on a large piece of waxed paper. Using a pair of tongs, dip each piece of chicken in the mustard mixture, then the bread crumbs, making sure all are fully coated. Gently pat the crumbs in place if they seem loose, but do not compact them too much. Arrange on a baking sheet lined with waxed paper.

4. Heat oil to a depth of ¼ inch in a large skillet. When it is hot enough to make a bread crumb sizzle, add the nuggets, placing them so they do not touch each other. Do not overcrowd the skillet—cook the pieces in batches, if necessary, turning once with tongs, until they are crisp and golden. Drain on paper toweling. Keep warm in a 250-degree oven while cooking additional batches. The nuggets can be served warm or at room temperature. It's best not to refrigerate them, since they'll lose their crispness, but they can be fried several hours in advance and held at room temperature. Reheat in a 400-degree oven for 6 minutes.

These have the same can't-stop-eating-them appeal of potato chips. Only they're better. Much better. And different, too. Chunky rounds of potatoes are baked so they're crisp outside, creamy and a little bit chewy inside. The sauces are purely for the sake of indulgence, turning a humble potato into a feast.

Southwestern Potato Slices

Preparation time: 10 minutes
Baking time: 25 to 27 minutes
Yield: 6 servings

1. 15 minutes before baking, place rack in center of oven and preheat to 450 degrees. Have 2 baking sheets ready.

2. Scrub the potatoes and cut them crosswise into ¼-inch slices, either with the thick (6mm) slicer of a food processor or by hand. Transfer to a bowl and toss first with the oil, then the cumin and salt. Spread in a single layer on the baking sheets.

3. Bake until light brown on the bottom, about 17 minutes. Turn with a spatula and cook until they are crisp and browned on both sides, 8 to 10 minutes longer. Serve hot.

The potatoes can be served as canapés, arranged in rows on a platter. Garnish the first row with guacamole, the second with salsa, the third with sour cream and so on. Or, serve the potatoes from a basket as chips, with the three garnishes offered in individual dishes.

6   medium Idaho potatoes
    (2¼ pounds total)
3   tablespoons safflower oil
1½ teaspoons ground cumin
1   teaspoon salt
    Guacamole (recipe
    follows)
    Salsa Cruda (see page
    332)
    Sour cream
    Cilantro leaves, for
    garnish

Guacamole

Preparation time: 10 minutes
Yield: 2½ cups

3 tablespoons cilantro leaves
1 jalapeño or serrano
   pepper, seeds and ribs
   removed
1 small piece onion (use ½
   ounce), peeled
3 very ripe dark-skinned
   avocados (1¼ pounds
   total)
1 to 1½ teaspoons fresh lime
   juice
   Salt

Mince the cilantro, hot pepper and onion together in a food processor or by hand. Add the avocados and mash to a chunky texture; do not overprocess. If you're using a processor, pulse it on and off. By hand, mash with the back of a fork. Add the lime juice and salt to taste. Guacamole should be made close to serving time. For short-term refrigeration, put it in a small bowl and place plastic wrap directly against its surface. Stir before using.

◆

Simple ingredients combine here to great effect, in both a visual and taste sense. Plum tomatoes are arranged over a cushion of soft cheese, then dappled with a Southwestern-inspired herbed oil. I've used frozen puff pastry to eliminate some of the work. Rolling it out is really the most time-consuming part of the recipe, and even that takes just minutes.

Tomato Cheese Tart

Preparation time: 20 minutes
Baking time: 25 to 30 minutes
Yield: 40 2-inch squares

¾ cup cilantro leaves
1 teaspoon cumin seeds
1 teaspoon dried oregano
1 teaspoon rubbed sage
2 medium garlic cloves,
   peeled
1 jalapeño pepper, seeded
⅓ cup light-tasting olive oil
1 teaspoon salt, or to taste
   Freshly ground black
   pepper

1. 15 minutes before baking, place rack in center of oven and preheat oven to 400 degrees.
2. Mince cilantro, cumin, oregano, sage, garlic and jalapeño pepper in a food processor or by hand. Mix with the oil, salt and pepper and set aside.
3. Shred the cheese in a processor or with a grater. Core tomatoes and cut them into ⅜-inch slices either with the all-purpose (4mm) slicer of a processor or by hand. If tomatoes are very ripe, it's best to slice them by hand.
4. Roll the puff pastry on a floured board to a 13-inch by 17-inch rectangle. Place in an ungreased 11½-inch by 15½-inch

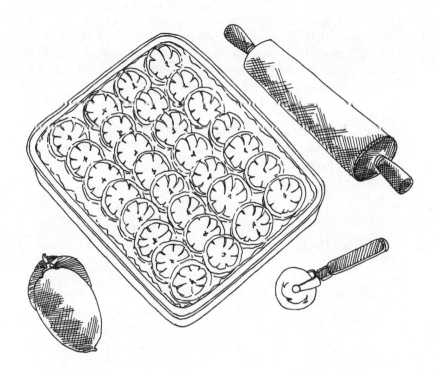

jelly roll pan and press lightly into the corners and up the sides of the pan. Roll the rolling pin over the top to cut away any excess dough.

    5. Brush mustard evenly over rolled dough, then sprinkle with cheese. Arrange tomatoes in slightly overlapping rows and brush with oil mixture.

    6. Bake until pastry is well browned, 25 to 30 minutes. Let rest for 5 minutes, then cut into 2-inch squares. A pizza cutter is good for this. Serve hot or at room temperature. Tart can be made a day in advance and refrigerated. To reheat, put pan in a cold oven and turn it to 350 degrees. Bake until heated through, about 15 minutes.

14 *ounces Monterey Jack cheese*

 6 *large plum tomatoes (1½ pounds total)*

 1 *sheet frozen puff pastry dough (8 to 8½ ounces), thawed*

2½ *tablespoons Dijon mustard*

One of my favorite impromptu lunches is a flour tortilla folded over some shredded cheese and cilantro, then baked so the cheese gets all gooey. Hardly unique, the same idea is seen all over Mexico, going by the name of *quesadillas*. Here is a clever appetizer version, adapted from that served at Trumps Restaurant in Los Angeles, where the sweetness of sliced grapes (yes, grapes) eases the richness of the cheese. Instead of being baked, these are sautéed so the edges are crisp and perfectly golden. I've also used papaya instead of grapes, with great success. The Sweet Pea Guacamole is heavenly with these quesadillas, and so, too, is a more typical guacamole made from avocados.

California Quesadillas

Preparation time: 10 minutes
Cooking time: 15 minutes
Yield: 6 to 8 servings

20 large tart seedless red or green grapes
1¼ pounds Monterey Jack cheese, chilled
10 7¼-inch flour tortillas
    Vegetable oil, for frying
    Sweet Pea Guacamole (recipe follows)
½ cup sour cream
10 sprigs fresh cilantro for garnish

1. Slice the grapes, either with the thick (6mm) slicer of a food processor or by hand. Set aside. Shred the cheese in the processor or with a grater.

2. Divide the cheese and grapes in an even layer among 5 tortillas, leaving a ½-inch border at the edge. Top each with another tortilla and press lightly to compress. The edges won't seal, but should stick together a bit.

3. Heat a thin film of oil in a large griddle or skillet over medium heat. When it is hot, cook the quesadillas, one at a time, turning once, until they are lightly browned on both sides, about 2 minutes total. Add more oil as necessary. Keep them warm in a 200-degree oven while you cook the rest.

4. To serve, cut each quesadilla into quarters or eighths with kitchen shears. Top each with a dollop of Sweet Pea Guacamole, 1 teaspoon sour cream and a sprig or leaf of cilantro.

Avocados have nothing over peas when it comes to guacamole, something you'll believe when you taste this rendition from chef Michael Roberts, owner of Trumps Restaurant in Los Angeles. With the sweet pea switch, you'll never again be dependent on unripe avocados. Creamy, smooth and sweet, this clever take-off stays bright green for several days. Don't use the more expensive tiny peas in this recipe. The larger ones work better since they have a greater flesh-to-skin ratio. Roberts serves this with California Quesadillas (see previous recipe). Home-fried corn tortilla chips are terrific, too.

Sweet Pea Guacamole

Preparation time: 15 minutes
Yield: 1¼ cups

1. Cook peas according to package instructions. Drain well and pat with paper towels to remove as much moisture as possible.

2. Mince the pepper in a food processor or blender. Scrape down the sides of the container, add oil and 1½ teaspoons lemon juice, and let machine run until pepper is even more finely minced. Add peas, cumin and salt and puree about 2 minutes, stopping several times to scrape down the sides of the container. Transfer to a small bowl.

3. Cut the onion into small dice and add to the pea mixture. Cover tightly and chill thoroughly up to 2 days before serving. Adjust the seasoning and lemon juice at serving time if necessary.

1 box (10 ounces) frozen peas
1 jalapeño pepper, seeded if desired
¼ cup extra-virgin olive oil
1½ to 2 teaspoons fresh lemon juice
¼ teaspoon ground cumin
¼ teaspoon salt
1-inch square red onion, peeled

Polenta, actually cooked cornmeal cereal, is country Italian food at its best—simple, rustic and sublime. Here, it is covered with cheese and coarsely cracked black pepper, making it an ideal nibble. Corn grits are coarser than yellow cornmeal and give the polenta more texture, which I like. Look for grits in health food or grocery stores that sell products in bulk. If you can't find them, use yellow cornmeal. Both are inexpensive ingredients that go a deliciously long way.

Polenta with Cheese and Cracked Peppercorns

Preparation time: 10 minutes
Cooking time: 12 minutes (Microwave: 14 minutes) + cooling time
Baking time: 10 minutes (Microwave: 4 minutes)
Yield: 32 triangles

2¼ cups water
3 tablespoons light-tasting olive oil
1 teaspoon salt
¾ cup yellow corn grits or cornmeal (3¼ ounces)
2½ tablespoons unsalted butter
3 ounces imported Parmesan (or cheese of your choice)
½ to ¾ teaspoon coarsely cracked black peppercorns

1. Butter a 9-inch square pan.
2. Bring the water, oil and salt to a boil in a 2½-quart pan. Whisk in the grits or cornmeal in a thin stream. Reduce the heat to low and cook, stirring occasionally, until the mixture has thick-

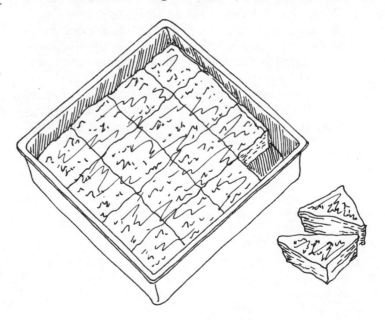

ened and there is a thin film on the bottom of the pan, 6 to 7 minutes. Off the heat, add the butter and stir until melted.

3. Pour the polenta into the prepared pan and smooth the surface with a spatula.

4. Mince or shred the cheese in a food processor or grate on the fine side of a grater. Sprinkle cheese over the top, then the pepper. Cool to room temperature. The polenta can be made in advance, covered tightly and refrigerated for up to 2 days, or frozen.

5. 15 minutes before baking, place the rack in the center of the oven and preheat oven to 400 degrees.

6. Cut polenta into 2-inch squares and transfer to a baking sheet. Cut the squares in half diagonally.

7. Bake until the cheese is soft, about 10 minutes, or 15 minutes if frozen. Serve hot or at room temperature.

MICROWAVE: Butter a 9-inch square microwave pan. Omit steps 1 and 2 above. Combine the water, oil, salt and grits in a 3-quart microwave casserole. Cover tightly with plastic wrap and pierce the plastic with a sharp knife so steam can escape. Cook on high power (100%) until thick, about 14 minutes, stirring once halfway through. Remove from the oven, add the butter, and stir until melted. Follow steps 3 and 4. Omit 5, 6 and 7. Cut into 2-inch squares and transfer to a microwave-safe plate. Cut in half diagonally. Cook, uncovered, on medium power (50%) until cheese is softened, but not runny, 3 to 4 minutes. Let rest 5 minutes before serving.

3 · Soups to Satisfy

At its very best, food is meant to gratify and soothe. Thus considered, soup never fails to succeed. I am totally captivated by the seemingly simple charms of soup, both the ritual of making it and the ultimate reward of eating it. Whether set out for supper in a tureen with a loaf of bread and wedges of cheese or poured into a thermos for a workday lunch, soup is always welcome and always appropriate.

Soups take on countless assorted forms, from a light vegetable puree to a substantial meal-in-a-bowl or a cup of icy-cold refreshment on a sweltering summer day. With so many guises, soup can be considered for almost any type of meal. While it is less common now, though still appropriate, to offer a separate soup course, informal styles of entertaining also encourage serving soup as the meal itself. And for those coming home after a long day at work, the satisfaction found in a bowl of soup is always welcome.

Making soup is easy and infinitely variable. For saving time, the food processor is terrific for soup-making chores, as many soups require lots of chopped, minced and sliced vegetables, a task that I gladly hand over to faster, more skilled "hands" than my own. Processors are great for just that. And if cooked vegetables are puréed into the broth, the processor is the best piece of equipment to handle that job. Blenders work well, too, except their capacity is smaller so it's necessary to puree in batches.

The soup kettle, in addition to being useful for turning leftovers into tasty soups, can also be a vehicle for indulging creative and seasonal whims. If turnips look better than parsnips, then feel free to make the change. The soup will have a subtly different character, unique and delicious in its own right. I have included the weights of the vegetables so adjustments are easy. Herbs are often interchangeable and a dash of spice adds its own stamp.

Most soups can be made ahead of time and reheated. A typical scenario may be to make a pot of soup on Sunday afternoon, then parlay it into several meals throughout the week. I'm eternally grateful to find soups tucked away in the freezer as well, especially in winter when their charms are all the more appealing.

In most soup recipes, making soup in the microwave oven takes more time than stove-top cooking and does not re-create the deep, rich flavors that come from long simmering. There are several recipes in this chapter where the microwave oven is a viable cooking alternative, but most often, it simply does not make sense. Reheating soups is another story. It is a pleasure to be able to ladle soup into bowls and reheat them in the microwave in just a few short minutes without even dirtying a pan.

If you're an avid soup maker, a pressure cooker is the equipment of choice. Pressure cookers have been vastly improved over the years and are now safe, quiet and odorless. They cook soup in a fraction of the time needed with an ordinary soup pot and produce the most wonderful, velvety purées and well-developed flavors.

In most cases, homemade stocks are not essential in making good soups. Canned broths are quite acceptable. In fact, the two are used interchangeably in these recipes. Homemade stocks lend richness and body that canned broths can't match, but the convenience of canned broths makes them an appealing choice. I find that most canned broths are somewhat saltier than I like, but that can usually be corrected by not adding any more salt to the soup. Canned broths can also be diluted with water to dissipate the saltiness. I'm most likely to do this when the soup base is just broth, without a vegetable purée or cream in it.

If you decide to prepare homemade stock, you'll be surprised to find that it is easy, with little hands-on attention. There are recipes for all the major types in the Basics chapter that produce pure, well-flavored stocks with no salt. The amount of bones needed and the lengthy cooking can make it look like a task of megalithic proportions, but it's not. A large stock pot is essential, though. It's not worth the effort of making a small recipe of stock since the yield is surprisingly small considering what you start out with. Most of the cooking is gentle, unattended simmering so you can go about your normal routine as the stock cooks, just checking in periodically. Stocks freeze very well, so you'll reap the benefits many times over.

Many treasured recipes are inspired by a celebrated chef or a new and innovative one; others come from the annals of classic cooking. Then there are those that come from pure ingenuity, the kind that's generated by what the cupboard and refrigerator have to offer. Such is the provenance of this soup, one of my favorites. Two humble root vegetables join forces in what I find to be a most harmonious combination.

Silky Carrot and Sweet Potato Soup

Preparation time: 15 minutes
Cooking time: 25 minutes
Yield: 8 cups

4 large shallots (2 ounces total), peeled
1 pound carrots, peeled
1 pound sweet potatoes, peeled
6 cups chicken stock (see page 339) or canned broth
1 teaspoon ground coriander
½ teaspoon ground ginger
Salt
Freshly ground white pepper
⅓ cup sour cream

1. Cut the shallots, carrots and sweet potatoes into very thin slices. This can be done with the thin (2mm) or medium (3mm) slicer of a food processor or by hand. Thinner slices will cook more quickly.

2. Put the vegetables in a 4-quart pan with the stock or broth, coriander, ginger, salt and pepper. Cover and bring to a boil. Reduce the heat and simmer until the vegetables are very soft, about 20 minutes from when the broth began to boil, or longer if the vegetables are thicker.

3. Strain the solids from the liquid, reserving both. Purée the solids in the processor or in batches in a blender, until completely smooth, about 2 minutes. Add the sour cream and mix until smooth.

4. Stir the puree into the cooking liquid and adjust the seasoning. Serve hot or chilled. The soup can be refrigerated for several days or frozen.

Fresh dill and mint are a delicious and invigorating mix of herbal essences that enhance the flavor of sweet peas. This sprightly green soup is light and refreshing, a welcome elixir on warm spring-into-summer days.

Garden Herb Pea Soup

Preparation time: 20 minutes
Cooking time: 25 minutes
Chilling time: Several hours
Yield: 4 cups

1. Mince the onion in a food processor or by hand.

2. Melt the butter in a 2½-quart pan. Add the onion and cook over medium heat until it is soft, about 5 minutes.

3. Add the peas and chicken stock or broth and bring to a boil. Cover and cook gently for 20 minutes.

4. Strain the vegetables from the cooking liquid, reserving both. Purée the vegetables, dill and mint in a processor or blender. Strain the puree, either through a food mill, a fine-mesh strainer or with the strainer attachment of a mixer or processor.

5. Stir the strained puree into the cooking liquid and add the half-and-half, salt, pepper and nutmeg. Chill before serving, or for up to 2 days. Before serving, adjust the seasoning and garnish each serving with a sprig of dill.

1 medium onion (4 ounces), peeled
2 tablespoons unsalted butter
2 boxes (10 ounces each) frozen peas
1¾ cups chicken stock (see page 339) or canned broth
½ cup fresh dill
½ cup fresh mint
1 cup half-and-half
Salt
Freshly ground white pepper
Freshly grated nutmeg
Fresh dill sprigs, for garnish

This milky-white soup is rich and soothing, as though it were amply endowed with cream. In truth, there's not a drop, only lots of low-calorie, high-impact vegetables. Parsnips are used as a body builder, adding a velvety finish and a hint of sweetness to the delicately flavored fennel.

Winter White Fennel Bisque

Preparation time: 10 minutes
Cooking time: 40 minutes
Yield: 6 cups

1 medium onion (4 ounces), peeled
1 tablespoon unsalted butter
2 large fennel bulbs (1¾ pounds total)
2 small parsnips (5 ounces total), peeled
2½ to 3 cups chicken stock (see page 339) or canned broth
Salt
Freshly ground white pepper

1. Cut the onion into very thin slices, with the thin (2mm) slicer of a food processor or by hand. Thinner slices will cook more quickly.

2. Melt the butter in a 3-quart pan. Add the onion and cook gently until it is soft, about 10 minutes.

3. Trim about ¼ of the feathery greens from the fennel and reserve as a garnish for the soup. Remove the slender stalks and the rest of the greens from the fennel, leaving only the bulb. Slice the fennel bulb and the parsnips as you did the onions.

4. Add the fennel and parsnips to the pan along with 2½ cups stock or broth. Cover and bring to a boil. When the mixture is boiling, reduce the heat and simmer until all the vegetables are very soft, about 25 minutes.

5. Strain the vegetables from the liquid, reserving both. Purée the vegetables and the reserved fennel greens in the processor or in batches in a blender.

6. Stir the puree into the cooking liquid and thin with additional broth if the soup is too thick. Add salt and pepper. The soup can be refrigerated up to 3 days, or frozen. Reheat gently and adjust the seasoning, if necessary, before serving.

I have a list of favorite eggplant recipes almost as long as my arm. High among them is this robust, nicely spiced soup in which I revel on cool fall days. The eggplant thickens the soup, giving it fullness and body, while sweet red peppers counteract any hint of bitterness. The hot pepper and curry powder turn up the temperature somewhat, though certainly not to the three-alarm level. Adjust them to your liking.

Curried Eggplant Soup

Preparation time: 15 minutes
Cooking time: 35 minutes
Yield: 7 cups

1. Mince the garlic and hot pepper in a food processor or blender. Chop the onion and red bell pepper in the processor or by hand. Trim the eggplants and cut them into ¾-inch cubes, without peeling them.

2. Heat the oil in a 3-quart pan. Add the garlic, hot pepper, onion, red bell pepper and curry. Cook over medium heat, stirring occasionally, until the onions and peppers are soft, about 6 minutes. Add the eggplant and cook 3 more minutes.

3. Add the stock or broth and water and heat to the boil. Cover and cook until all the vegetables are very soft, about 20 minutes.

4. Strain the solids from the liquid, reserving both. Purée the solids in the processor or in batches in a blender until smooth, about 2 minutes. Stir the puree into the cooking liquid. Strain, then add the cream. The soup can be served hot or cold. It will last in the refrigerator for up to 4 days and freezes well.

2 *large garlic cloves, peeled*
1 *jalapeño or serrano pepper*
1 *large onion (8 ounces), peeled*
1 *medium red bell pepper (6 ounces)*
2 *medium eggplants (1½ pounds total)*
3 *tablespoons light-tasting olive oil*
4 *teaspoons curry powder, or to taste*
3⅓ *cups chicken stock (see page 339) or canned broth*
1 *cup water*
⅓ *cup whipping cream*

Lentil soup—or just about any soup made from legumes—has the potential for being too heavy for my taste. This one avoids that pitfall yet still serves as a potent elixir. I've used many different types of sausage and have finally decided that *andouille,* the marvelously spicy Cajun sausage, is my favorite for this soup. It is hard to find, though, so be assured that kielbasa, Thuringer, even smoked bratwurst, are delicious. And if you're off sausage entirely, dice 2 whole chicken breasts and add them with the celery along with a pinch of crushed red pepper flakes.

_____Lentil Soup with Sausage and Swiss Chard_____

Preparation time: 20 minutes
Cooking time: 45 minutes
Yield: 8 cups

1	large garlic clove, peeled
2	medium leeks (10 ounces total)
2	tablespoons light-tasting olive oil
6	cups chicken stock (see page 339) or canned broth
⅔	cup lentils (4½ ounces)
⅓	cup tomato paste
1	tablespoon light brown sugar
2	bay leaves
1½	teaspoons dried thyme
6	small celery stalks (12 ounces total)
12	ounces smoked sausage
6	ounces Swiss chard or spinach
	Salt
	Freshly ground black pepper

1. Mince the garlic in a food processor or by hand. Cut the leeks into ¼-inch slices, with the all-purpose (4mm) slicer of a processor or by hand.

2. Heat the oil in a 4-quart pan. When it is hot, add the garlic and leeks and cook over medium heat until softened, about 4 minutes.

3. Add the stock or broth, lentils, tomato paste, sugar, bay leaves and thyme. Cover and cook until the lentils are almost tender, about 35 minutes.

4. Cut the celery into ¼-inch slices as you did the leeks. Cut the sausage into ¾-inch slices.

5. Add the celery and sausage to the soup and continue to cook until the celery is tender, about 10 minutes longer.

6. Cut the stems and leaves of the chard, or the spinach leaves, into ¼-inch slices. Stir into the soup and remove the pan from the heat. Add salt and pepper to taste. The soup can be refrigerated for up to 4 days, or frozen. Reheat and adjust the seasoning, if necessary, before serving.

◆

This is a fall favorite of mine, the first soup I'm apt to think of when the air turns cool. Unlike most broccoli soups, this one is very light, yet satisfying just the same. A confetti of vitamin-packed vegetables colors and flavors the milky broth that forms the base of the soup. While many soups freeze well, this one doesn't, though it can be refrigerated for several days.

Broccoli Soup with Red Peppers and Mushrooms

Preparation time: 15 minutes
Cooking time: 25 minutes (Microwave: 15 minutes)
Yield: 6 cups

1. Mince the onion and celery in a food processor or by hand.

2. Melt the butter in a 4-quart pan. Add the onion and celery and cook over medium heat until soft, about 5 minutes. Stir in the flour and cook 1 minute, stirring often so it does not brown.

3. Roughly chop the broccoli in the processor or by hand. Cut the red pepper and mushrooms into ¼-inch dice.

4. Add the broccoli to the pan along with the stock or broth, curry powder, tarragon, salt and pepper. Bring to a boil, then cook, uncovered, until the broccoli is tender, about 10 minutes.

5. Add the red peppers and mushrooms and continue to cook just until the peppers begin to soften, about 4 minutes longer. Add the cream and cook gently until heated through. Do not boil after the cream is added or it will curdle. Serve immediately or refrigerate up to 3 days. Reheat gently and adjust the seasoning before serving.

MICROWAVE: Follow step 1 above. Put butter, onion and celery in a 2-quart microwave casserole. Cover tightly with plastic

1 *small onion (3 ounces), peeled*
1 *medium stalk celery (2 ounces)*
1½ *tablespoons unsalted butter*
3 *tablespoons unbleached all-purpose flour*
1 *medium stalk broccoli (10 ounces)*
1 *medium red pepper (6 ounces)*
5 *medium-sized mushrooms (2½ ounces total)*
3½ *cups chicken stock (see page 339) or canned broth*
¾ *teaspoon curry powder*
½ *teaspoon dried tarragon*
   Salt
   Freshly ground white pepper
1 *cup whipping cream*

wrap and pierce the plastic with a sharp knife so steam can escape. Cook on high power (100%) for 3 minutes. Stir in flour and cook, uncovered, for 1 minute. Follow step 3 above. Add broccoli and only 2 cups of stock or broth and the seasonings. Cover and cook on high power (100%) until broccoli is tender, 7 minutes. Add the red pepper and mushrooms, cover and cook on high power (100%) until peppers are softened, 4 minutes. Add cream and remaining stock or broth and cook until heated through, 1 to 2 minutes.

◆

Sweet potatoes are used to enrich this chowder, sans cream, and color it a deep, sprightly orange. Hominy and big chunks of chicken add substance, while fresh cilantro and hot peppers lend Southwestern sparkle. Given its hearty nature, this soup is best used as a main dish, served with a basket of warmed flour tortillas or corn muffins.

Runaway Ranch Chicken Chowder

3 whole boneless chicken breasts (1¾ pounds), split

3 tablespoons unsalted butter

1 medium onion (5 ounces), peeled

1 large sweet potato (12 ounces), peeled

4½ to 4¾ cups chicken stock (see page 339) or canned broth

2 serrano peppers, seeded

½ teaspoon ground coriander

¼ teaspoon ground cumin

1 can (16 ounces) hominy, drained

⅔ cup fresh cilantro leaves Sour cream, if desired, as garnish

Preparation time: 15 minutes
Cooking time: 40 minutes
Yield: 7 cups

1. Remove the skin and fat from the chicken. Cut the meat into ¾-inch cubes.

2. Melt the butter in a 5-quart pan. Add the chicken and cook over high heat, stirring often, until the meat is no longer pink. Be careful not to overcook it since it will continue to cook when it's returned to the soup. Remove from the pan with a slotted spoon and set aside.

3. Cut the onion and sweet potato into thin slices, either with the thin (2mm) or medium (3mm) slicer of a food processor or by hand. Thinner slices will cook more quickly.

4. Add them to the same pan along with 4½ cups of the stock or broth. Cover and bring to a boil. Reduce the heat and simmer until the vegetables are very soft, about 20 minutes.

5. Strain the solids from the liquid, reserving both. Puree the solids with the serrano peppers, coriander and cumin either in a processor or in batches in a blender.

6. Return the purée to the pan and add the cooking liquid, chicken and hominy. The soup can be prepared in advance to this point and refrigerated for up to 2 days or frozen. To serve, cook the soup just until heated through. Thin with the remaining broth if it is too thick. Add the cilantro leaves and adjust the seasoning just before serving. Garnish with sour cream, if desired.

◆

This is a very cool and refreshing soup, perfect to serve on sunny summer days. The buttermilk is lighter than cream and lends a sprightly tang to the sweet, succulent mangoes. There are many different types of mangoes, some juicier and more aromatic than others. The right ones will make a big difference—select soft mangoes with a sweet, flowery fragrance.

Orange Mango Soup

Preparation time: 10 minutes
Chilling time: Several hours
Yield: 4 cups

1. Remove the zest, the colored part only, from the orange with a zester or grater and set it aside. Cut a flat top and bottom on the orange. Stand it on a board and remove the white pith, cutting from top to bottom with a paring knife. Cut the orange into ⅛-inch slices and refrigerate them until serving time.

2. Peel the mangoes and cut the flesh away from the pits. Puree the flesh with the orange zest in a food processor or blender until smooth.

3. Transfer to a 1½-quart refrigerator container. Stir in the buttermilk, orange juice and honey. The soup should have the consistency of whipping cream. If it is too thick, add more buttermilk. Chill thoroughly, up to 2 days before serving.

4. Just before serving, adjust the tart/sweet balance by adding lemon juice and more honey, if necessary. Pour into chilled dishes. Float an orange slice on top and garnish with a mint leaf.

1 large navel orange
3 large, very ripe mangoes (2¼ pounds total)
1½ cups buttermilk
1½ cups orange juice
1 to 3 teaspoons honey
Fresh lemon juice, if necessary
8 small fresh mint leaves

With its Spanish origins, gazpacho has many of the same flavors found in Mexican cuisine. With that in mind, I've tampered with this classic summer soup by adding some of the Mexican ingredients I love so much. Three different kinds of peppers are used, from hot to sweet. Some are roasted, some not, so they add textural contrast and lots of flavor. Include some cooked shrimp, scallops or lobster if you want to turn the soup into a more substantial main course for summer.

Flamenco Pepper Gazpacho

Preparation time: 25 minutes
Chilling time: Several hours
Yield: 10 cups

1½ cups cilantro leaves
1 large garlic clove, peeled
1 to 3 jalapeño peppers, seeded if desired
1 large yellow pepper (6 ounces)
1 small cucumber (10 ounces)
3 medium tomatoes (1 pound total)
2 large stalks celery (6 ounces total)
2 large red peppers (12 ounces total), roasted (see page 336)
1 large poblano pepper (3 ounces), roasted (see page 336)
1 medium red onion (5 ounces)
1 can (46 ounces) tomato juice
½ cup catsup
2 tablespoons red wine vinegar
½ teaspoon salt

1. Mince the cilantro, garlic and jalapeño peppers in a food processor or by hand. Transfer to a large bowl.

2. Remove the seeds and membrane from the yellow pepper. Seed the cucumber. Remove the seeds and all membrane from the inside of the tomatoes. (When good, locally grown tomatoes are available, just remove the seeds.) Split the celery lengthwise into ¼-inch strips.

3. Cut these vegetables plus the red and poblano peppers and the onion into small, uniform dice, about ¼-inch. Add to the bowl.

4. Add the tomato juice, catsup, vinegar and salt and stir to combine. Refrigerate until well chilled, up to 4 days. Adjust the seasoning before serving, if necessary.

As I thought of what I like about chili—the gutsy, rich flavor, fiery spicy bite, the complexity of long-simmered ingredients—it occurred to me that not one of them had anything to do with meat. So, here you have it, a robust chili, chock-full of beans, vegetables and wheat berries and not an iota of meat. You won't miss it a bit. Serve it in big bowls, or try it over pasta shells, corn bread or polenta.

Chili Non Carne

Preparation time: 20 minutes
Cooking time: 1 hour, 10 minutes
Yield: 3 quarts

1. Seed the hot pepper if desired. Mince the hot pepper, garlic and onions in a food processor or by hand.

2. Heat the oil in a 5-quart pan. Add the minced vegetables and the wheat berries. Cook gently until the onions are soft, about 5 minutes.

3. Meanwhile, roughly chop the carrots and bell peppers, either in batches in a processor or by hand.

4. Add the carrots, peppers and juice from the tomatoes to pan. Roughly chop the tomatoes and add them to the pan along with the tomato paste and seasonings. Simmer, uncovered, until the wheat berries are soft, but still chewy, about 45 minutes.

5. Rinse both cans of beans under cold water and drain well. Quarter the mushrooms. Add beans and mushrooms to pan and cook until flavors are blended, about 15 minutes longer. Serve immediately or refrigerate up to 4 days. Reheat and adjust seasonings, if necessary, before serving. Serve with cheese and sour cream.

Note: Wheat berries add a nice, chewy bite to the chili. They are available at health food stores. If you are unable to locate them, they can be omitted.

1 *serrano or jalapeño pepper*
1 *large garlic clove, peeled*
2 *large red onions (12 ounces total), peeled*
3 *tablespoons light-tasting olive oil*
½ *cup wheat berries (see Note)*
2 *medium carrots (5 ounces), peeled*
2 *medium bell peppers (12 ounces total), preferably 1 red and 1 green*
2 *cans (28 ounces each) plum tomatoes*
1 *can (6 ounces) tomato paste*
2 *teaspoons dried oregano*
2 *teaspoons ground cumin*
½ *teaspoon salt*
½ *teaspoon cayenne pepper*
2 *cans (15 ounces each) kidney or pinto beans, or 1 can of each*
4 *ounces mushrooms*

GARNISH:
Shredded longhorn or Colby cheese
Sour cream

Though this hearty soup is far from being 100 percent authentic, I have no doubts that everyone will give it an enthusiastic thumbs up when it's tasted. It's a light broth filled to capacity with a garden of fresh vegetables, little meatballs and cheese-filled pasta. It's not one of those soups that needs a long simmer to develop its character. Once it's in the pot, it cooks in a snappy 25 minutes.

—— Italian Meatball Soup with Tortellini ——

Preparation time: 20 minutes
Cooking time: 25 minutes
Yield: 9 cups

MEATBALLS:

1½ ounces Parmesan cheese, preferably imported
1 slice white bread
1 small onion (1½ ounces), peeled
3 tablespoons milk
¼ teaspoon salt
8 ounces ground meat, preferably a mix of beef, pork and veal

SOUP:

2 small onions (3 ounces total), peeled
2 small carrots (3 ounces total), peeled
4½ cups chicken stock (see page 339) or canned broth
¾ cup fresh or frozen cheese-filled tortellini
1½ teaspoons dried basil
⅛ teaspoon crushed red pepper flakes
1 small zucchini (3 ounces)
3 ounces Swiss chard or spinach
Freshly ground black pepper

1. For the meatballs: Mince the cheese, bread and onion in a food processor or blender. Add the milk, salt and, if you are using a processor, the meat. Mix just until combined. If you're using a blender, transfer the cheese mixture to a bowl and mix in the meat by hand with a fork. Roll into 25 small meatballs.

2. For the soup: Cut the onions and carrots into ¼-inch slices with the all-purpose (4mm) slicer of a processor, or by hand. Transfer to a 4-quart pan and add the stock or broth, tortellini, basil and pepper flakes. Heat to a boil, then reduce to a simmer and add the meatballs. Cook until the tortellini are almost tender, about 10 minutes, depending on the type of tortellini you're using. Some brands may take longer.

3. While the soup is cooking, cut the zucchini and chard or spinach into ¼-inch slices with the all-purpose (4mm) slicer of a processor, or by hand. Add them to the pan and cook until tortellini are tender, 3 to 4 more minutes. Add ground pepper and adjust the seasoning. The soup can be made up to 3 days in advance and reheated. Thin with water if it is too thick.

Cabbage is one of my favorite vegetables. I love its earthy taste and marvel at how well it melds with other flavors. Here, tart apples and smoky undertones of bacon are its enhancements in the soup pot. The result? A substantial soup that is a pure comfort on blustery days. This is one soup that can be made in the microwave oven with a significant saving in cooking time.

Cabbage and Apple Chowder

Preparation time: 20 minutes
Cooking time: 45 minutes (Microwave: 26 minutes)
Yield: 6½ cups

1. Cut the onion, apples and potato into very thin slices, either with the thin (2mm) or medium (3mm) slicer of a food processor, or by hand. Thinner slices will cook more quickly.

2. Melt the butter in a 4-quart pan. Add the onion, apples and potato, cover and cook over high heat, stirring occasionally, until they begin to soften, about 7 minutes. Add 2 cups of the stock or broth and bring to a boil. Cover and cook until all the ingredients are very soft, about 20 minutes.

3. Strain the solids from the liquid, reserving both. Puree the solids with the parsley in a food processor, or in batches in a blender, until completely smooth, about 2 minutes.

4. Cut the bacon into ½-inch pieces. Core the cabbage and cut into ½-inch slices either with the all-purpose (4mm) slicer of a processor, or by hand.

5. Cook the bacon in same pan as the vegetables and stock, until it is crisp. Add the cabbage and cook over medium-high heat until it begins to soften, about 8 minutes. Add the puree, the cooking liquid, 2 cups stock or broth, salt and pepper, and cook until heated through. Serve hot. The soup can be made 2 days in advance. Reheat gently and adjust the seasoning before serving.

MICROWAVE: Follow step 1. Melt the butter in a 2-quart microwave casserole. Add apple, onion and potato, making sure none of the potato slices stick together. Cover tightly with plastic wrap and pierce the plastic with a sharp knife so steam can escape. Cook on high power (100%) for 2 minutes. Stir, then push the ingredients to the edge of the dish, leaving the center empty. Cover and cook 3 minutes more. Add 2 cups stock or broth, cover and cook on high power (100%) until the ingredients are very soft, 10 minutes. Follow steps 3 and 4. Cook the bacon in the

1 medium onion (4 ounces), peeled
2 medium tart apples (10 ounces total), peeled, cored
1 small Idaho potato (4 ounces), peeled
1½ tablespoons unsalted butter
3 to 4 cups chicken stock (see page 339) or canned broth
½ cup parsley leaves
2 ounces slab bacon
1 small head green cabbage (12 ounces)
   Salt
   Freshly ground white pepper

81 •

same pan on high power (100%) until browned, about 2 minutes. Add cabbage and cook, uncovered, on high power (100%) until wilted, about 6 minutes, stirring once halfway through. Add purée, 1 cup of stock or broth, cooking liquid, salt and pepper. Cook on high power (100%) until hot, 2 minutes. If the soup is too thick, add more broth. Serve hot.

◆

This is one of my favorites, a delicious and refreshingly down-to-earth fish soup. So often, recipes for fish soups ask you to get fish frames, with heads attached, to make stock and then go on from there. While making such a stock is a worthy endeavor, it's hardly something I think of making on a tight schedule. Instead, I turn to this quick tomato-based chowder. Its "stock" is made from bottled clam juice, a quick alternative. The orange rind and curry powder add an aromatic undertone to the soup, while the red bell pepper adds sweetness. If you're serving this for dinner, count on 2 generous servings. For a lighter meal, it will serve 3 to 4.

Bahamian Fish Chowder

Preparation time: 10 minutes
Cooking time: 20 minutes
Yield: 5 cups

1. Mince the garlic and onion in a food processor or by hand. Cut the red pepper into ¼-inch dice.

2. Heat the oil in a 4-quart pan. When it is hot, add the garlic, onion and red pepper and cook over medium heat, stirring occasionally, until the pepper is soft, about 10 minutes.

3. Drain the tomatoes and add the liquid to the pan. Coarsely chop the tomatoes in the processor or by hand. Add them to the pan along with the clam juice, orange zest, curry powder, salt and pepper. Bring to a boil over high heat, then cook, uncovered, for 5 minutes. The soup can be prepared in advance to this point and refrigerated for 3 days or frozen. Bring stored soup to a boil again before continuing with the recipe.

4. Cut the fish into 1-inch cubes. Lower the heat so the soup is at a simmer, and add the fish. Cover and cook just until the fish turns opaque, 2 to 3 minutes, shaking the pan several times rather than stirring, so the fish does not break up. Thin with additional clam juice or water if the broth is too thick. Remove from the heat and stir in the butter.

5. Cut the green onions into thin rings. Ladle soup into shallow soup bowls. Garnish with green onions and serve immediately.

Note: 1 pound of large shrimp or sea scallops or a combination of both can be used in place of the fish. Shell the shrimp, leaving the tail intact and remove the vein. Add shrimp and/or scallops to the soup and cook according to the method for the fish, as above.

1 small garlic clove, peeled
1 medium onion (4 ounces), peeled
1 medium red bell pepper (6 ounces)
2 tablespoons light-tasting olive oil
1 can (16 ounces) whole tomatoes
2 bottles (8 ounces each) clam juice
Zest of 1 orange, removed with a zester or grater
½ teaspoon curry powder
½ teaspoon salt
Freshly ground black pepper
1 pound firm white fish fillets (monkfish, snapper and sea bass are good)
1 tablespoon unsalted butter
4 large green onions (2 ounces total)

4·Significant Starters

In planning this chapter, I mused long and hard over the very nature of entertaining. There is no question that home entertaining has changed, evolved and become more of a personal statement. A new, casual approach is welcome and refreshing for it opens up so many possibilities. Yet at the same time, I am struck by how the more things change, the more they stay the same.

Formal entertaining is still practiced by many and is even enjoying a renaissance of sorts, introducing it to a whole new generation of hosts. China, silver and damask cloths are back, bringing with them the stated elegance of a multi-course sit-down dinner. Such meals are typically inaugurated with a separate first course. Besides their obvious role, first courses serve an important function that heightens their importance: they set the tone for the flow of the meal, so select them with a careful eye to the other courses and to the image you want to convey.

This collection of recipes is undeniably festive. Some may involve a bit more work than other recipes within these pages, but they are not difficult, and many can be made ahead of time. And all fit other menu slots as well. Consider them also as part of a light lunch or supper or as a selection of *tapas*. At the same time, don't limit your search for first courses to this chapter alone. The Pasta, Vegetable, Salad and Nibbles chapters all include dishes that can add sparkle to a special meal.

Tangy rounds of goat cheese are sautéed in olive oil, giving them a velvety, soft texture. The melted inside contrasts with a crisp sheath of bread crumbs on the outside. A pool of garlic-scented Marinara Sauce and a jade-green basil leaf set it off to perfection.

Fried Goat Cheese With Italian Tomato Sauce

Preparation time: 10 minutes
Cooking time: 5 minutes
Yield: 4 servings

1. Reheat the Italian Tomato Sauce on the stove or in the microwave oven.

2. Cut the cheese into 8 equal-sized disks.

3. Beat the egg in a small dish. Put the bread crumbs in another dish. Dip the cheese first in the egg, then in the bread crumbs.

4. Heat the oil in a large skillet. When it is hot, add the cheese and cook, turning once, until very lightly browned, about 2-3 minutes. Do not cook too much or the cheese will melt through the bread crumbs. Drain on paper toweling. The cheese can be sautéed several hours in advance and held at room temperature. Reheat in a preheated 350-degree oven for 5 to 7 minutes.

5. To serve, divide the sauce between 4 salad plates, spreading it in a pool over the bottom. Top with 2 disks of warm cheese and garnish with basil. Serve immediately.

1 *cup Italian Tomato Sauce (see page 226)*
1 *log soft goat cheese such as Montrachet or Lezay (4 ounces)*
1 *large egg*
¾ *cup soft bread crumbs*
1 *tablespoon light-tasting olive oil*
4 *fresh basil leaves for garnish*

Peruvian food isn't talked about too much in food circles, though frankly, I don't know why. As ethnic cuisines go, it's as interesting and varied as the best of them. Here, in a liberal adaptation of a Peruvian classic, sweet, meaty pieces of sea bass are marinated and tossed with a multicolored mix of sweet potatoes, corn and green onions.

_____Ceviche of Sea Bass with Corn and Sweet Potatoes

Preparation time: 20 minutes
Marinating time: 6 to 8 hours
Yield: 6 servings

2 serrano peppers, seeded
  Zest of 1 orange, removed
  with a zester or grater
1 large garlic clove, peeled
½ cup fresh lime juice
2 tablespoons sherry
  vinegar
1 teaspoon sugar
¾ teaspoon salt
12 ounces sea bass
1 medium sweet potato (12
  ounces), peeled
4 medium green onions
  (1½ ounces total)
2 tablespoons light-tasting
  olive oil
¾ cup fresh or frozen sweet
  corn kernels
½ cup cilantro leaves
2 tablespoons mayonnaise

1. Mince the peppers in a food processor or blender. Remove half the peppers and set aside. Add the orange zest and garlic to the half still in the container and mince. Mix in the lime juice, vinegar, sugar and ½ teaspoon salt. Transfer to a large plastic food bag.

2. Remove the skin from the fish and cut the flesh into ½-inch cubes. Add the fish to the marinade. Seal the bag tightly and turn it over several times so the fish is well coated with the marinade. Refrigerate for 6 to 8 hours.

3. Cut the sweet potato into ¼-inch dice. Cut the green onions into ¼-inch rings.

4. Heat the oil in an 8-inch skillet. When it is hot, add the sweet potatoes and cook, uncovered, stirring occasionally, just until they begin to soften, about 5 minutes. Add the green onions and corn and remove the skillet from the heat. Transfer the vegetables to a mixing bowl and let cool.

5. Drain the marinade from the fish. Add the fish to the vegetables along with the cilantro, mayonnaise, the rest of the minced hot pepper and the remaining ¼ teaspoon salt. Mix together gently. Serve immediately or cover tightly and refrigerate overnight. To serve, stir gently and adjust the seasoning if necessary.

MICROWAVE: Follow steps 1 through 3 above. The sweet potato can be cooked in the microwave oven. Combine the oil and sweet potato in a shallow 10-inch round microwave dish, stirring so the potato is coated with oil. Push to the edge of the dish, leaving the center empty. Cook, uncovered, on high power (100%) until the potato begins to soften, about 4 minutes, stirring twice. Remove from the oven and add the green onions and corn. Transfer to a mixing bowl and let cool. Finish step 5 above.

◆

These exotic rolls, called *goi cuon* in their native land, are cool in every sense of the word. Full of clear flavors, crisp textures and vibrant colors, they're very refreshing and don't require any cooking at all—a real plus in the summertime. They're rolled so that the curled shrimp show through the transparent rice papers, which makes for a very inviting presentation.

Vietnamese Shrimp Rice Paper Rolls

Preparation time: 20 minutes
Soaking time: 20 minutes
Yield: 6 servings

1. For the rolls, put the rice vermicelli in a 3-quart bowl and pour 3 cups boiling water over. Soak for 20 minutes to soften the noodles, then drain thoroughly. They can be soaked up to 3 days in advance and refrigerated in a plastic bag.

2. Fill a jelly roll pan with hot tap water. Moisten the rice papers by immersing them in the water for about 15 seconds. Transfer each one to a separate 12-inch piece of plastic wrap.

3. Mince the ginger in a food processor or by hand. Cut the green onions into thin rings. Split the shrimp in half lengthwise, cutting them through the back. Remove the thick center ribs from each lettuce leaf.

4. To assemble the rolls, arrange 4 shrimp halves across the center of each paper going from the 9 o'clock to the 3 o'clock position. Top with a lettuce leaf, with the stem end of the lettuce at the 6 o'clock position. The lettuce should be slightly smaller than the rice paper. Trim as necessary. Sprinkle with minced ginger followed by a portion of rice vermicelli, green onions, bean sprouts, mint and cilantro.

5. Using the plastic wrap to help you, fold the bottom half of the rice paper up over the filling. Then, roll them up as tight as possible, tucking in the filling as you go along. The rolls can be made several hours in advance and refrigerated.

6. For the sauce, combine the hoisin sauce, ⅓ cup of water,

ROLLS:
3 ounces rice vermicelli (see Note)
6 8-inch round rice papers (see Note)
1 piece fresh ginger (¾ inch by 1 inch), peeled
3 large green onions (2 ounces total)
12 large cooked, peeled shrimp
6 large leaves green leaf lettuce
1½ cups bean sprouts
24 fresh mint leaves
36 cilantro leaves

DIPPING SAUCE:
½ cup hoisin sauce
⅓ to ½ cup water
2 tablespoons plum sauce
½ to ¾ teaspoon chili paste (see Note)
⅓ cup unsalted dry roasted peanuts
1 large carrot (4 ounces)
6 large lettuce leaves

plum sauce and chili paste in a small bowl. Add more water if mixture is too thick. Coarsely mince the peanuts and shred the carrot in a processor or with a grater. Add the peanuts and carrots to the sauce just before serving.

7. To serve, unwrap the rolls and place on a lettuce-lined plate so the shrimp are facing up. Pass Dipping Sauce separately. To serve as hors d'oeuvres, carefully cut into thirds with a serrated knife.

Note: Rice vermicelli, rice papers and chili paste are available at Vietnamese, Thai and other Asian markets.

◆

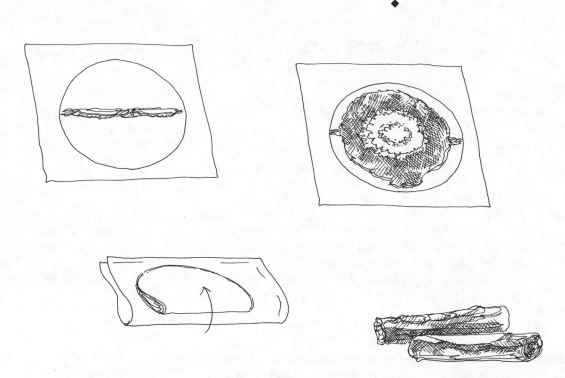

Shrimp is still one of the most popular seafood offerings for entertaining. Here, coral-colored shrimp, swathed in a light, herb-flecked dressing, are curled over a bed of fuchsia cabbage. Raspberry vinegar adds a lively and refreshing edge to both the shrimp and the cabbage. The overall effect is exciting, both visually and in taste.

Herbed Shrimp on Spicy Red Cabbage

Preparation time: 20 minutes
Cooking time: 6 minutes (Microwave: 5½ minutes)
Marinating time: 4 hours or overnight
Yield: 6 servings

1. Peel the shrimp, leaving the tail intact. Slit down the back and remove the black vein. Rinse and pat dry.

2. Mince the jalapeño pepper and dice the onion.

3. Heat the oil and half of the hot pepper in a large skillet. Add the shrimp and cook over high heat, turning once, just until shrimp turn pink, about 3 minutes. Remove with tongs and transfer to a large plastic bag. Add the onions to the skillet and cook just until they are warmed through, about 30 seconds.

4. Add the onions to the shrimp along with the mayonnaise, lime juice, vinegar, tarragon, dill and salt to taste. Seal tightly, placing the twist tie right next to the shrimp so there is no air space, and refrigerate 4 hours or overnight.

5. Cut the cabbage into ⅛-inch-wide ribbons, with the thin (2mm) slicer of a processor, or by hand.

6. Cook the cabbage in 4 quarts boiling water for 45 seconds. Drain and rinse under cold water to stop the cooking. Wrap it in a towel and squeeze out as much water as possible.

7. Mix the remaining hot pepper, the oil, vinegar and salt in a medium bowl, then add the cabbage and mix well. The cabbage can be made a day in advance, covered tightly and refrigerated.

8. To serve, add salt to taste to the shrimp and cabbage. (Be careful—some shrimp are very salty.) Place a cluster of cabbage on each of 6 plates, top with 3 shrimp, a portion of red onions and a drizzle of marinade. Garnish the top of the shrimp with a few snips of dill and each dish with 2 large sprigs dill.

MICROWAVE: Follow steps 1 and 2 above. Put the oil and one half of the hot pepper in a shallow 10-inch round microwave dish. Cook, uncovered, on high power (100%) for 1 minute. Arrange the shrimp around the edge of the dish, with the tails pointing to the center. Cover tightly with microwave plastic wrap, piercing wrap once with the tip of a sharp knife so steam can escape. Cook on medium power (50%) until the shrimp turn pink, about 3 minutes. If not fully cooked, 20 to 30 seconds longer. Follow steps 4 and 5 above. Wrap the sliced cabbage in a tight packet of microwave plastic wrap, piercing wrap so steam can escape. Place on a paper plate and microwave on high power (100%) until limp, about 1 minute and 10 seconds. Follow steps 7 and 8 above.

SHRIMP:

18 *jumbo shrimp, about 1¼ pounds*
1 *jalapeño pepper, seeded*
1 *medium red onion (5 ounces), peeled*
2½ *tablespoons light-tasting olive oil*
2½ *tablespoons mayonnaise*
2 *tablespoons fresh lime juice*
2 *tablespoons raspberry vinegar*
1½ *tablespoons minced fresh tarragon*
1½ *tablespoons minced fresh dill*
Salt

CABBAGE:

1 *wedge red cabbage, cored, about ¼ of a large head*
Jalapeño pepper, from above
1½ *tablespoons light-tasting olive oil*
1 *tablespoon raspberry vinegar*
¼ *teaspoon salt*
Fresh dill sprigs, for garnish

Served hot or at room temperature, this simple preparation flatters asparagus without overpowering its delicate taste.

_____ Warm Asparagus Mimosa _____

Preparation time: 20 minutes
Cooking time: 3 to 10 minutes (Microwave 3 to 10 minutes)
Yield: 6 servings

2　*pounds asparagus*
1　*large hard-cooked egg*

DRESSING:
1　*small shallot (½ ounce),*
　　peeled
¼　*cup extra virgin olive oil*
2　*tablespoons rice wine*
　　vinegar
1　*tablespoon orange juice*
1　*teaspoon Dijon mustard*
¼　*teaspoon Oriental sesame*
　　oil
¼　*teaspoon salt*

1. Peel the asparagus stems with a vegetable peeler and remove the woody ends.

2. Bring lightly salted water to a boil in a skillet large enough to hold the asparagus. Add the asparagus and cook just until they are tender, from 3 to 8 minutes depending on thickness. Watch carefully—do not overcook. Drain and hold under cold water to stop further cooking. Drain and pat dry.

3. Peel the egg and separate the yolk and white. Mince the egg white in a food processor or by hand. Mince the yolk, separately from white.

4. For the dressing, mince the shallot in the processor or by hand. Mix with the olive oil, vinegar, orange juice, mustard, sesame oil and salt. The dish can be prepared a day in advance to this point. Place asparagus in a plastic bag and refrigerate. Keep egg white and yolk separate and refrigerate. Refrigerate dressing. Bring all the ingredients to room temperature before finishing.

5. Just before serving, gently heat the dressing. Add the asparagus and toss gently so it is well coated with dressing. Cook only until warm, not hot, about 1 minute.

6. Divide between 6 plates and garnish with egg white, then yolk. Serve warm or at room temperature.

MICROWAVE: Follow step 1 above. Bunch the asparagus together. Wrap tightly in plastic wrap and place the packet on a paper plate. Cook on high power (100%) until tender, 3 to 8 minutes, turning the packet over once after 2 minutes. To test for doneness, pierce through the plastic with the tip of a sharp knife into one of the center spears. If it is not tender, cook in short time increments (30 seconds) until tender. Carefully unwrap and hold the asparagus under cold water to stop the cooking. Follow steps 3 and 4. Just before serving, cook the dressing on high power in a shallow, 10-inch round microwave casserole just until warmed, 1 minute. Add the asparagus and toss gently to coat with dressing. Cook 1 minute longer. Serve as in step 6.

This luscious layering of jade green avocado and orange-hued salmon is the creation of Pierre Pollin, owner and chef of Le Titi de Paris, a charming restaurant just outside of Chicago. The balance of flavors is superb, with the rich, smoky flavor of the salmon playing off the more neutral flavor of avocado. Pollin serves it with a dab of mustardy mayonnaise. But it's good served plain as well. The terrine is easy to assemble, requiring no cooking. It can be made the day before, but no longer, as the avocado tends to discolor.

Avocado and Smoked Salmon Terrine

Preparation time: 30 minutes
Chilling time: 6 hours or overnight
Yield: 8 servings

1. Line a 5-cup terrine or loaf pan with plastic wrap, leaving enough overhang at the ends to cover the top of the terrine later.

2. Mix the water and lemon juice in a small dish and sprinkle the gelatin over. When the liquid is absorbed, dissolve the gelatin by setting the dish in a pan of hot water or microwave on medium power (50%) for 50 seconds. Be sure there aren't any undissolved gelatin granules. Cool slightly.

3. Whip 1¼ cups cream with an electric mixer until it holds soft peaks.

4. Purée the avocados, the dissolved gelatin, salt and pepper in a food processor or blender. Gently fold the purée into the whipped cream.

5. Wash the processor bowl or blender. Purée 7 ounces of the salmon, then slowly pour in egg white and the remaining ½ cup cream and mix until smooth, about 10 seconds.

6. Spread ⅓ of the avocado mixture in an even layer in the terrine, then—carefully—½ of puréed salmon mixture. Arrange remaining 3 ounces of sliced salmon in a single layer over the puréed salmon. Continue layering with ⅓ of the avocado mixture, ½ of the puréed salmon and ⅓ of the avocado mixture. Bang terrine on the counter several times to settle the mixture. Cover tightly with the plastic wrap and refrigerate 6 hours or overnight.

7. To serve, uncover and carefully invert the terrine onto a platter. Remove the plastic and use a small spatula to smooth the surface. Dip a sharp knife into warm water and cut into ¾-inch slices. Transfer to individual plates. Serve with a dollop of Mustard Mayonnaise, if desired, and garnish with watercress.

2 tablespoons water
2 tablespoons fresh lemon juice
2 teaspoons unflavored gelatin (1 package)
1¾ cups whipping cream
2 large, ripe dark skinned avocados (1 pound total), peeled
Pinch of salt
Freshly ground white pepper
10 ounces smoked salmon
1 large egg white
Mustard Mayonnaise (see page 327), optional
Watercress, for garnish

Charlie Trotter, the owner and chef of the Chicago restaurant of the same name, has had a remarkable range of training both here and abroad. His experiences have become part of his cooking, which is very creative and well thought out, as evidenced by this salad. The richness of smoked duck is enhanced by sweet, tropical fruits and delicately flavored raspberry vinegar. The fruits must be perfectly ripe, full of juicy sweetness and flavor. I serve the salad either as a first course for 6 or as a light, wonderful lunch for 4.

Charlie Trotter's Smoked Duck Salad

Preparation time: 20 minutes
Yield: 6 servings

DRESSING:
9 tablespoons walnut oil
4¼ tablespoons peanut oil
¼ cup raspberry vinegar
¾ teaspoon salt

SALAD:
½ small red onion, peeled (use 1½ ounces)
1¼ cups mango, peeled, cut in ¾-inch cubes
1¼ cups papaya, peeled, cut in ¾-inch cubes
1¼ cups cantaloupe, cut in ¾-inch cubes
4 smoked duck or chicken breasts or smoked turkey breast (12 ounces total), cut in ½-inch cubes
12 cups mixed sweet and bitter greens (Boston lettuce, Bibb lettuce, watercress, curly endive, arugula)
½ cup toasted minced walnuts (see page 338)
¼ cup raspberries, optional

1. For the dressing, mix both oils, the vinegar and salt. The dressing can be made up to 3 days in advance and refrigerated. Bring to room temperature before using.

2. For the salad, cut the onion into very fine juliennes. Combine with the mango, papaya, cantaloupe, duck, greens and walnuts. Gently toss with the dressing. Divide between 6 salad plates and garnish with raspberries, if you are using them. Serve immediately.

This is a dazzling first-course salad, just the right beginning for an elegant meal. A bed of crisp greens and julienned fennel is topped with medallions of milky white scallops, softly sautéed red onions and slivers of wilted radicchio. A fruity, sweet/sour dressing is used both to cook the onions and dress the greens, resulting in a delicious amalgamation of flavors.

Warm Scallop Salad

Preparation time: 25 minutes
Cooking time: 10 minutes (Microwave: 8 minutes)
Yield: 6 servings

1. For the dressing, mince the orange zest and ginger in a food processor or by hand. Mix with the oil, vinegar, honey, mustard, tarragon, dill, salt and pepper. Set aside.

2. For the salad, remove the slender stalks of the fennel down to the bulb. Save to use in a salad, soup, or discard. Separate the bulb into layers. Trim any brown spots and remove any coarse outer strings with a vegetable peeler. If the layers are thick, especially the outer ones, split them in half. Cut into ⅛-inch slivers and put in a serving bowl. Tear the lettuce into bite-size pieces. Remove the stems from the watercress. Add the greens to the fennel and refrigerate. Cut the onion into very thin rings, either with the thin (2mm) slicer of a processor or by hand.

3. Heat half the dressing in a 10-inch skillet. When it is hot, add the onions and cook over medium heat until they are very soft, about 6 minutes. The onions can be cooked a day in advance and refrigerated. Reheat gently before finishing the recipe.

4. While the onions are cooking, cut the scallops horizontally into thirds to make thin circles. Cut the radicchio into ½-inch slivers.

5. Add the scallops and radicchio to the onions, increase the heat to high and cook, stirring several times, just until the scallops turn opaque, 1 to 2 minutes.

6. To serve, toss the greens with the remaining dressing. Adjust the vinegar and seasoning to taste. Divide among 6 salad plates. Carefully arrange the scallop-radicchio-onion mixture over the top and serve immediately.

MICROWAVE: Follow steps 1 and 2. Cook half the dressing in a shallow, 10-inch round microwave dish on high power (100%) for 1 minute. Stir in the onions and cook, uncovered, on high

DRESSING:
Zest of ½ orange, removed with a zester or grater
1 *small piece fresh ginger (⅜-inch cube), peeled*
½ *cup extra virgin olive oil*
2 *tablespoons raspberry vinegar*
1 *teaspoon honey*
½ *teaspoon Dijon mustard*
½ *teaspoon dried tarragon*
½ *teaspoon dried dill*
½ *teaspoon salt*
Freshly ground white pepper

SALAD:
1 *small fennel bulb (8 ounces)*
1 *small head romaine lettuce (6 ounces), washed and crisped*
⅔ *cup watercress leaves*
2 *small red onions (3 ounces each), peeled*
12 *ounces sea scallops*
2 *large radicchio leaves (1 ounce total)*

power until they are soft, about 4 minutes, stirring once after 3 minutes. Follow step 4. Stir the scallops and radicchio into the onions so they are coated with dressing, then push the scallops to the edge of the dish. Cook, uncovered, on medium power (50%) just until the scallops are cooked, 2-3 minutes, stirring once after 1½ minutes. Finish as in step 6.

◆

This is a delicate presentation of mushrooms, cooked in a balsamic vinaigrette and served over greens. The hot mushrooms and vinaigrette wilt the greens slightly but still leave them crisp enough to provide a welcome contrast to the mushrooms. I serve this as a first course when other choices seem too dominant for the meal that follows. This is appropriate for vegetarian meals as well as those with a rich main course.

_____Warm Medley of Mushrooms on Mixed Greens

Preparation time: 15 minutes
Cooking time: 5 minutes (Microwave: 5 minutes)
Resting time: 5 minutes
Yield: 4 servings

2 heads Boston lettuce (12 ounces total)
1 head radicchio (3 ounces)
¾ pound fresh wild mushrooms—porcini, shiitake and morels are all good
¾ cup extra virgin olive oil
⅓ cup balsamic vinegar
1½ tablespoons Armagnac or cognac
½ teaspoon salt
Freshly ground black pepper
2 tablespoons minced fresh chives

1. Wash and crisp the lettuce and radicchio and tear into bite-size pieces. Divide among 4 salad plates and refrigerate until serving time.

2. Gently brush the dirt from mushrooms and cut them into ½-inch slices.

3. Place the oil, vinegar, Armagnac or cognac, salt and pepper in a 10-inch skillet over high heat. When mixture is very hot, add the mushrooms and cook, stirring constantly, until they are soft, about 3 minutes. Remove the pan from the heat, add the chives and adjust the seasoning.

4. Divide the mushrooms and pan juices among the plates. Let rest at room temperature for 5 minutes before serving so the flavors develop.

MICROWAVE: Follow steps 1 and 2. Combine the oil, vinegar and Armagnac or cognac in a shallow, 10-inch round microwave dish. Cook on high power (100%) for 2 minutes. Add the mush-rooms and cook on high power, stirring once, just until they soften, about 3 minutes. Add the salt, pepper and chives. Serve as in step 4.

◆

This lusty dish conjures up images of a *trattoria* in Italy, where it would be one of many choices on an antipasto table. The fennel is softly cooked and boldly flavored with garlic, lemon juice and black pepper. Thin slices of prosciutto add richness, which plays off of the astringent lemon taste. I also serve this as a cold vegeta-ble, without the prosciutto.

_____Italian Fennel with Lemon and Prosciutto_____

Preparation time: 15 minutes
Cooking time: 8 minutes (Microwave: 8 minutes)
Yield: 4 servings

1. Remove the slender stalks and greens from fennel, down to the bulb, and save for a soup, salad, or discard. Trim the bulb with a paring knife, leaving the core intact. Trim any brown spots and remove coarse outer strings with a vegetable peeler. Cut bulb in half vertically, then cut each half into 4 equal-sized wedges.

2. Cook the fennel in boiling water until it is tender enough to pierce easily with a sharp knife, 6 to 8 minutes. Drain and set aside.

3. While the fennel is cooking, mince the parsley in a food processor or by hand and set aside. If you're using a processor, put the lemon zest, pepper and salt in the work bowl, turn on the machine and drop the garlic through the feed tube to mince. Add the oil and lemon juice. Or mince the lemon zest and garlic by hand and mix with the oil, lemon juice, salt and pepper.

4. Put the oil mixture in a large bowl and add the warm fennel. Toss gently with 2 spoons, being careful so the fennel doesn't fall apart. Refrigerate at least 3 hours or up to 3 days. Bring to room temperature before serving.

5. To serve, arrange 2 wedges on each of 4 plates, with a

1 large fennel bulb (1 pound)
2 tablespoons parsley leaves
Zest of ½ lemon, removed with a zester or grater
¼ teaspoon coarsely cracked black pepper
¼ teaspoon salt
1 large garlic clove, peeled
1 tablespoon light-tasting olive oil
2 teaspoons fresh lemon juice
4 thin slices prosciutto
1 ounce minced Parmesan cheese, preferably imported

slice of prosciutto next to them. Sprinkle the fennel with the cheese and some minced parsley.

MICROWAVE: Follow step 1 above. Arrange the fennel in a shallow, 10-inch round microwave dish, with the narrower top of the bulb pointing to the center of the dish. Cover tightly with plastic wrap. Cook on high power (100%) until the fennel is tender, about 8 minutes. Test by piercing through the plastic with a sharp knife. Carefully remove the plastic and drain any liquid that has accumulated. Follow steps 3, 4 and 5.

5 · More Than Green Salads

When I consider why I love salads so much, lots of things come to mind. Freshness, color, verve, variety and good taste just begin to sum up their appeal. Most meals are enhanced by the addition of a salad, and for that matter there are many salads that can make a meal. Their improvisational spirit and free-form stance is hard to resist, or match.

I shudder to think that salads are all too often a routine and uninspired part of the meal. Iceberg lettuce torn into a bowl and covered with bottled dressing is not my idea of salad. (I might add here that, unlike many, I have nothing against iceberg lettuce and occasionally make a salad of it with the Sweet and Sour Dill Dressing on page 120.) Salads should practically jump off the plate with freshness and excitement!

Freshness is critical to salads that aspire to greatness. Make sure all your ingredients are fresh and well cleaned. The best way to clean greens is to put them in a sink filled with cold water—the most surefire method of getting all the dirt that hides deep inside. Soggy lettuce is sure to ruin a salad by diluting the dressing, so clean the greens ahead of time, then dry them thoroughly. I am partial to salad spinners, though I know several people who swear by shaking the lettuce in a pillow case. That's fine, too—whatever it takes to get the job done. Once cleaned, I wrap the greens in paper towels, then put them in a plastic bag and seal it. Depending on how fresh they are to begin with, salad greens can last in the refrigerator for up to 5 days.

Those salads not based on greens alone should also be made from the freshest ingredients available. To me, it's worth cooking a chicken to moist perfection with the express purpose of turning it into a salad. It's so much nicer to have big pieces of meat rather than little, overcooked shreds. Certainly it's okay to use leftovers —meat, fish, shellfish and vegetables—in salads, if none are over-cooked. All the other ingredients should be similarly fresh and inviting.

Presentation is important to me and I find that the simple act of adding a sprig of fresh herbs, a shower of minced herbs, or occasionally a handful of edible flowers, at serving time, makes a big difference. I'm not saying salads should look precious—but they should look inviting. Meat and pasta salads are more appealing when they're placed on a chiffonade of lettuce or leafy greens, even on slivered red cabbage.

I've added several all-purpose dressings to the end of the chapter. But don't overlook the dressings that are paired with salads throughout the chapter. All of these can be used on salads of your own creation. When matching a dressing to a salad, select one that compliments and enhances with a light touch. The object is not to overwhelm or mask flavors—rather, to flatter. And while we're on the subject of improvisation, feel free to change the salad ingredients according to what's freshest and best at the market. I've included weights so adjusting ingredients will be easy.

◆

Even the simplest salads should be as fresh and inviting as a summer garden. This one is just that. A colorful collage of vegetables is minced right into the peppermint-scented vinaigrette.

Romaine Salad with Vegetable Vinaigrette

Preparation time: 20 minutes
Yield: 8 servings

1. Tear the lettuce into bite-size pieces and put in a large salad bowl. Refrigerate until serving time.

2. To make the vinaigrette in a food processor, cut the cucumbers and green onions into 1-inch pieces and combine half of each in the processor. Add the oil, mint leaves, vinegar, mustard, salt and pepper and chop roughly by pulsing the machine on and off several times. Transfer to a bowl and chop the rest of the cucumbers and green onions. Seed the tomato and dice by hand; add, along with the cucumbers and green onions, to the bowl with the other vegetables that have been processed.

3. To make the vinaigrette by hand, seed the tomatoes. Mince the cucumbers, green onions, mint leaves and tomato. Mix with the oil, vinegar, mustard, salt and pepper.

4. Just before serving, toss the vinaigrette with the lettuce and adjust the seasoning, if necessary.

3 *small heads romaine lettuce (2 pounds total), washed and crisped*

VINAIGRETTE:
3 *small pickling cucumbers (12 ounces total)*
2 *large green onions (3 ounces total)*
¾ *cup extra virgin olive oil*
¾ *cup fresh peppermint leaves*
¼ *cup sherry vinegar*
4 *teaspoons Dijon mustard*
¾ *teaspoon salt*
   Freshly ground black pepper
1 *large tomato (8 ounces)*

101 •

This refreshing, light salad of greens and herbs is delicately garnished with thin shavings of Parmesan cheese. It is a great opener when served as a separate course, and is perfectly suited to serving with simply roasted meat, poultry or broiled fish. Most often, though, I serve it with grilled thin-crusted pizzas for a delightful meal.

Italian Garden Salad with Shaved Parmesan

CHEESE AND VINAIGRETTE:

2¼ ounces imported Parmesan cheese at room temperature, rind removed

1 small clove garlic, peeled

½ cup extra virgin olive oil

4 teaspoons fresh lemon juice

2 teaspoons balsamic vinegar

1½ teaspoons Dijon mustard

¼ teaspoon salt
Freshly ground black pepper

SALAD:

2 medium red bell peppers (10 ounces total)

1 small, sweet red onion (3½ ounces), peeled

9 cups chilled mixed greens (I use 1 cup of combined basil, peppermint and oregano leaves, 2 cups arugula, 1 cup watercress, 1 small head of radicchio, 1 medium romaine lettuce heart, washed and crisped)

Preparation time: 20 minutes
Yield: Makes 4 servings

1. For the cheese and vinaigrette, slice the cheese with the ultra-thin (1mm) slicer of a food processor. It can also be sliced by hand as thin as possible, which will take a very steady hand. Set the slices of cheese aside.

2. To make the dressing, put the broken pieces of cheese in a processor or blender. Add the garlic and run the processor or blender until the cheese and garlic are finely minced. Add the oil, lemon juice, vinegar, mustard, salt and pepper and mix well. Set aside.

3. For the salad, peel the red peppers with a swivel-bladed vegetable peeler, removing as much of the skin as possible. Don't worry if you can't get to all the bits of skin from the folds of the peppers. Cut the peppers into ½-inch strips. Cut the onion into ⅛-inch slices, either with the thin (2mm) slicer of a processor or by hand. Tear the greens into bite-size pieces.

4. The salad can be prepared a day in advance to this point. Wrap the cheese, cover the dressing and refrigerate both. Refrigerate the greens and sliced vegetables separately, in airtight plastic bags. To serve, bring the vinaigrette and cheese to room temperature. Toss the chilled greens and vegetables with the vinaigrette and adjust the seasonings and lemon/vinegar balance, if necessary. Divide among large salad plates, tucking the cheese slices into the greens. Let rest a few minutes before serving.

This is a cross between a salad and cole slaw, combining ribbons of crisp romaine lettuce with delicate slivers of red cabbage, all dressed with a tangy, non-creamy version of blue cheese dressing. The dressing is so delicious that you'll use it on other salads as well.

Romaine and Red Cabbage Slaw with Banker's Blue Cheese Dressing

Preparation time: 15 minutes
Yield: 6 servings

1. For the slaw, cut the lettuce into ½-inch ribbons, with the thick (6mm) slicer of a food processor or by hand. Cut the cabbage into paper-thin slices with the ultra-thin (1mm) slicer or by hand. Toss together in a salad bowl and refrigerate until serving time.

2. For the dressing, mince the green onion in a processor or by hand. Mix with the oil, vinegar, mustard, salt and pepper, then fold in the cheese. The dressing can be made up to 3 days in advance and refrigerated.

3. At serving time, toss the dressing with the chilled slaw and adjust seasoning if necessary.

SLAW:
1 large head romaine lettuce (1 pound), washed and crisped
1 wedge red cabbage (5 ounces, approximately ¼ of a medium head)

DRESSING:
1 large green onion (1 ounce)
¾ cup safflower oil
3 tablespoons red wine vinegar
1½ tablespoons Dijon mustard
¼ teaspoon salt
Freshly ground black pepper
1½ ounces crumbled blue cheese

For one of my newspaper columns, I asked several chefs what salad was quintessentially autumn to them. This was Carolyn Buster's contribution. As owner and chef of The Cottage restaurant in the Chicago suburbs, she constantly creates salads, some of them quite elaborate. Yet she named this simple salad as a favorite one she turns to time and again. It's just the kind of recipe you're glad to have in your files—simple, easy and very tasty. A comment on the pepper: Measure it—don't just add a few twists of the mill. A teaspoon seems like a lot, but it offsets the sweetness of the dressing, bringing to it a perfect balance.

——Broccoli Salad with Sweet Mustard Dressing——

Preparation time: 20 minutes
Cooking time: 6 minutes
Yield: 4 to 6 servings

DRESSING:
1 medium garlic clove, peeled
¾ cup safflower oil
1 small or ½ large egg yolk
2 tablespoons Dijon mustard
2 tablespoons sugar
1 teaspoon salt
1 teaspoon freshly ground pepper
1½ tablespoons fresh lemon juice
1 tablespoon white vinegar

SALAD:
1 large bunch broccoli (1½ pounds)
1 head red or green leaf lettuce
2 tablespoons pomegranate seeds, optional

1. For the dressing, mince the garlic in a food processor or by hand. Mix with the oil, egg yolk, mustard, sugar, salt and pepper. Slowly drizzle in the lemon juice and vinegar and mix until smooth. Dressing can be made 3 days in advance and refrigerated.

2. For the salad, cut the broccoli into 3-inch lengths, then split them so the spears are no thicker than ¾ inch. Peel the stems with a vegetable peeler.

3. Cook the broccoli in boiling salted water just until tender, about 6 minutes.

4. Drain immediately and hold under cold water until cool. Drain well and pat dry, especially the flowerets. Broccoli can be cooked a day in advance and refrigerated. Bring to room temperature and pat dry again before using.

5. To serve, arrange lettuce on salad plates and divide broccoli spears among them. Spoon 2½ to 3 tablespoons of dressing over each serving and sprinkle with pomegranate seeds, if desired.

Note: Avid microwave users will be surprised to see that I don't use it here, where it seems so logical. Boiled broccoli is preferable in taste, texture and color, and there isn't a big time-saving advantage to the microwave. So, here, I stand by convention.

Sweet, juicy pears and richly flavored walnut oil favor this sophisticated dinner salad. Bitter greens, such as watercress, arugula or endive, will offset the sweetness of the pear, so add at least one to your mix of greens. The pear, of course, must be ripe and juicy but still firm for the salad to succeed. A creamy, mild goat cheese spread on toasted French bread or Melba toast is a perfect partner.

Pears and Walnuts with Mixed Greens

Preparation time: 25 minutes
Yield: 4 servings

1. For the dressing, mince the shallot in a food processor or by hand. Add both oils, the vinegar, mustard, sugar, salt and pepper and mix well. Use immediately or refrigerate up to 3 days.

2. For the salad, cook the walnuts in the walnut oil in a small skillet until they are light brown and fragrant, 4 to 5 minutes. Don't let them burn. Set aside to cool.

3. Cut the pear in half lengthwise and remove the core, but do not peel. Cut lengthwise into ¼-inch slices. Place in a shallow bowl and cover with the dressing.

4. Tear the greens into bite-size pieces and toss together in

DRESSING:
- 1 medium shallot (¾ ounce), peeled
- ½ cup extra virgin olive oil
- 1½ tablespoons walnut oil
- 1½ tablespoons red wine vinegar
- 1 tablespoon Dijon mustard
- ½ teaspoon sugar
- ¼ teaspoon salt
  Freshly ground white pepper

SALAD:
- ½ cup walnuts (2 ounces)
- 1 tablespoon walnut oil
- 1 large Bartlett or Comice pear (8 ounces)
- 10 cups mixed greens, including watercress, arugula, Boston and leaf lettuce, washed and crisped

a salad bowl. The salad can be made 2 hours in advance to this point, if desired. Cover the greens and the pear and refrigerate.

5. At serving time, drain the dressing from the pear and pour it over the greens. Toss gently. Adjust the seasoning and add freshly ground white pepper. Divide the greens among 4 salad plates. For each portion, fan 3 to 4 slices of pear across the greens and sprinkle with walnuts.

◆

This is a lively relish-like vegetable salad, just the ticket to go alongside a big bowl of soup or a casserole. The dressing and salad can be prepared in advance, then tossed together just before serving. That way, the mushrooms stay white and keep their texture. Emmantaler cheese is excellent, but you can also use Gruyère or Swiss, which have a similar nutty flavor.

Mushroom Salad with Peppers and Green Onions

DRESSING:
- ½ cup parsley leaves
- ½ cup plus 1 tablespoon safflower oil
- 3 tablespoons white wine vinegar
- 1½ tablespoons Dijon mustard
- ¾ teaspoon dried tarragon
- ½ teaspoon salt

SALAD:
- 8 small green onions (4 ounces)
- 1 medium red bell pepper (5 ounces)
- 1 pound mushrooms
- 5 ounces Emmantaler or other Swiss cheese, chilled

Preparation time: 20 minutes
Yield: 6 servings

1. For the dressing, mince the parsley in a food processor or by hand. Add the oil, vinegar, mustard, tarragon and salt and mix well.

2. For the salad, cut the green onions, including the green tops, into thin rings. Cut the red pepper into ¼-inch dice. Cut the mushrooms into thin slices, either with the thin (2mm) slicer of a processor or by hand. Shred the cheese, using the processor or a grater. Mix the green onions, red pepper, mushrooms and cheese together in a large bowl. To make the salad in advance, keep the salad dressing separate, cover the salad and dressing and refrigerate.

3. Just before serving, toss the salad with the dressing and adjust the seasoning.

Summer hardly seems like summer without cole slaw. It's terrific at picnics and barbecues, since it goes with so many summertime favorites, from fried chicken to steaks to boiled lobster and corn on the cob. This version stands out because it calls for less oil than most others. Boiled dressing is an old-fashioned formula, proving that sometimes it's a good idea to look back into the annals of cooking for a great "new" idea.

Summer Slaw with Boiled Dressing

Preparation time: 20 minutes
Cooking time: 8 minutes
Yield: 6 to 8 servings

1. For the dressing, combine the oil, vinegar, sugar, mustard and salt in a small pan and bring to a boil. Lower heat and cook at medium-high until the sugar has dissolved, about 3 minutes.

2. Mix the water, cornstarch and horseradish until smooth, using a food processor or a whisk. If you use a processor, let it run as you pour the hot liquid in the pan through the feed tube. By hand, slowly add the hot liquid to the water-cornstarch-horseradish mixture, whisking constantly.

3. Return this mixture to the same pan and cook over medium heat, stirring often, until thickened, 3 to 4 minutes. Cool before using. The dressing can be refrigerated for up to 3 days.

4. Core the cabbage and cut it into wedges. The easiest and neatest way to shred it is with the ultra-thin (1mm) slicer or medium shredder of a processor, but it can also be done by hand. If you're using a processor, it isn't necessary to wash the work bowl after making the dressing. Shred the carrot in the processor or with a grater.

5. Toss the carrots and cabbage with the dressing. The slaw can be made a day in advance and refrigerated. Before serving, stir well, then drain excess liquid. Add the herbs and adjust the seasoning if necessary.

Note: For Tex-Mex flavor, add 1 cup minced cilantro leaves and a minced hot pepper to the slaw. For an Oriental touch, mince 4 small scallions and a 1-inch piece of peeled fresh ginger root and toss in with the cabbage.

DRESSING:
½ *cup safflower oil*
⅓ *cup cider vinegar*
2 *tablespoons sugar*
1 *teaspoon Dijon mustard*
1 *teaspoon salt*
⅓ *cup water*
1 *tablespoon cornstarch*
1 *tablespoon well-drained prepared horseradish*

SLAW:
1 *small head green cabbage (1¼ pounds)*
¼ *large head red cabbage (8 ounces)*
1 *large carrot (4 ounces), peeled*
¼ *cup minced fresh herbs, such as basil, tarragon, lovage, dill and/or parsley*

This crisp, colorful salad offers just the right kind of refreshment that a spicy Southwestern meal calls for. Jícama, a sweet, juicy root vegetable from Latin America, is a wonderful foil for spicy foods. Here, this white-fleshed vegetable is tossed amid a mass of multicolored bell peppers, diced orange and green onions and glossed over with a citrusy dressing.

—————South of the Border Jícama Salad—————

Preparation time: 25 minutes
Chilling time: Several hours
Yield: 8 servings

SALAD:
- 3 medium navel oranges (1¼ pounds total)
- 1 small jícama (12 ounces), peeled
- 2 medium red bell peppers (10 ounces total)
- 2 medium yellow bell peppers (10 ounces total)
- 6 large green onions (3 ounces total)

DRESSING:
- 1 small garlic clove, peeled
- 1 small jalapeño or serrano pepper, seeded
- ¼ cup cilantro leaves
- 3 tablespoons safflower oil
- 1½ tablespoons lime juice
- 1 tablespoon cider vinegar
- ½ teaspoon salt

1. For the salad, trim the ends of the oranges to leave a flat top and bottom on them. Stand them on a board and remove all the peel and white pith, cutting from top to bottom with a paring knife. Turn them over and trim the pith from the bottom. Working over a bowl to catch the juice, segment the oranges by cutting between the membrane. Cut the segments into ½-inch dice and add them to the bowl. Cut the jícama and bell peppers into ½-inch dice and green onions into ¼-inch-thick rings and add to oranges.

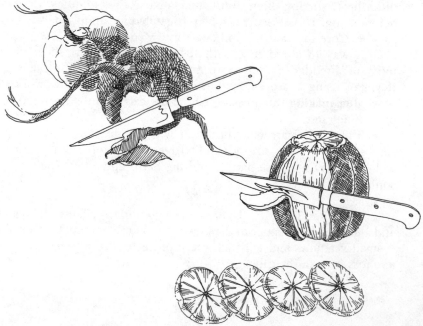

2. For the dressing, mince the garlic, hot pepper and cilantro together in a food processor or by hand. Mix with the oil, lime juice, vinegar and salt.

3. Toss the dressing, vegetables and oranges together, cover and refrigerate several hours or overnight. Stir well and drain any excess liquid. Adjust the seasoning and add more lime juice, if necessary, before serving.

◆

Translated, the name means red salad, which will hardly be a mystery once you see this ruby-colored jewel. Raw beets and juicy pears sweeten the red cabbage slaw and are likely to elicit such queries as "What's in this salad?" I like to serve this with sandwiches, roast pork loin and duck.

Salade Rouge

Preparation time: 20 minutes
Yield: 6 to 8 servings

1. For the salad, core the cabbage and slice into very thin ribbons, either with the ultra-thin (1mm) or thin (2mm) slicer of a food processor or by hand. Cut the pear in half lengthwise and remove the core. Shred the pear and beets with a processor or a grater. Combine in a large mixing bowl.

2. For the dressing, mix the oil, vinegar, honey, salt, cinnamon and pepper. Add to the mixing bowl along with the walnuts and toss thoroughly. Adjust the seasoning. Serve immediately or cover tightly and refrigerate up to 3 days. If refrigerated, before serving, toss to coat the vegetables with the vinaigrette, then adjust the seasoning.

SALAD:
1 *small head red cabbage (1 pound)*
1 *large firm, ripe pear (8 ounces), peeled*
2 *medium raw beets (8 ounces), peeled*

DRESSING:
1 *cup safflower oil*
½ *cup raspberry vinegar*
1 *tablespoon honey*
1½ *teaspoons salt*
1 *teaspoon cinnamon
Freshly ground black pepper*
1 *cup toasted walnuts (4 ounces) (see page 338)*

Celery root, or celeriac, is that rather unattractive addition to the produce bins that shows up in late fall. It's dark brown, gnarled and shaggy-looking, not something you're apt to try if you judge a book solely by its cover. But its taste more than compensates for what it lacks in beauty. Inside, celery root is creamy white. Though the texture is different, the flavor is not unlike that of celery, only more intense. Here, it's prepared as a winter-white salad, combined with sweet juicy pears, walnuts and tangy blue cheese.

———Julienned Celery Root and Pear Salad———

Preparation time: 15 minutes
Chilling time: 2 to 3 hours
Yield: 4 to 6 servings

½ cup mayonnaise (see page 327 or store-bought)
1½ tablespoons fresh lemon juice
2¼ teaspoons Dijon mustard
2 small celery roots (1 pound total)
1 large firm, ripe Bartlett pear (8 ounces)
2 ounces blue cheese, crumbled
3 tablespoons toasted, minced walnuts (see page 338)

1. Mix the mayonnaise, lemon juice and mustard in a large mixing bowl and set aside.

2. Peel the celery root and pear and core the pear. Cut both into fine shreds, either with the shredder or 3mm julienne disc of a food processor, or with a grater.

3. Add the celery root and pear to the mixing bowl and toss gently. Refrigerate for 2 to 3 hours before serving.

4. Just before serving, toss in the cheese and sprinkle walnuts over the top.

Mayonnaise and sour cream, common components of old-fashioned potato salad, send the calorie count skyrocketing. Here, yogurt and reduced-calorie mayonnaise are used for an overall saving of more than 1,000 calories. The results? A deliciously rich and creamy-tasting salad that's perfect for sleek summertime dining. The recipe makes enough for a good-sized crowd; you may want to cut it in half.

Spud Light Potato Salad

Preparation time: 25 minutes
Cooking time: 18 minutes (Microwave: 18 minutes)
Yield: 8 to 10 servings

1. Put the potatoes in 8 quarts of water. Bring to a boil, then cook until just tender, 15 to 18 minutes. Do not overcook. Drain well. When they are cool enough to handle, cut them into ¾-inch dice and place in a large bowl.

2. Split the celery stalks lengthwise into ¼-inch strips, then cut them into small dice. Cut the green onions into thin rings.

3. Gently toss the celery, green onions, yogurt, mayonnaise, mustard, dill, tarragon, salt and pepper with the potatoes. The salad can be served immediately or covered tightly and refrigerated up to 2 days. Adjust the seasoning before serving.

3 pounds tiny red potatoes
4 large celery stalks
  (12 ounces total)
6 large green onions
  (3 ounces total)
½ cup plain low-fat yogurt
½ cup reduced-calorie
  mayonnaise
1 tablespoon Dijon mustard
2 teaspoons dried dill
1 teaspoon dried tarragon
¼ teaspoon salt, or to taste
  Freshly ground pepper

MICROWAVE: Cut potatoes into ¾-inch dice. Arrange half of them in a circle around the inside edge of a shallow, 10-inch round microwave dish. Add ¼ cup water, cover tightly with plastic wrap and pierce wrap once with the point of a sharp knife so steam can escape. Cook on high power (100%) for 4 minutes. Stir and push back to the edge of the dish. Cover and cook on high power just until tender, 5 more minutes. Drain well. Cook remaining potatoes the same way. Finish the recipe as above.

Note: The actual cooking time for the potatoes in the microwave oven is the same as stovetop cooking. However, you do not have to boil a pot of water first and the kitchen stays cooler, which are both big pluses in the summer. If you cut the recipe in half, the microwave cooking time will also be cut in half since the potatoes are cooked in batches.

As fond as I am of potato salads and sweet potatoes, I find it hard to believe it took me so long to think of sweet potato salad. Here, in the spirit of better late than never, is a lively-looking salad of orange potatoes flecked with green onions and yellow bell peppers. It goes well with almost anything casual, from Cajun-spiced food to burgers to bratwurst.

The potatoes are sliced before cooking so they cook in almost no time. Watch carefully so they don't get mushy.

———Sweet Potato Salad with Honey Citrus Dressing

Preparation time: 10 minutes
Cooking time: 2 minutes (Microwave: 5 minutes)
Chilling time: 1 hour
Yield: 4 servings

2 medium sweet potatoes (1 pound), peeled
1 small piece fresh ginger (½-inch cube), peeled
1 jalapeño or serrano pepper
2 tablespoons safflower oil
2 to 3 tablespoons fresh lemon juice
1 tablespoon orange juice concentrate, thawed
1 teaspoon honey
½ teaspoon salt
1 medium yellow or red bell pepper (4 ounces)
3 large green onions (2 ounces total)

1. Cut the sweet potatoes into matchstick pieces, about ¼ inch by 2 inches. It is easiest to do this with the thick (6mm) slicer of a food processor. Lay the potatoes in the feed tube, trimming them, if necessary, so they fit. Slice with firm pressure. Remove the slices from the work bowl of the processor and stack them so they more-or-less resemble the original shape of the potato. Insert them again into the feed tube with the cut side perpendicular to the slicer, and slice again. Or cut them into matchsticks by hand.

2. Cook the sweet potatoes in boiling water just until they are tender-crisp, 1½ to 2 minutes. Drain, refresh under cold water and transfer to a large bowl.

3. Mince the ginger and hot pepper. If you are using a processor, use the same work bowl into which you sliced the potatoes. Mix with the oil, 2 tablespoons lemon juice, orange juice concentrate, honey and salt. Pour the dressing over the potatoes while they are still hot and toss gently. Refrigerate at least 1 hour.

4. Cut the red or yellow pepper into ½-inch dice. Cut the green onions into thin rings. Add to the chilled potatoes and mix well. The salad can be prepared 2 days in advance to this point, covered tightly and refrigerated. Just before serving, adjust the seasoning, adding the remaining lemon juice, if necessary. Serve at room temperature.

MICROWAVE: Follow step 2. Arrange the potatoes in a shallow, 10-inch round microwave dish, pushing them to the edge of the dish so the center is empty. Cover tightly and cook on high power

(100%) until tender, about 4 minutes, stirring once halfway through. Drain and transfer to a large bowl. Finish as in steps 4 and 5.

Note: It takes longer to cook the sweet potatoes in the microwave oven, but you do not have to boil a pot of water first.

◆

This is a cross between a chef's salad and a Waldorf salad, a pairing that sounds a bit like the odd couple of the salad world. Apples, raisins and nuts are joined by pieces of chicken and a big bowl of cabbage. The surprise element is sorrel, a tender and tangy green that pokes up in the early spring.

California Waldorf Salad

Preparation time: 20 minutes
Yield: 6 servings

1. For the dressing, remove the stems and large ribs from the sorrel before measuring. Put the leaves in a food processor or blender and mix with the oil, vinegar, mayonnaise, mustard, sugar and salt until the sorrel is finely minced. If you're using a processor, leave the dressing in the work bowl and slice the cabbage right into the dressing. Otherwise, transfer the dressing to a large bowl.
2. For the salad, remove the core from the cabbage and cut it into wedges. Slice it into ½-inch ribbons, either with the thick (6mm) slicer of a processor or by hand. Add the cabbage to the dressing.
3. Cut the apples in half lengthwise and remove the core with a melon baller. Cut each half into 6 wedges. Then cut the wedges into ½-inch-wide pieces. Cut the green onion into thin rings. Cut the red pepper into ¼-inch dice. Add these vegetables to the cabbage.
4. Remove the skin, bones and all little bits of fat from the chicken and cut the meat into ½-inch cubes. Toss with the cabbage, vegetables, raisins and walnuts. The salad can be served immediately or covered tightly and refrigerated overnight. Adjust the seasoning before serving.

Note: When sorrel is not available, substitute 1 cup of

DRESSING:
- *1 cup sorrel leaves (see Note)*
- *½ cup plus 1 tablespoon safflower oil*
- *¼ cup cider vinegar*
- *3 tablespoons mayonnaise*
- *1½ teaspoons Dijon mustard*
- *¾ teaspoon sugar*
- *¾ teaspoon salt*

SALAD:
- *1 small head Savoy cabbage (1 pound)*
- *2 small Red Delicious apples (12 ounces)*
- *1 small green onion (½ ounce)*
- *1 medium red bell pepper (5 ounces)*
- *4 cooked chicken breast halves*
- *⅔ cup raisins (4 ounces)*
- *½ cup toasted walnuts (see page 338)*

113 •

loosely packed spinach leaves. When the dressing is made, taste and add fresh lemon juice to your liking—start out by adding 2 teaspoons. The dressing should be tart but not puckery.

◆

This salad, loosely based on Middle Eastern cooking, makes partners of couscous, a beadlike type of pasta, and a confetti of minced vegetables, nuts and currants. Be sure to use quick-cooking couscous.

Moroccan Couscous and Vegetable Salad

Preparation time: 20 minutes
Cooking time: 15 minutes
Yield: 4 to 6 servings

⅔ cup chicken stock (see page 339) or canned broth
1 cup quick-cooking couscous (6½ ounces)
1 cup dried currants (1½ ounces)
1 medium zucchini (5 ounces)
3 medium green onions (2 ounces total)
1 large shallot (1 ounce), peeled
1 small red bell pepper (4 ounces)
3 tablespoons light-tasting olive oil
3 tablespoons pine nuts
½ teaspoon salt
2 to 3 tablespoons fresh lemon juice
½ teaspoon ground cumin

1. Bring the stock or broth to a boil. Combine the couscous and currants in a mixing bowl and pour the stock over. Fluff with a fork and let rest until the couscous is tender and the broth is absorbed, about 5 minutes.

2. Split the zucchini lengthwise and scoop out the inside, leaving only a ¼-inch-thick shell. Cut the shell into small pieces in a food processor or by hand and set aside. (The inside of the zucchini is not used in this recipe.) Mince the green onions and the shallot in a processor or by hand. Cut the red pepper into small pieces, either in the processor or by hand.

3. Heat the oil in a 10-inch skillet. When it is hot, add the pine nuts and cook over medium heat until they are golden brown. Remove them with a slotted spoon and set aside.

4. Add the shallot, green onions, zucchini and salt to the skillet and cook over high heat, stirring often, just until the vegetables begin to soften, about 2 minutes. Add the peppers and cook 1 minute longer. Add the couscous, currants, 2 tablespoons of lemon juice and the cumin. Cook just enough to heat through, about 1 minute. Remove from the heat and add the pine nuts. Taste and adjust the seasoning, adding the remaining tablespoon of lemon juice if it is needed. Adjust the seasoning before serving. Serve chilled or at room temperature. The salad can be refrigerated for up to 3 days.

This salad mirrors an antipasto platter, offering roasted peppers, Italian salami and cheese tossed with cheese-filled tortellini. It packs easily, so it is a good choice for al fresco meals or as a take-along for potluck dining.

Antipasto Tortellini Salad

Preparation time: 20 minutes
Cooking time: 10 minutes
Yield: 6 servings

1. For the dressing, mince the onion in a food processor or by hand. If you're using a processor, add the basil, oil, vinegar, salt and red pepper flakes and process for several seconds. Transfer to a mixing bowl. By hand, mince the basil and put it in a bowl with the minced onion, oil, vinegar, salt and pepper flakes.

2. For the salad, cut the bell peppers into ½-inch dice and add to the bowl.

3. Cut the salami into ⅛-inch by 1½-inch strips and the cheese into ¼-inch cubes. Add them to the bowl and toss gently.

4. Cook the tortellini according to the package instructions. Drain and toss gently with the salad. Serve immediately or cover and refrigerate overnight. Adjust the seasoning before serving. Serve at room temperature.

DRESSING:
1 small red onion
   (4 ounces), peeled
½ cup fresh basil leaves
¼ cup extra virgin olive oil
2 tablespoons red wine
   vinegar
¾ teaspoon salt
⅛ teaspoon crushed red
   pepper flakes

SALAD:
3 large bell peppers (1½
   pounds total), preferably
   1 each of red, yellow
   and green, roasted
   (see page 336)
2 ounces thinly sliced
   Genoa salami
2 ounces Fontinella cheese
8 ounces fresh or frozen
   cheese-filled tortellini

The addition of shrimp carries this vibrant pasta salad into the main course category. I especially enjoy it as part of a buffet or in summer when its light, fresh flavor is especially welcome. Try to use fresh herbs—it makes a tremendous difference.

Athenian Pasta Salad

Preparation time: 20 minutes
Cooking time: 12 minutes
Yield: 4 servings

DRESSING:

1 small red onion
   (4 ounces), peeled
1 large garlic clove,
   peeled
¾ cup fresh dill
½ cup fresh mint leaves
⅔ cup extra virgin olive oil
3 tablespoons fresh lemon
   juice
¼ teaspoon salt
   Freshly ground black
   pepper

SALAD:

16 medium cooked shrimp,
   peeled, with tail left on
8 ounces dried fusilli
   (corkscrew) pasta
12 cherry tomatoes
16 oil-cured black olives
6 ounces feta cheese
   Additional mint leaves,
   for garnish

1. For the dressing, mince the onion, garlic, dill and mint in a food processor or by hand. Mix with oil, lemon juice, salt and pepper. Toss ¼ cup of the dressing with the shrimp and refrigerate. Set the rest aside.

2. Bring 6 quarts salted water to a boil. Cook the pasta until al dente. Drain and toss with the remaining dressing while the pasta is still hot.

3. Cut the tomatoes in half and add them to the pasta along with the olives. Toss thoroughly and adjust the seasoning. The salad can be made a day in advance to this point, covered tightly and refrigerated. Bring to room temperature before serving.

4. Just before serving, cut the cheese into ⅓-inch dice and add it to the salad; toss very gently so the cheese doesn't crumble. Garnish the salad with the shrimp and the mint leaves. Serve warm or at room temperature.

Note: If fresh herbs are not available, use 2 tablespoons dried dill and 2 teaspoons dried mint, minced together with ¼ cup of fresh parsley leaves.

This sumptuous chicken salad comes from Convito Italiano, a pair of carry-out shop/restaurants in the Chicago area. Owned by Nancy Barocci, they convey integrity, commitment and a style that is most definitely Italian. Artichokes, sun-dried tomatoes, green pepper and a bit of smoked ham are the flavorful additions to big, moist pieces of white and dark chicken dressed with mayonnaise.

___Chicken and Artichoke Salad Convito Italiano___

Preparation time: 15 minutes
Cooking time: 25 minutes (Microwave: 20 minutes)
Yield: 4 servings

1. For the salad, place the chicken in a shallow pan, season with salt and pepper and cover tightly with aluminum foil. Bake in a preheated 425-degree oven until the breast portions are cooked, about 20 minutes. Remove the breasts and continue to cook the leg and thigh portions until the juice from the thigh runs clear, about 5 minutes longer. When cool enough to handle, remove the skin and cut the meat into 1-inch pieces. Transfer to a mixing bowl.

2. Gently squeeze the water from the artichokes, then quarter lengthwise. Cut the ham into ½-inch squares and the green pepper into 1½-inch by ⅛-inch strips. Add these ingredients to the bowl.

3. For the dressing, combine the mayonnaise, tomatoes, lemon juice and salt in a food processor or blender and mix until the tomatoes are minced.

4. Add to the salad and mix gently. Can be prepared 2 days in advance, covered and refrigerated. Mix well and adjust the seasoning before serving.

MICROWAVE: Arrange the chicken in a shallow, 10-inch round microwave dish, placing the thicker part around the edge of the dish. Cover tightly and cook on high power (100%) for 10 minutes. Turn the pieces over, cover and cook until the breast portions are cooked, about 5 minutes. Remove them and continue to cook the thigh and leg portions until the juices run clear instead of pink, about 5 minutes longer. Complete as in steps 2 through 4.

Note: I prefer the flavor of dried tomatoes that are not packed in oil because they have little or no added salt. If you

SALAD:
1 large frying chicken (about 3¼ pounds), quartered
Salt
Freshly ground pepper
1 can (14 ounces) artichokes in water, rinsed and drained
2 ounces thinly sliced smoked ham
½ of a medium green pepper (use 2 ounces)

DRESSING:
¾ cup mayonnaise (see page 327 or store-bought)
6 sun-dried tomatoes, softened in water (see Note)
1 to 2 teaspoons fresh lemon juice
¼ teaspoon salt, or to taste

117 •

cannot find them, use oil-packed with the least amount of added salt. If you do use oil-packed tomatoes it will not be necessary to soften them in water.

◆

Colorful and bold, this salad is Southern in inspiration, universal in appeal. Apple is a surprise ingredient, adding a crunchy, sweet-tart bite. A lot of black pepper is used to counter the sweet dressing and add a piquant edge.

Sweet and Sour Ham Salad with Black-eyed Peas

Preparation time: 15 minutes
Yield: 4 to 6 servings

DRESSING:

- ⅓ cup safflower oil
- 3 tablespoons cider vinegar
- 1 tablespoon Dijon mustard
- 2 teaspoons sugar
- 2 teaspoons coarsely cracked black pepper
- ½ teaspoon salt

SALAD:

- 1 large Granny Smith apple (7 ounces), unpeeled
- 1 large red pepper (7 ounces)
- 6 medium green onions (3 ounces total)
- 1¼ pounds smoked ham, sliced ½-inch thick
- 1 can (15 ounces) black-eyed peas, rinsed and drained

1. For the dressing, mix the oil, vinegar, mustard, sugar, pepper and salt.

2. For the salad, place the ingredients in a mixing bowl as they are cut. Cut the apple into small dice. Cut the red pepper into 1½-inch by ⅛-inch strips. Cut the green onions into rings. Cut the ham into ½-inch cubes.

3. Add the black-eyed peas and the dressing to the bowl and mix gently. The salad can be served immediately or covered tightly and refrigerated for several hours. Mix well and adjust the seasoning before serving if necessary.

Succotash, a thoroughly American dish of corn and lima beans, is enlivened with shrimp and a creamy dill dressing in a colorful summer salad. It is a delightful way to use leftover corn on the cob should it be your good fortune to have some.

Shrimp and Succotash Salad with Creamy Dill Dressing

Preparation time: 15 minutes
Cooking time: 10 minutes (Microwave: 9 minutes)
Yield: 4 to 6 servings

1. For the salad, cook the lima beans in boiling water just until they begin to soften, 5 to 10 minutes, depending on their size. Drain and set aside until cool.

2. Cut the bacon into ¼-inch dice. Fry in a small skillet until crisp.

3. Mince the onion and transfer to a large bowl. Reserve 6 shrimp for garnish and cut the rest crosswise into thirds. Add them to the onion along with the lima beans, corn and bacon.

4. For the dressing, mix the mayonnaise, orange juice, cream, dill and salt.

5. Toss the dressing into the salad. Serve immediately or cover tightly and refrigerate overnight. Mix well and adjust the seasoning, if necessary, before serving. Serve garnished with whole shrimp and dill sprigs.

MICROWAVE: Wrap the lima beans in plastic wrap and place on a paper plate. Cook on high power (100%) just until they begin to soften, 4 to 7 minutes. Test for doneness through the plastic with the tip of a sharp knife. Set aside to cool. Cut the bacon into ¼-inch dice. Place on a paper plate lined with several thicknesses of paper toweling. Cover with a paper towel and cook on high power until crisp, 2 to 2½ minutes. Finish as in steps 3, 4 and 5.

SALAD:
1½ cups fresh baby lima beans (or a 10-ounce box frozen)
2 ounces slab bacon
1 small red onion (2 ounces), peeled
1¼ pounds large shrimp, cooked and peeled
1½ cups corn (fresh-cooked or frozen)

DRESSING:
½ cup mayonnaise (see page 327 or store-bought)
¼ cup orange juice
2 tablespoons whipping cream
3 tablespoons minced fresh dill, or 2 teaspoons dried
¼ teaspoon salt, or to taste
Dill sprigs, for garnish

This basic dressing has a wide range of uses and can be the foundation of many variations you may wish to make. Which oil and vinegar you select will change its character to suit any salad. Safflower oil is tasteless, but very light, so it's a good oil to mix with other more flavorful oils such as walnut or hazelnut. Sometimes olive oil alone will seem too heavy, so, again, you might mix it with safflower oil.

For the vinegar, use red wine, sherry, white wine or cider vinegar—or lemon juice instead. The dressing can be used plain or flavored with herbs or savory condiments.

Basic Vinaigrette Dressing

¾ cup oil of your choice or a combination as suggested above
¼ cup vinegar, as suggested above
1 teaspoon salt
Freshly ground black pepper

Preparation time: 5 minutes
Yield: 1 cup

Mix the oil, vinegar, salt and pepper. The dressing can be refrigerated for up to 2 weeks.

◆

Sweet and Sour Dill Dressing

1 small shallot (¼ ounce), peeled
¾ cup safflower oil
¼ cup cider vinegar
2 tablespoons mayonnaise (see page 327 or store-bought)
1½ tablespoons Dijon mustard
2 teaspoons sugar
1½ teaspoons dried dill
½ teaspoon salt
½ teaspoon coarsely cracked black pepper

Preparation time: 5 minutes
Yield: 1 cup

Mince the shallot in a food processor or by hand. Add the oil, vinegar, mayonnaise, mustard, sugar, dill, salt and pepper and mix until smooth. Can be refrigerated up to 1 week.

Blue Cheese Dressing

Preparation time: 10 minutes
Yield: ¾ cup

¼ cup parsley leaves
½ cup safflower oil
2 tablespoons sherry vinegar
1 teaspoon Dijon mustard
Salt
Freshly ground white pepper
2½ ounces crumbled blue cheese

Mince the parsley in a food processor or by hand. Mix with the oil, vinegar, mustard, salt and pepper. Add the blue cheese. If you're using a processor, pulse it on and off several times, just enough to mix the ingredients. Do not overprocess—the cheese should stay in small pieces. By hand, mix cheese in with a fork, using the back of the fork to break up some of the cheese so it is creamy. The dressing can be refrigerated for up to 1 week.

◆

With its slightly sweet flavor, this dressing is delicious on meat salads and cole slaw or used as a dip.

Honey Mustard Dressing

Preparation time: 10 minutes
Yield: About 1 cup

1 medium shallot (¾ ounce), peeled
½ cup safflower oil
3 tablespoons cider vinegar
2½ tablespoons Dijon mustard
1½ tablespoons honey
1 large egg white
¼ teaspoon salt
Freshly ground pepper

Mince the shallot in a food processor or by hand. Add the oil, vinegar, mustard, honey, egg white, salt and pepper and process or mix with a whisk until well combined. Dressing can be refrigerated for up to 3 days.

6 · Fish and Shellfish

The continuing emphasis on fresh, light meals puts the spotlight right on fish and shellfish. To its positive nutritional stance, add the fast, easy cooking and the wide variety that mark fish, and it clearly is the food of choice for many meals. People are now very receptive to fish, not only to savoring the all-time favorites such as salmon, shrimp and scallops, but also to trying the lesser-known species that are now widely available. All but unheard of a decade ago, mahi-mahi, orange roughy, tilefish and shark are sought after and appreciated for their varied tastes. And the energetic distributors who fly fish and other fresh ingredients around the country can be thanked for the incredible variety to be found even in landlocked cities.

People are much more comfortable about cooking fish at home than they once were. Fish is actually among the easiest foods to cook. The most common mistake is overcooking. For years, the oft-quoted rule was to cook fish until it flaked with a fork. In fact, fish cooked until it flakes is hopelessly overdone, dry and lacking in flavor. Instead it should be cooked just to the point that its flesh loses its translucence and turns opaque. Unlike meat, all species of fish are tender and will cook quickly. A simple and fairly accurate guide to fish cooking has been developed by the Canadian Department of Fisheries. Their recommendation is to cook fish 10 minutes for every inch of thickness. It is a good guideline, but keep in mind that it is just that—a guide. There will always be fluctuations in cooking time. It pays to be attentive to the fish as it cooks, to catch it at the perfect point between done and overdone. As you gain experience, you may find that testing for doneness is most easily done by feeling the fish. Properly cooked, it will be firm in the center, though not hard. This takes practice, but once learned, I find it to be the easiest way.

I can't say enough about buying fresh fish and then using it quickly. It is now possible to buy fresh fish in all large urban areas. Once home, keep it in the coldest part of the refrigerator and plan on cooking it that day, if possible. I make a habit of calling the fish store to see when they are getting new shipments so I can be sure the fish is fresh.

Many cooking methods are appropriate for fish and shellfish. Grilling is one of my favorites. The ease, the delicate taste imparted and the sheer simplicity—to say nothing of the natural exhaust system in the great outdoors—are all weighted equally in my preference. Except for the harshest days in January, I find I can grill outdoors all year long, even in the Midwest, where I live. Broiling is always an alternative to grilling, though it doesn't impart quite the same flavor to the fish.

Other methods to consider are poaching, baking, sautéing and steaming, all of which yield fine results.

No discussion of fish cookery would be complete without mentioning the microwave oven. When cooking for one or two persons, it does a masterful job in a short amount of time. Across the board, I've had consistently good results with both fish and shellfish by arranging them so the thicker parts are at the edge of the dish where they'll cook more quickly. I then cover the dish with plastic wrap and cook on medium power (50%). Even though the total cooking time is slightly longer than when cooked on high power, there's more control and less chance of overcooking the fish.

When you're cooking for more than two persons, or adding a sauce to the fish, conventional cooking is often as fast as, or faster than, cooking in the microwave oven. For this reason, many of these recipes do not include microwave oven directions. Do consider the microwave, however, for quick, after-work meals or when cooking fish and shellfish for salads.

The briny, slightly sweet taste of shrimp and the pungent tang of feta cheese share a natural affinity. Here, they shape the character of this simple to make, yet elegant, main course. Most of the work can be done in advance so that only a final, brief heating in the oven or microwave oven is needed before serving. Doubling or tripling the recipe is no problem, making this a good choice for entertaining.

Baked Shrimp, Greek Style

Preparation time: 15 minutes
Cooking time: 20 minutes
Yield: 6 servings

36 large shrimp, shells on
   (about 2 pounds)
4 fresh plum tomatoes
   (12 ounces total)
3 large garlic cloves, peeled
6 tablespoons unsalted
   butter
¾ teaspoon dried oregano
   Scant ½ teaspoon salt, or
   to taste
¼ teaspoon crushed red
   pepper flakes
¾ cup dry vermouth
3 ounces feta cheese
3 tablespoons minced fresh
   dill and/or parsley

1. Peel the shrimp, leaving the tail attached. Make a slit down the back and remove the vein. Rinse under cold water and pat dry. Core the tomatoes, cut in half crosswise and squeeze gently to remove the seeds. Cut into ½-inch dice. Mince the garlic in a food processor or by hand.

2. Melt the butter in a large skillet over medium-high heat. Add the garlic, shrimp, oregano, salt and pepper flakes and cook, turning once, until the shrimp are almost but not quite cooked, 3 to 4 minutes. The shrimp will be cooked again in the oven, so be

sure they are still a bit undercooked at this stage. Remove the shrimp from the skillet and transfer them to a shallow casserole just large enough to hold the shrimp in a single layer, or to 6 individual baking dishes.

3. Add the vermouth to the skillet and boil over high heat until it is reduced by half, about 3 minutes. Add the tomatoes and cook just until heated through, about 30 seconds. Add the tomatoes and the cooking liquid to the shrimp, dividing it equally if you are using individual dishes. Crumble the cheese over the top. The recipe can be prepared a day in advance to this point, covered and refrigerated. Bring to room temperature before finishing.

4. 15 minutes before baking, place the rack in the center of the oven and preheat oven to 350 degrees.

5. Bake until bubbly, about 15 minutes. Sprinkle with dill or parsley and serve immediately.

MICROWAVE: You can cook the shrimp in the microwave if you prefer, though it will take longer in the end since this must be done in two batches on medium power. I recommend stovetop cooking of the shrimp as in steps 1, 2 and 3 above, then finishing the recipe in the microwave oven. Be sure to put the cooked shrimp in a microwave-safe dish or dishes. Skip steps 4 and 5. Cook, uncovered, on medium power (50%), until hot, 4 to 5 minutes. Sprinkle with dill or parsley and serve immediately.

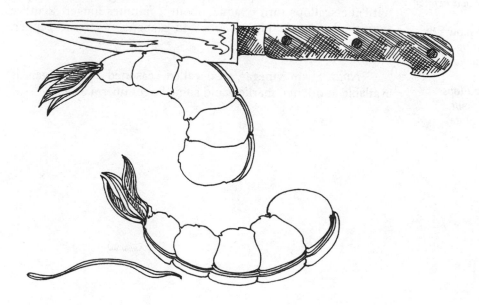

Here I've tapped the influences of both Asian and American cooking. Red, green and yellow vegetables and a mix of fresh herbs add splashes of color and flavor to sweet bay scallops. I especially like this served with white rice or linguine noodles. Then, if I'm lucky enough to have leftovers, I toss it all together and serve it on lettuce greens as a delicious salad the next day.

Cooking in the microwave oven offers no advantages so I've not included instructions. Feel confident that stovetop cooking time here is very short and cleanup is easy.

East-West Scallops

Preparation time: 15 minutes
Cooking time: 6 minutes
Yield: 3 to 4 servings

¼ *cup fresh mint leaves*
¼ *cup cilantro leaves*
½ *small jalapeño or serrano pepper*
1 *small red onion (2 ounces), peeled*
1 *small red bell pepper (3 ounces)*
1 *small yellow bell pepper (3 ounces)*
¼ *pound small snow peas*
¼ *cup light-tasting olive oil*
½ *teaspoon Oriental sesame oil*
1 *pound bay scallops*
2½ *tablespoons sushi vinegar (see Note)*

1. Mince the mint, cilantro and jalapeño or serrano pepper together, either in a food processor or by hand and set aside. Mince the onion, either in the processor or by hand. Cut the bell peppers into ½-inch dice. Remove the strings from the snow peas.

2. Heat the oils together in a large skillet or wok. When hot, add the bell peppers and onion and cook over medium-high heat, stirring often, until softened, about 3 minutes.

3. Add the snow peas, scallops and vinegar and cook just until the scallops turn opaque, about 2 minutes longer. Remove from the heat and add the herbs and jalapeño or serrano pepper. Serve immediately.

Note: Sushi vinegar, also called seasoned rice vinegar, is available at oriental markets and some large supermarkets.

Talk about fast! Not many dishes cook in just 2 minutes but this one does, with superb results. Salmon fillets, sliced so thin they're almost transparent, are cloaked in a citrusy dressing. Then they are arranged right on dinner plates and popped into a very hot oven. This is also good served at room temperature. Most china and ceramic plates can withstand the heat for the short amount of time they're in the oven, but very fine bone china should not be used.

_____Two-Minute Baked Salmon Scaloppine_____

Preparation time: 5 minutes
Marinating time: 10 minutes
Cooking time: 2 minutes
Yield: 2 servings

3 tablespoons fresh orange juice
2 tablespoons extra virgin olive oil
1 tablespoon dry vermouth
1 tablespoon fresh lemon juice
1 teaspoon soy sauce
1 teaspoon finely minced orange zest
¼ teaspoon salt
10 to 12 ounces salmon fillets, skinned, cut on the bias as thin as possible, about ¹⁄₁₆ inch (see Note)
1 teaspoon snipped fresh chives or minced parsley

1. 15 minutes before baking, place the rack in the center of the oven and preheat oven to 500 degrees.

2. Mix the orange juice, oil, vermouth, lemon juice, soy sauce, orange zest and salt in a large plastic food bag. Add the salmon and seal the bag tightly with a twist tie, right against the salmon. Turn the bag over several times so the fish is well coated with the marinade. Let marinate for 10 minutes.

3. Arrange the fish on 2 china dinner plates, covering the entire surface of the plate, except the rim, overlapping the fish as little as possible. Brush lightly with a small amount of the remaining marinade.

4. Bake just until the surface of fish lightens in color, about 2 minutes. Sprinkle with chives or parsley and serve immediately.

Note: It's best to have the fish market cut the fish for you. Explain that you would like it cut as for gravlax. If you slice it yourself, place it in the freezer until it is firm, but not completely frozen, so that the slicing will be easier. In either case, if the fish is not quite thin enough, you can flatten it by pressing it firmly but gently between 2 pieces of plastic wrap.

Many people look for an alternative to beef hamburgers. This is the best one yet, a "meaty" and juicy swordfish burger that's every bit as good as, if not better than, its beefy counterpart. It's also a lesson in economy, stretching what would normally serve 2 people into 4 generous burgers. Try them on a big onion roll with lettuce, tomato and mustardy mayonnaise—delicious!

Grilled Swordfish Burgers

Preparation time: 10 minutes
Grilling time: About 6 minutes
Yield: 4 3½-inch burgers

1. Mince the onion in a food processor. Add the bread, butter, cream, mustard, paprika and salt and process until smooth. Add the fish and purée, stopping several times to scrape down the sides of the work bowl.

2. Lightly flour your hands and gently shape the mixture into 4 patties, about ¾-inch thick, 3½ inches in diameter. The patties can be cooked immediately or refrigerated for several hours.

3. Cook over a hot charcoal fire, turning once, until cooked through. Swordfish burgers can also be broiled or sautéed in equal parts of butter and oil. Serve immediately.

1 *small onion (2 ounces), peeled*
2 *slices good-quality white bread*
3 *tablespoons unsalted butter, softened*
2 *tablespoons whipping cream*
2 *teaspoons Dijon mustard*
½ *teaspoon Hungarian paprika*
½ *teaspoon salt*
14 *ounces well-trimmed swordfish, cut in 1-inch cubes*
Flour, for shaping

129 •

Swordfish is one of my favorite ocean teasures, mild-tasting, meaty and substantial. It does, however, require some thought in preparation, since it can be somewhat bland. Brushing the steaks with a mustard glaze before they are cooked overcomes that obstacle and adds a delicious savory tang at the same time. Then they are topped with a lively relish that is just as good on other seafood —shrimp, mahi-mahi and scrod are all good bets. The fish can be served hot or at room temperature, making it ideal for warm weather dining.

Mustard-Glazed Swordfish with Tomato Feta Relish

Preparation time: 20 minutes
Cooking time: 5 to 10 minutes
Yield: 4 servings

1. For the relish, core the tomato, cut in half crosswise and remove the seeds and membrane, leaving only the outer shell. Cut the shell into ¼-inch dice and place in a small bowl. Slice the green onion into ¼-inch rings and add to tomatoes. Cut the cheese into ¼-inch cubes. Add to the bowl along with oil, lemon juice, dill and pepper, mixing gently so the cheese doesn't crumble. Relish can be made a day in advance and refrigerated. Bring to room temperature before using.

2. For the fish, mix the mustard, oil, vinegar, oregano and salt until smooth. The mixture can be refrigerated for up to 4 days.

3. Prepare a hot grill or preheat the broiler. Generously brush 1 side of each piece of fish with mustard glaze. Broil, glazed side up; or grill over charcoal, glazed side down, to desired doneness. Cook other side, brushing with glaze, until done, taking care not to overcook.

4. To serve hot, transfer the fish to warm plates, spoon 3 tablespoons relish over top and garnish with fresh dill. Or serve at room temperature. If you're serving the fish at room temperature, it can be cooked a day in advance and refrigerated. Remove from the refrigerator about 25 minutes in advance to remove the chill and garnish with relish and dill as above.

RELISH:
- 1 medium tomato (6 ounces)
- 1 small green onion (½ ounce)
- 1½ ounces feta cheese
- ¼ cup extra virgin olive oil
- 1 tablespoon fresh lemon juice
- 3 tablespoons fresh dill or 1 teaspoon dried dill
- Freshly ground pepper

FISH:
- ¼ cup Dijon mustard
- ¼ cup extra virgin olive oil
- 2½ tablespoons red wine vinegar
- 1 teaspoon ground oregano
- ½ teaspoon salt
- 4 swordfish steaks (approximately 10 ounces each)
- Sprigs of fresh dill for garnish

Shrimp is always a popular choice for entertaining. Here they're treated rather exotically with a fragrant and spicy blend of Indian spices. The spiciness of the shrimp is countered with sweet orange-flavored onions, though the overall effect is still fairly hot. To tone it down a bit, use the smaller amount of cayenne pepper.

For a main dish, I serve this over a bed of cooked leaf spinach or with white rice. It's also a great choice on a buffet, or as a first course or part of an assortment of *tapas*.

Punjab Spiced Shrimp with Sweet Cooked Onions

Preparation time: 15 minutes
Cooking time: 13 minutes
Yield: 3 to 4 servings

1 pound large shrimp, shells on (24 count)
2 teaspoons cider vinegar
¾ to 1 teaspoon cayenne pepper
1 teaspoon ground cumin
½ teaspoon salt
2 medium sweet onions (14 ounces total), peeled
¼ cup light-tasting olive oil
2 teaspoons Oriental sesame oil
½ cup orange juice

1. Peel the shrimp, leaving tail attached, and remove the vein. Rinse and pat dry. Transfer to a plastic bag.

2. Mix the vinegar, cayenne, cumin and ¼ teaspoon salt to a smooth paste. Add to the shrimp. Working through the bag, mix the spice mixture with the shrimp, coating them completely. Set aside to marinate while you cook the onions.

3. Cut the onions into thin slices, either with the medium (3mm) slicer of a food processor or by hand.

4. Heat the oils together in a 10-inch skillet. When hot, add the onions and remaining ¼ teaspoon salt and cook over high heat until they are very soft and light brown, about 7 minutes. Add the orange juice and cook until most of the juice has evaporated. Add the shrimp and cook, stirring several times, until they turn opaque, about 3 minutes. Serve warm or at room temperature. This can be made a day in advance and reheated gently in a large skillet.

Crab cakes are a special treat either as an entree or a first course. This particular rendition, one of the best, comes from Henry Markwood of the Winnetka Grill in Winnetka, Illinois. The Dusseldorf mustard and Asiago cheese are the lively secrets. Shaping and sautéing them takes a little time, though hardly too much for someone who loves crab cakes.

Pan-Fried New Orleanian Crab Cakes

Preparation time: 20 minutes
Cooking time: 25 minutes
Yield: 12 3-inch cakes (4 main-course or 6 first-course servings)

1. Finely crumb 6 slices of the bread in a food processor or blender. Transfer the crumbs to a shallow pie plate.

2. Finely mince the cheese and parsley together in the processor or blender. Mix with eggs, oil, the 2 tablespoons mayonnaise, Worcestershire, lemon juice, mustard and salt.

3. Trim the crusts from the remaining 4 slices of bread and tear into ¼-inch pieces. Add the bread pieces to the cheese mixture along with the crab meat. If you are using a processor, combine with 3 to 4 pulses. Otherwise, transfer the cheese mixture from the blender to a bowl and mix in the bread and crab meat with a fork until they are uniformly moistened.

4. Shape into patties, using about ¼ cup of the mixture for each. The mixture will be loose—don't worry. If it is too sticky, dust your hands with flour. Roll the patties in the bread crumbs, then reshape, pressing the crumbs into the surface and forming a neat, compact patty about 3 inches in diameter. Roll in crumbs again, completely coating both sides and the edges. The patties can be shaped several hours in advance, arranged on a baking sheet lined with wax paper and refrigerated. Reshape gently before frying.

5. Heat vegetable oil to a depth of ½ inch in a frying pan until a bread crumb sizzles. When it is hot, add patties in batches, so they will not be crowded. Cook, turning once, until deep brown on both sides. Total cooking time is 6 to 8 minutes. Drain on paper towels. Keep cooked cakes warm in a single layer on a cookie sheet in a 250-degree oven while you cook the rest. Serve hot, with Mustard Mayonnaise.

10 slices good-quality white bread (8 ounces total)
1½ ounces Asiago cheese
¼ cup parsley leaves
2 large eggs
¼ cup extra virgin olive oil
2 tablespoons mayonnaise
2 teaspoons Worcestershire sauce
2 teaspoons fresh lemon juice
1 teaspoon Dusseldorf mustard
½ teaspoon salt
12 ounces lump crab meat, picked through to remove shell and cartilage
Vegetable oil, for cooking
Mustard Mayonnaise (see page 327)

Light and delicately flavored, this is a beautiful presentation, ideal for summer meals. The smoky taste of grilled tuna is enhanced by garden-fresh tomatoes, sweet onion and tender spinach leaves. Lemon adds a lively, fresh note, basil the fragrance of a summer herb garden. Like so many of the seafood recipes, this can be served hot or at room temperature, making it as versatile as it is delicious. And despite the long list of ingredients, it's quite easy to prepare.

—— Grilled Tuna with Lemon Fettuccine ——

Preparation time: 25 minutes
Grilling time: 8 to 10 minutes
Cooking time: 12 minutes
Yield: 6 servings

1¾ pounds fresh tuna steaks
⅓ cup plus 1 tablespoon garlic oil (see page 333) or 1 small garlic clove, minced, added to ⅓ cup plus 1 tablespoon light-tasting olive oil
Salt
Freshly ground white pepper
1 medium red onion (6 ounces), peeled
2 medium tomatoes (14 ounces total)
3 cups loosely packed baby spinach leaves (3 ounces)
4 ounces Parmesan cheese, preferably imported
9 ounces dried fettuccine
Zest of ½ lemon, removed with a zester or grater
½ to 1 cup chicken stock (see page 327) or canned broth
2 tablespoons fresh lemon juice
⅓ cup julienned fresh basil leaves
6 lemon wedges

1. Prepare a hot grill, the fire preferably made with a mix of charcoal and 1 cup soaked mesquite wood chips. Or place the broiler rack 6 inches from the heat and preheat the broiler.

2. Rinse and dry the tuna. Brush with 1 tablespoon garlic oil and season with salt and pepper. Grill or broil, turning once, just until barely cooked in the center. Do not overcook. Carefully break the fish into ¾-inch chunks.

3. Cut the onion into ¼-inch dice. Core the tomatoes and cut them in half crosswise. Gently squeeze each half to remove the seeds. Cut into ½-inch dice. Cut the spinach into ½-inch ribbons. Shred the cheese finely, either with the fine shredder of a food processor or the fine side of a grater.

4. Bring a large pot of salted water to a boil. Add the pasta and cook until it is *al dente*. Drain well. The recipe can be prepared a day in advance to this point. In that case toss the cooked pasta with several teaspoons oil. Wrap each ingredient separately and refrigerate.

5. To finish the recipe, heat the remaining ⅓ cup garlic oil in a large sauté pan. When it is hot, add the onion dice and cook over medium heat, stirring often, until they are softened, about 3 minutes. Add the tomatoes, lemon zest, ¾ cup stock or broth and lemon juice and bring to a simmer. Toss in the pasta and cook until heated through. Gently toss in the tuna and spinach and cook until hot. Moisten with more stock or broth, if necessary. Remove from the heat, gently toss in the basil and adjust the seasonings.

6. To serve, divide among 6 plates and arrange the cheese in

a circle around the edge of the pasta. Serve hot or at room temperature with a lemon wedge.

◆

When it's sparkling fresh, scrod is a remarkably sweet and mild-tasting fish. Here its pure taste is reinforced in a simple preparation, without heavy sauces or spices. Instead it's set off with a crisp sheath of bread crumbs. The crumbs must be coarsely textured, so be sure not to use packaged crumbs. Some people like tartar sauce with this, others like lemon wedges.

Crispy Broiled Scrod

Preparation time: 10 minutes
Broiling time: 6 to 10 minutes
Yield: 4 servings

1. 15 minutes before cooking, place the rack 8 inches from the heat source and preheat the broiler. Line a baking sheet with aluminum foil.

2. Shred the bread with the shredder of a food processor or on the large side of a hand grater. Transfer to a large piece of wax paper.

3. Mix the oil, lemon juice and salt in a small dish. Rub over both sides of fillets. It's easiest to do this with your fingers, but it can be brushed on if you prefer. Coat both sides with the bread crumbs.

4. Broil, watching closely, just until the fish is opaque in the center. Timing will depend on the thickness of the fish, and should be no longer than 10 minutes for the thickest fillet. Do not overcook.

5. Sprinkle with dill, if desired, and serve immediately.

3-inch piece stale French bread
4 teaspoons light-tasting olive oil
4 teaspoons fresh lemon juice
1/8 teaspoon salt
4 scrod fillets, 6 to 7 ounces each
2 tablespoons minced fresh dill, optional
Tartar Sauce, optional (see page 327)
Lemon wedges
Dill sprigs, optional

This boldly flavored sauce is from a recipe that was shared with me by Leslee Reis of Café Provençal in Evanston, just north of Chicago. It's a perfectly orchestrated balance of tartness and assertiveness, tempered by the sweetness of butter and cream. Besides salmon, the sauce can be used on veal scaloppine.

Grilled Salmon with Lemon Caper Sauce

Preparation time: 20 minutes
Marinating time: 2 hours or overnight
Cooking time: 25 minutes
Yield: 4 servings

FISH:
¼ cup parsley leaves
¼ cup fresh basil leaves
2 large shallots
(1½ ounces total),
peeled
⅓ cup extra virgin olive oil
⅓ cup safflower oil
4 salmon fillets

SAUCE:
2½ tablespoons fresh lemon juice
¼ cup dry white wine
¼ cup fish stock (or 2 tablespoons each of water and clam juice)
¼ cup whipping cream
1 anchovy fillet
1 teaspoon Dijon mustard
6 tablespoons unsalted butter, softened
1½ tablespoons capers, drained
Salt
Cayenne pepper

1. For the fish, mince the parsley, basil and shallots in a food processor or by hand. Transfer to a large plastic bag. Add both oils and the salmon. Seal the bag with a twist tie right against the fish, and turn it over several times to coat the fish with the marinade. Refrigerate for 2 hours or overnight, turning over occasionally.

2. Prepare the sauce. Cook the lemon juice, wine and stock in a 1-quart non-aluminum pan until liquid is reduced to 2 tablespoons, about 12 minutes. Add the cream and boil until it is reduced to ¼ cup, 2 to 3 minutes longer.

3. Purée the reduction with the anchovy and mustard in a mini-chopper or blender. (A standard-sized processor is too large for this small amount.) Return the mixture to the pan.

4. Over low heat, whisk in the butter, 1 tablespoon at a time, waiting until each piece is incorporated before adding another. Remove from heat and add 1 tablespoon capers, salt and cayenne pepper to taste. Place the sauce in a warm spot while you cook the fish.

5. Place the oven rack 8 inches from the heat source and preheat the broiler. Remove fish from the marinade and gently pat dry with a paper towel. Arrange the fillets on the broiler pan, skin side down. Broil until the flesh is opaque, about 8 minutes, depending on the thickness of the fish—be careful not to overcook it. Nap each fillet with about 2 tablespoons sauce and garnish with remaining capers.

In Italy, this type of sauce is often paired with seafood. In keeping with that, I've partnered it with fresh mussels for a simple and utterly delightful supper. A loaf of Italian bread to soak up the sauce and a jug of red wine are all that's necessary to complete the meal.

Mussels with Italian Tomato Sauce

Preparation time: 10 minutes
Soaking time: 30 minutes
Cooking time: About 10 minutes (Microwave: About 12 minutes)
Yield: 2 servings

1. Pull the beards from the mussels. Put the mussels in a 3-quart pan with cold water to cover; set aside to soak for 30 minutes. Drain mussels and rinse the grit from the pan. Discard any mussels that feel unusually heavy because these are full of sand. Discard any whose shells are open.

2. Put the mussels back in the pan without any additional water, cover and cook over high heat just until the shells open, 5 to 7 minutes. Drain as much liquid as possible from the mussels without removing them from their shells. Discard any mussels that do not open. Divide between 2 large, shallow soup bowls, cover with foil and keep warm. Discard liquid and rinse the pan to get rid of grit.

3. Heat the tomato sauce in the same pan. When hot, stir in the oil and remove from the heat.

4. To serve, spoon the sauce over the mussels and garnish with parsley. Serve immediately.

MICROWAVE: Follow step 1. Cook mussels in 2 batches as follows. Put half in a shallow, 10-inch round microwave dish. Cover and cook on high power (100%) until shells open, 4 to 5 minutes. Using a slotted spoon, transfer to a large, shallow soup bowl. Cook the other half and place in another soup bowl. Cover and keep warm. Discard liquid and rinse the dish. Add the tomato sauce and cook on high power until hot, about 1½ minutes. Stir in the oil and serve as in step 4.

2 *dozen mussels*
2 *cups Italian Tomato Sauce (see page 226)*
1 *tablespoon full-flavored olive oil*
2 *tablespoons minced parsley*

This is a very simple preparation with great visual appeal. Its success depends on first-rate seafood, fresh and sea-sweet. The recipe comes from Avanzare, one of Chicago's premier Italian restaurants. There, it's served on skewers that are actually long stems of fresh rosemary with all the leaves removed except a tuft at one end.

Skewered Seafood with Arugula Butter

BUTTER:
- 1 medium clove garlic, peeled
- 6 tablespoons unsalted butter, chilled, cut into 6 pieces
- ¾ cup arugula
- 2 tablespoons fresh parsley, preferably flat leaf
- ½ teaspoon fresh lemon juice
- ¼ teaspoon brine-packed or water-packed green peppercorns, rinsed
- Salt
- Freshly ground black pepper

SEAFOOD:
- ¼ cup light-tasting olive oil
- ¼ cup fresh lemon juice
- 1 teaspoon dried rosemary
- Salt
- Freshly ground black pepper
- 12 fresh jumbo shrimp, peeled, tails intact
- 12 sea scallops
- 1½ pounds swordfish or tuna, cut into pieces the same size as the scallops

Preparation time: 20 minutes
Marinating time: 4 hours or overnight
Cooking time: 5 minutes
Yield: 6 servings

1. For the butter, mince the garlic in a food processor or blender. Add the butter, arugula, parsley, lemon juice, green peppercorns and salt and pepper to taste. Mix until smooth, stopping as necessary to scrape down the sides of the container. The butter can be refrigerated for 5 days, or frozen. Soften to room temperature before using.

2. For the seafood, mix the oil, lemon juice, rosemary, salt and pepper in a large plastic bag. Add the shrimp, scallops and fish and seal tightly, right against the seafood. Refrigerate at least 4 hours or overnight.

3. Arrange the shrimp, scallops and fish on 6 skewers, alternating each item. Leave a small space between each piece so they will cook evenly. The skewers can be assembled several hours in advance, covered tightly and refrigerated.

4. Prepare a hot charcoal or wood fire or preheat a broiler. Cook, turning the skewers once, just until fish turns opaque. Do not overcook. Spread each skewer with 1 tablespoon of the softened butter and serve immediately.

Note: Spinach can be substituted for the arugula.

The relish is a colorful, sweet-sour combination that I love as much for its versatility as for its wonderful, fresh taste. Here it is used to contrast with the richness of salmon steaks, a near-perfect partnership for summer meals. If you grill the salmon, either use an oiled fish basket or put the steaks on pieces of aluminum foil so they don't stick to the grill, which can be a very frustrating experience.

____Salmon Steaks with Sweet Cucumber Relish____

Preparation time: 20 minutes
Marinating time: 30 minutes
Cooking time: 10 minutes
Yield: 6 servings

1. For the marinade, mince the ginger and green onions in a food processor or by hand. Mix with the vinegar and mustard. Transfer to a large plastic bag, add the salmon and seal tightly, right next to the fish. Refrigerate for 30 minutes, turning the bag over several times.

2. For the relish, seed the cucumber but do not peel it. Cut the cucumber along with all the other relish vegetables into ⅛-inch dice. Mince the mint. Place the vegetables and mint in a bowl and mix with the vinegar and oil. The relish can be refrigerated up to 2 days in advance. Adjust the seasoning and the vinegar balance, if necessary, before using.

3. Prepare a hot charcoal fire on a barbecue grill or place the broiler rack 8 inches from the heat and preheat the broiler. Remove the salmon from the marinade. Let the excess drip off, but do not pat dry. Grill or broil, turning once, until fish lightens in color in the center and feels firm to the touch. Be careful not to overcook. Serve hot or at room temperature, topped with the relish.

Note: Sushi vinegar, also called seasoned rice vinegar, is available at oriental groceries, many large markets and specialty stores.

MARINADE:
1 *piece fresh ginger
(1-inch cube), peeled*
6 *small green onions
(2 ounces total)*
½ *cup sushi vinegar (see
Note)*
1 *teaspoon Dijon mustard*
6 *salmon steaks (about
8 ounces each)*

RELISH:
½ *medium English,
"gourmet", or "burpless"
cucumber (use 8 ounces)*
½ *small red bell pepper
(use 2 ounces)*
½ *small green bell pepper
(use 2 ounces)*
1 *small red onion
(2 ounces)*
1 *cup fresh peppermint
leaves*
¼ *cup sushi vinegar*
1 *tablespoon extra virgin
olive oil*

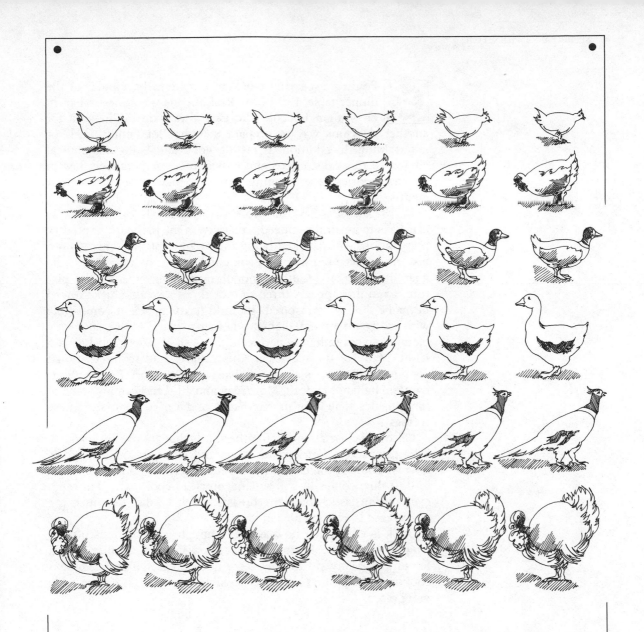

7 · Poultry

Poultry, especially chicken, is extremely popular at the dinner table. I can't think of anyone who doesn't like it, or of a single cook who isn't always on the lookout for another delicious way to prepare it, either for family meals or entertaining. In addition to tasting good and being economical compared to steaks, chops and roasts, it is comparatively low in fat and calories, a compelling reason to have it as part of our menus.

In 1825, Brillat-Savarin wrote that poultry is to the cook as canvas is to a painter. Indeed, creativity is the hallmark of poultry preparation, with chicken being the premier player. There is not just one or even ten ways to cook chicken, but literally hundreds, guaranteeing that mealtime monotony will never enter the picture. Even if it appears three to four times a week, chicken need never be dull or uninspired. Its mild flavor makes it compatible with many other ingredients, whether a marinade or an exotic blend of spices to lightly permeate the flesh or a fiery relish to top it off. Many of the recipes in this chapter nod to international cooking, and there is almost global representation. French, Vietnamese, Italian, Mexican, Moroccan and all-American are some of the cuisines that have inspired new and varied flavors in these recipes.

I also pay close attention to other birds that are readily available in supermarkets. Turkey has transcended its seasonality and is now welcome at the table all year long. Once sold only as a whole bird, it now comes in convenient, quick-to-cook parts. I'm especially enthusiastic about the breast, which I value for much the same reasons as I do chicken.

Duck is as popular now as ever, though its cooking is often a lengthy procedure. Fortunately there's a solution, similar to that for turkey. Many stores now carry duck breasts, a clever, quick-cooking strategy that makes it possible to put duck on the table more often.

When Bill Rice, author of *Feasts of Wine and Food,* started writing a weekly food and wine column for the *Chicago Tribune Sunday Magazine,* he debuted with a simple recipe, so simple, in fact, that it almost seemed too basic. But that was precisely his point. Life's most simple pleasures often get lost in the shuffle. So to Bill, and to everyone who remembers just how good a perfectly roasted chicken can be, I dedicate this, my own rendition, based on his.

Perfectly Roasted Chicken

Preparation time: 15 minutes
Baking time: 45 minutes
Yield: 3 to 4 servings

1. 15 minutes before roasting, place the rack in the center of the oven and preheat oven to 450 degrees. Line a shallow roasting pan with aluminum foil.
2. Wash the chicken and pat dry.
3. Mince the garlic in a food processor or by hand. Mix with the mustard, thyme, ½ teaspoon salt and pepper.
4. Starting at the breast and working down to the thigh area, separate the skin from the meat with your fingers, being careful not to tear the skin. Carefully spoon the mustard mixture into the space between the skin and the meat. Massage the breast and thigh area to disperse the mustard mixture evenly. Season the outside and the cavity with salt and pepper. The chicken can be baked immediately or covered and refrigerated overnight.
5. Place, breast side up, in the roasting pan. Bake in the preheated oven until the juice runs clear rather than pink when the thigh is pierced with a knife. This will take about 45 minutes. Let rest for 10 minutes before serving.

Note: A 5-pound roasting chicken can also be used. Double all the other ingredients and bake the chicken 20 minutes longer.

1 *large frying chicken, about 3½ pounds (see Note)*
2 *large garlic cloves, peeled*
3 *tablespoons Dijon mustard*
½ *teaspoon dried thyme*
Salt
Freshly ground black pepper

My fascination with Vietnamese food led me to the kitchens of Mekong Restaurant in Chicago, where I learned some tricks of their chef's culinary trade. Fascination, such as it is, grew into adoration and I rate the cuisine of Vietnam among my favorites. This dish is typical—hot, sweet and pungent all at the same time. Some of the ingredients, like the lemon grass, chili paste and *nuoc mam,* will require a special trip to an Asian market, a worthwhile adventure in and of itself. Rice is a typical side dish, but I like udon noodles or linguine just as well.

——Spicy Chicken with Lemon Grass——

Preparation time: 20 minutes
Marinating time: 2 to 12 hours
Cooking time: 5 minutes
Yield: 6 to 8 servings

2 stalks lemon grass
2 large egg yolks
¼ cup oyster sauce
1½ tablespoons nuoc mam (Vietnamese fish sauce)
2 teaspoons honey
2 teaspoons hoisin sauce
1½ teaspoons chili paste
4 whole boneless chicken breasts (about 3 pounds total), split
6 medium green onions (4 ounces total)
2 tablespoons peanut oil
Fresh cilantro leaves for garnish

1. Discard the coarse outer leaves of the lemon grass and cut the soft white center, about 3 inches, into ½-inch pieces. Mince it as fine as possible in a mini-chopper, blender or by hand and transfer to a small bowl. Mix with the egg yolks, oyster sauce, *nuoc mam,* honey, hoisin and chili paste. Transfer to a large plastic bag.

2. Remove the skin from chicken and cut the meat crosswise into ¾-inch strips. Add to the marinade, seal the bag tightly, close against the chicken, and refrigerate from 2 to 12 hours, turning the bag over occasionally.

3. Cut the green onions into ¼-inch-long rings.

4. Heat the oil in a wok or large skillet. When it is hot, add the chicken and marinade. Stir-fry over high heat just until the meat turns opaque, 2 to 3 minutes. Remove from heat and toss in the green onions. Serve immediately, garnished with cilantro.

Poulet au vinaigre is a classic recipe from the French country kitchen, so simple in its charms that it has become a fixture on bistro menus in France and now in the States as well. This version is inspired by Au Petit Truc, a bistro just outside Beaune in the Burgundian region of France. Edith Remoissent, owner and chef, has simplified the typical preparation and enlivened it with a bit of tarragon. Complete the meal and the mood with Mashed Potatoes Niçoise (see page 202).

Chicken in Vinegar with Tarragon

Preparation time: 15 minutes
Cooking time: 25 minutes
Yield: 4 servings

1. Wash the chicken and pat it dry. Season with salt and pepper.
2. Mince the garlic and shallots in a food processor or by hand. Core the tomatoes, cut them in half crosswise and squeeze gently to remove the seeds. Cut into ½-inch dice.
3. Melt the butter in the oil in a 12-inch skillet. When it is sizzling, add the chicken, skin side down. Brown over high heat, turning once, about 12 minutes. Remove from the pan and set aside. Pour off the fat from the skillet.
4. Return the skillet to high heat and carefully pour in the vermouth. Cook for 15 seconds, stirring constantly to scrape up any browned bits of chicken from the pan. Add the garlic, shallots and half the diced tomatoes and cook until the shallots are softened and most of the liquid has cooked away, about 3 minutes.
5. Add the vinegar and beef broth and bring to a boil. Add the legs and thighs, the accumulated meat juices and the tarragon. Cover and cook over medium heat for 6 minutes. Add the breasts and wings, cover and cook until all the chicken is cooked, about 4 minutes more. Toss in the remaining tomatoes during the last 2 minutes of cooking. Adjust the seasoning and serve immediately. The recipe can also be prepared 2 days in advance. If so, do not add the breasts, wings and remaining tomatoes as indicated above. To finish, arrange all pieces in a casserole along with sauce and remaining tomatoes. Cover with foil and bake in a preheated 375-degree oven until hot, about 20 minutes.

1 *large frying chicken (about 3¼ pounds), cut into serving pieces*
½ *teaspoon salt*
Freshly ground black pepper
1 *medium garlic clove, peeled*
4 *large shallots (2 ounces total), peeled*
4 *large plum tomatoes (14 ounces total)*
1½ *tablespoons unsalted butter*
1½ *tablespoons light-tasting olive oil*
½ *cup dry vermouth*
¼ *cup red wine vinegar*
¼ *cup beef stock (see page 390) or canned broth*
½ *teaspoon dried tarragon*

Cooking in airtight packets has several noteworthy advantages. For one thing, you get a wonderful concentration of flavors, since nothing escapes during cooking. For another, the packets can be made up in advance and refrigerated for up to a day. And, cooking time is short and does not require careful watching.

Oven-Steamed Chicken Breasts with Sun-Dried Tomatoes

Preparation time: 20 minutes
Baking time: 12 minutes (Microwave: 8 minutes)
Yield: 4 servings

6 sun-dried tomatoes, preferably dry-packed
1 teaspoon dried dill
¼ teaspoon dried tarragon
2 medium shallots (1 ounce total), peeled
4 tablespoons unsalted butter
½ cup whipping cream
1 teaspoon fresh lime juice
Salt
Freshly ground black pepper
2 whole boned and skinned chicken breasts (about 1¼ pounds), split

1. Place rack in center of oven and preheat to 500 degrees. Cut four 15-inch squares of heavy-duty aluminum foil or parchment paper.

2. Soak dry-packed tomatoes in hot water for 10 minutes, then drain and pat dry. If you're using tomatoes packed in oil, rinse them under hot water and pat dry (do not soak these). Whichever you use, cut them into ⅛-inch strips.

3. Mince the dill, tarragon and shallots together in a food processor or by hand.

4. Melt the butter in a 1-quart, non-aluminum pan. Add the shallot mixture and cook gently until the shallots are soft, about 5 minutes.

5. Add the tomatoes to the pan along with the cream, lime juice and salt and pepper to taste. Simmer over medium heat, stirring often, until thickened, about 5 minutes. Set aside, off the heat.

6. Place each chicken breast between 2 pieces of plastic wrap and press with a meat pounder or the bottom of a heavy pot to a uniform thickness. They don't need to be thin, just even.

7. Spread 1 tablespoon of the sauce on the center of each foil or parchment square. Top with a chicken breast and season with salt and pepper. Spoon another tablespoon of sauce over the chicken. Fold packets closed so they are airtight, leaving a little air space between the chicken and the foil. The packets can be assembled a day in advance and refrigerated; let them come to room temperature before cooking.

8. Place packets on a baking sheet. Bake for 12 minutes. Fold back foil and serve directly from the packets, or transfer the chicken and sauce to heated serving plates.

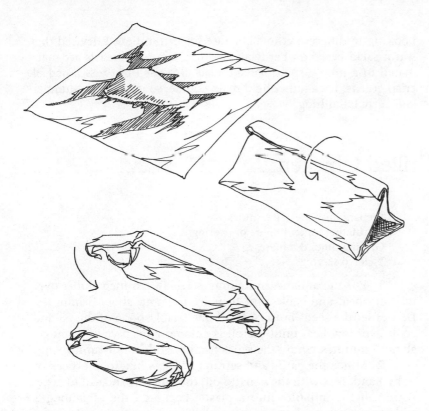

MICROWAVE: Cut four 12-inch squares of parchment paper. Follow steps 2 and 3 above. Combine the butter and shallot mixture in a 4-cup microwave dish. Cook, uncovered, on high power (100%) until softened, about 2 minutes. Add ⅓ cup cream only, the tomatoes and the lime juice. Cook, uncovered, on high power for 2 minutes. Follow steps 6 and 7, using parchment paper—do not use foil. Fold the paper in half to cover the chicken, then cut the folded paper into ovals about 2 inches larger all around than the chicken breast. Fold the edges and crimp them so they're airtight. Arrange one on each side of a 9-inch square microwave-proof baking dish, with the rounded edges facing the center of the dish. Cook, uncovered, on high power for 7 to 8 minutes, turning them over once halfway through.

Looking to different ethnic cuisines for inspiration, I devised this warm salad based on Peruvian cooking. Chicken breasts are marinated in a mildly spicy sauce that is also used to dress a bed of crisp greens. It's a rather light main course, so it's nice for summer and early fall dining.

Peruvian Grilled Chicken

Preparation time: 20 minutes
Marinating time: 4 hours or overnight
Grilling time: 8 minutes
Yield: 6 servings

1 tablespoon annatto seeds (see Note)
1½ teaspoons cumin seeds
½ cup light-tasting olive oil
2 medium garlic cloves, peeled
2 serrano peppers, seeded
¾ cup red wine vinegar Salt
3 whole boneless chicken breasts (about 2¼ pounds), split
1 large head red leaf lettuce (6 ounces)
8 medium green onions (3 ounces total)
1 cup cilantro leaves

1. Put the annatto and cumin seeds in a 6-inch skillet over medium heat and cook until they are fragrant, about 3 minutes. Do not let the seeds burn. Add all but 1 tablespoon of the oil and cook over low heat until the oil is colored a deep yellow-orange, about 5 minutes. Strain the seeds from the oil and discard them.

2. Mince the garlic and serrano peppers in a food processor or by hand. Mix with the annatto oil, the vinegar, and salt to taste. Pour half this mixture into a plastic bag. Add the remaining 1 tablespoon olive oil to the other half and set aside to use for dressing the greens.

3. Remove the skin and fat from the chicken. Add the breasts to the bag and seal tightly, against the chicken. Refrigerate at least 4 hours or overnight, turning the bag over several times.

4. Prepare a barbecue grill, preferably with a mix of charcoal and 1 cup of soaked mesquite wood chips; or place the broiler rack 6 inches from the heat and preheat the broiler.

5. Remove the chicken from the marinade, letting the excess drip off. Season lightly with salt. Grill or broil, turning once, just until the meat is no longer pink, about 8 minutes.

6. While the chicken is cooking, cut the lettuce and green onions into ¼-inch slices either with the thick (6mm) slicer of a processor or by hand.

7. Set aside 1 tablespoon of the reserved salad dressing. Toss the rest with the lettuce, green onions and cilantro. Divide the dressed greens among 6 plates. Cut each chicken breast horizontally into ⅜-inch strips. Reassemble to their original shape and place over lettuce. Moisten the chicken with the reserved dressing and serve immediately.

Note: Annatto seeds, also called achiote, are available at Latin

American groceries and many large supermarkets. If they are not available, they can be omitted. Add a pinch of turmeric instead, if desired, to achieve the gold color.

◆

Come summer, the barbecue grill puts in more hours than my stove. Besides being such a seasonal pleasure, grilling imparts nuances of flavor to foods that nothing else comes close to. This skewered mix of chicken and vegetables is a simple preparation, a prime candidate for summer grilling. Kabobs are terrific for casual outdoor eating, since everything is bite-size. The spices in the marinade are mild, though well defined, not at all overpowering to the delicate flavor of chicken. I've marinated a whole chicken this way, too, and reveled in adding the leftovers to a salad.

Chicken and Vegetable Brochettes

Preparation time: 20 minutes
Marinating time: 4 hours or overnight
Cooking time: 12 minutes
Yield: 6 servings

1. Mince the garlic and 1 ounce of onion in a food processor or by hand. Mix with the oil, lime juice, paprika, oregano, thyme, salt and cayenne. Transfer to a plastic bag and add the chicken. Seal bag tightly against the meat and turn it over several times so the chicken is well coated with the marinade. Refrigerate at least 4 hours or overnight, turning the bag over several times.

2. Prepare a hot barbecue fire, preferably with a mix of charcoal and 1 cup of soaked mesquite wood chips; or place a broiler rack 6 inches from heat and preheat the broiler.

3. Cut each chicken breast into 5 equal pieces. Slice the limes. Cut the onion lengthwise into 6 wedges, then separate each wedge into 2 pieces.

4. Arrange 6 skewers with the ingredients in this order: chicken, lime, chicken, onion, mushroom, chicken, tomato, chicken, onion, mushroom, chicken, tomato. Brush with marinade. The kabobs can be assembled several hours in advance and refrigerated.

5. Grill or broil, turning once, until the chicken turns opaque, about 12 minutes. Serve hot or at room temperature.

1 *medium garlic clove, peeled*
½ *small onion (use 1 ounce), peeled*
¼ *cup safflower oil*
1 *tablespoon lime juice*
2 *teaspoons sweet paprika*
1 *teaspoon ground oregano*
1 *teaspoon ground thyme*
1 *teaspoon salt*
⅛ *teaspoon cayenne pepper*
3 *whole boned and skinned chicken breasts, split (about 2 pounds total)*
2 *limes*
1 *large sweet onion (12 ounces), peeled*
12 *small mushrooms (4 ounces)*
12 *cherry tomatoes*

Steaming is a method of cooking that we most often associate with vegetables. Certain types of poultry and fish do well, too, especially chicken, as you'll see here. The steam generated from a large steamer is very intense and cooks food quickly with moist, flavorful results. You'll need a large steamer—at least 12 inches in diameter. Bamboo steamers sold with woks are fine to use, or fashion one yourself with a metal colander placed over an opened tuna fish can in a large, covered pot. Make sure there is enough water in the bottom of the steamer but not so much that it touches the food.

Here, a garden of colorful summer vegetables is joined by big, juicy chunks of chicken in a delicious main-course dish, full of freshness, style and verve. Once the cooking is under way, the dish is on the table in about 30 minutes. It can be served either hot or at room temperature.

Steamed Chicken and Vegetable Ratatouille

1 large frying chicken (3 pounds), cut into serving pieces
1 whole boneless chicken breast (about 14 ounces)
Salt
Freshly ground black pepper
2 large garlic cloves, peeled
1 large eggplant (1¼ pounds)
3 medium red bell peppers (14 ounces total)
2 small red onions (5 ounces total), peeled
1 small zucchini (4 ounces)
1 small yellow squash (4 ounces)
3 tablespoons light-tasting olive oil
¼ cup tomato paste
1 teaspoon balsamic vinegar
1 cup julienned fresh basil leaves

Preparation time: 20 minutes
Cooking time: 20 minutes
Yield: 6 servings

1. Wash the chicken and pat dry. Season with salt and pepper. Arrange in a single layer, skin side down, including the breast, in a large steamer over rapidly boiling water. Cover and cook, turning once, until cooked, about 8 minutes. Use tongs to remove chicken from the steamer and set aside on a plate, but do not discard the water. When the chicken is cool enough to handle, remove the skin from all the pieces and tear or cut the meat off the bones into large chunks.

2. While the chicken is cooking, prepare the vegetables. Mince the garlic in a food processor or by hand. Cut the eggplant, peppers and onions into ¾-inch dice. Cut the zucchini and yellow squash into ¼-inch slices, either with the thick (6mm) slicer of a processor or by hand.

3. Add the eggplant, pepper and onions to the steamer, cover and cook, stirring several times, until they are tender/crisp, about 8 minutes. Transfer the vegetables to a large bowl.

4. Remove the steamer insert and discard the water from the bottom of steamer. Add the oil and garlic to the pan or wok and cook over medium heat until garlic is soft but not brown, about 4 minutes. Add tomato paste and vinegar and stir until smooth. Add the vegetables and the chicken with any juices that have collected.

Cook until heated through. Remove from the heat, add the basil and adjust the salt and pepper to taste. Serve hot or at room temperature. This can be made in advance, short of adding the basil, and reheated on the stove or in the microwave oven.

◆

Occasionally I am overwhelmed with a desire for crispy fried chicken, biting through a crunchy, mildly seasoned coating and finding tender, juicy chicken underneath. Making the desire a reality stops me in my tracks. When I think of how fattening and cholesterol-laden it is, I turn to an alternative. This one delights me on all counts. Same great taste, crispy coating and eat-with-your-fingers pleasure, but with a fraction of the fat and calories. The skin is removed from the chicken before it's coated with crumbs, eliminating a significant amount of the fat right there. Then it's baked instead of fried.

Crispy Oven-Fried Chicken

Preparation time: 20 minutes
Baking time: 55 minutes
Yield: 4 servings

3 slices soft white bread (3 ounces total)
1 -ounce piece Parmesan cheese, preferably imported
2 tablespoons yellow cornmeal
1 large garlic clove, peeled
1½ teaspoons rubbed sage
¼ teaspoon cayenne pepper
¼ teaspoon salt
2 teaspoons light-tasting olive oil
1 large frying chicken (3 pounds), cut into serving pieces
3 tablespoons Dijon mustard
1½ teaspoons water

1. 15 minutes before baking, place the rack in the center of the oven and preheat to 375 degrees. Lightly grease a jelly roll pan.

2. Combine the bread, cheese, cornmeal, garlic, sage, cayenne and salt in a food processor or blender. Let the machine run until the mixture is finely crumbed, about 1 minute. Add the oil and mix just enough to moisten the crumbs. Transfer the crumbs to a shallow pie plate.

3. Remove the skin and fat from the chicken pieces, except the wings.

4. Stir the mustard and water together and spread over the chicken. Dip the chicken in the crumb mixture to coat with an even layer of crumbs—the coating should not be too thick. If it is, gently brush away the excess. Gently pat the crumbs in place.

5. Arrange the chicken in the pan with the meatier side up. Bake until crisp and golden, about 55 minutes. Serve hot or at room temperature.

Paillard is a French term, thought to be the name of a Parisian restaurateur, that now describes very thinly pounded meat. Because the meat is so thin, it cooks in under 2 minutes, fast by anyone's standards. Here, and in the recipe that follows, I use the same principle: pounding the meat, searing in a skillet and saucing very simply. For last-minute convenience, flattened chicken breasts freeze very well and defrost in almost no time.

Chicken Paillards with Pesto Cream and Balsamic Vinegar

Preparation time: 15 minutes
Cooking time: 5 minutes
Yield: 2 servings

1 *whole boned and skinned chicken breast (about 10 ounces), split*
3 *tablespoons Pesto Sauce (see page 330)*
1 *tablespoon balsamic vinegar*
⅓ *cup whipping cream*
Salt
Freshly ground black pepper

1. Flatten each chicken breast half into a paillard as follows: Carefully remove the tendon. Place each breast half between 2 sheets of plastic wrap. Flatten with a meat pounder until the breast is a uniform thickness of about ⅛ inch, or even slightly less. I find it works best to start in the center and work outward, pounding the meat rather than pressing it. The paillards can be cooked right away or frozen. To freeze, stack them between the sheets of plastic, then wrap in a plastic bag.

2. Set a 10-inch skillet over medium heat. As it is heating, brush 1 side of each breast with 2 teaspoons Pesto Sauce. When the pan is warm, but not hot, add the chicken, with the pesto side down. Brush the top of each breast with the remaining pesto. Cook until the bottom is done, about 45 seconds. Turn and cook the other side, 45 to 60 seconds. Set on a warm platter and cover with aluminum foil.

3. With the pan over medium-high heat, add the vinegar and stir up any brown bits from the bottom. Add the cream and any juice that has accumulated on the platter from the chicken and cook until the sauce has thickened enough to coat the back of a wooden spoon, 2 to 3 minutes. Add salt and pepper to taste. Pour the sauce over the chicken and serve immediately.

These pounded chicken breasts employ the same quick-cooking technique as the preceding recipe except in this one they are flavored and sauced with a mildly spicy mix of peppers and cilantro and garnished with a sprinkling of fresh vegetables.

Chicken Paillards with Tex-Mex Flavors

Preparation time: 15 minutes
Cooking time: 5 minutes
Yield: 2 servings

1. Flatten the chicken breasts as in the preceding recipe.
2. Mince the cilantro and serrano pepper in a food processor or by hand. Mix with the oil, mustard, sage and ¼ teaspoon salt. Brush one side of each paillard with ¼ of the mixture.
3. Cut the green onions into thin rings. Core the tomato, cut in half horizontally and squeeze gently to remove the seeds. Cut into ⅜-inch dice.
4. Set a 10-inch skillet over medium heat. When the pan is quite warm, but not too hot, add the chicken, placing it with the herbed side down. Brush the top of each piece with the rest of the herb mixture. Cook until the bottom is done, about 45 seconds. Turn with tongs and cook the other side just until done, 45 to 60 seconds. Set the meat aside on a warm platter and cover with aluminum foil.
5. With the pan over medium-high heat, add the vinegar and scrape up any browned bits that may be clinging to the bottom of the pan so they dissolve into the sauce. Pour in any juice that has collected on the meat platter, then whisk in the butter. Remove from the heat and add the green onions, tomato and salt and pepper to taste. Pour this mixture over the paillards and serve immediately.

1	whole boned and skinned chicken breast (about 10 ounces), split
¼	cup cilantro leaves
1	small serrano pepper, seeded
2	tablespoons extra virgin olive oil
1	teaspoon Dijon mustard
½	teaspoon dried sage Salt
3	medium green onions (1 ounce total)
1	medium plum tomato (3 ounces)
1½	teaspoons rice vinegar
1	tablespoon unsalted butter

This is an updated version of *pot au feu,* a classic French family dish, providing soup, chicken, sausage and a wonderful variety of vegetables, all at the same time from the same pot. Whether you serve it from the pot it is cooked in, or in an elegant tureen, or on a platter with the broth passed separately, you will find it as warm and welcoming on a bleak, cold day as I did in Paris at Coconnas, a distinguished bistro in the Place des Vosges. I think it is best cooked just before serving, but it is easy enough, so that is no problem. It requires no attention and the ingredients are all cooked together in the same pot.

_____ Chicken and Sausage Pot au Feu _____

Preparation time: 20 minutes
Cooking Time: 45 minutes
Yield: 4 servings

2 large garlic cloves, peeled
1 large Spanish onion (8 ounces), peeled
4 small turnips (8 ounces total)
4 whole cloves
4 small zucchini (10 ounces total)
½ small head of cabbage (use 14 ounces)
6 small new red potatoes (10 ounces total)
4 medium carrots (8 ounces total)
4 chicken legs with thighs attached (2½ pounds total)
1 tablespoon light-tasting olive oil
4 smoked sausages (12 ounces total)
6 cups chicken stock (see page 339) or canned broth
1 bay leaf
Horseradish Sauce (recipe follows)

1. Prepare the vegetables. Mince the garlic and onion in a food processor or by hand. Peel the turnips and stick one end of each with a clove. Trim the ends of the zucchini and cut into 1-inch chunks. Cut the cabbage into 4 wedges. Remove 1 strip of the skin from around the center of each potato. Peel the carrots and cut them in thirds. This can be done several hours in advance.

2. Separate the chicken legs from the thighs. Heat the oil in a 6-quart pot. When it is hot, add the chicken and cook until it is browned on all sides. When it is browned, push the chicken to the edge of the pot and add the sausages. Cook, turning as necessary, until they are browned. Remove the sausages from the pot and set them aside. Leave the chicken in the pot, still pushed off to the side.

3. Stir the garlic and onions into the pot and cook over high heat until softened, about 2 minutes. Skim and discard the fat from the stock or broth. Add the stock or broth, all the vegetables and the bay leaf to the pot, and stir gently. Bring to a boil over high heat, then cover and reduce the heat. Simmer gently until all the vegetables are tender, about 25 minutes. Return the sausages to the pot during the last 10 minutes of cooking.

4. Bring the pot to the table, or transfer contents to a large tureen and use tongs and a ladle to serve. Or remove the chicken and sausages with tongs and transfer them to a warmed platter. With a slotted spoon, remove the vegetables and arrange them on the platter in groups, keeping each kind of vegetable together. Skim the surface fat from the broth—a gravy strainer works very

well. Moisten the meat and vegetables with some of the broth and pass the rest separately. Because of the broth, shallow soup bowls are the most suitable serving dishes. Serve with Horseradish Sauce.

Horseradish Sauce

Preparation time: 5 minutes
Yield: ¾ cup

Stir all the ingredients together. If it is too sharp for your taste, add more cream or a pinch of sugar. The sauce can be made up to 2 days in advance and refrigerated.

Note: To drain horseradish, put it in a fine-mesh strainer and press with the back of a spoon to remove as much liquid as possible. Measure the horseradish after it has been drained.

½ *cup whipping cream*
3 *tablespoons Dijon mustard*
3 *tablespoons well-drained horseradish (see Note)*

This is a great-tasting, all-purpose marinade with wide appeal. Here I've used it on chicken pieces, but it's delicious on a whole turkey breast, as well as on pork tenderloin and flank steak. All of the Oriental ingredients will easily be found in most large supermarkets.

Grilled Chicken with Ginger and Soy

Preparation time: 10 minutes
Marinating time: 12 to 24 hours
Cooking time: 25 to 30 minutes
Yield: 3 to 4 servings

1 *piece fresh ginger (¾-inch cube), peeled*
2 *large garlic cloves, peeled*
¼ *cup safflower oil*
3 *tablespoons rice wine vinegar*
2 *tablespoons soy sauce*
2 *tablespoons hoisin sauce*
2 *tablespoons light brown sugar*
1 *large frying chicken (3 pounds), cut into serving pieces*
    Salt

1. Mince the ginger and garlic in a food processor or by hand. Mix with the oil, vinegar, soy sauce, hoisin sauce and brown sugar.

2. Transfer the marinade to a large plastic food bag and add the chicken. Seal bag tightly, against the chicken, place in another bag and seal again. Refrigerate from 12 to 24 hours, turning the bag over occasionally.

3. Prepare a hot barbecue fire, preferably with a mix of charcoal and 1 cup soaked mesquite woodchips; or place the broiler rack 8 inches from the heat and preheat the broiler.

4. Remove the chicken from the marinade and season lightly with salt. Grill or broil, turning once, until done, 25 to 30 minutes. Serve hot or at room temperature.

Cornish hens have an elegance that makes them an excellent choice for entertaining. At the same time, they are certainly easy enough to cook any day of the week. A whole hen is a large serving for many people, though a half doesn't seem quite enough. I usually plan on one per person, then use the leftover meat in a salad.

Honey-Glazed Game Hens

Preparation time: 10 minutes
Cooking time: 45 minutes
Yield: 4 servings

1. 15 minutes before baking, place rack in center of oven and preheat to 425 degrees. Line a shallow roasting pan with aluminum foil.

2. With kitchen shears, cut down both sides of the backbone of each hen to remove it. Cut through the center of the breast bone to cut the hens in half.

3. Mix the salt, thyme and red pepper flakes together. Sprinkle over the tops and bottoms of the hens. Arrange the halves in the pan, skin side up. Bake for 20 minutes.

4. Stir the orange juice and honey together. After the hens have baked for 20 minutes, pour this mixture onto the foil in the bottom of the roasting pan. Bake for 5 minutes to melt the honey, then begin brushing the hens with the juice and pan drippings every 5 minutes until the juices run clear from the thigh, about 20 minutes longer, for a total baking time of about 40 minutes. Serve hot or at room temperature.

4 Cornish game hens, thawed, if frozen
2 teaspoons salt
2 teaspoons dried thyme
½ teaspoon crushed red pepper flakes
1⅓ cups orange juice
¼ cup honey

Many markets now carry boneless duck breasts, a bonanza to those who savor that particular portion. It also gives the option of cooking duck at home without all the fat that comes from cooking the whole bird. Here, they are pan-cooked with a sweet-tart sauce.

_____ Sautéed Duck Breasts with Ginger and Lime Sauce _____

Preparation time: 15 minutes
Cooking time: 10 minutes
Yield: 4 servings

4 boneless duck breast halves (about 1¼ pounds total), split
¾ teaspoon ground coriander
¾ teaspoon salt
Freshly ground black pepper
1 piece fresh ginger (¾-inch cube), peeled
5 tablespoons unsalted butter
⅓ cup sweet white wine, such as muscat blanc, California Riesling or sauterne
¼ cup beef stock or broth
3 tablespoons lime juice
1 tablespoon white wine vinegar

1. Remove the skin and fat from the duck breasts. Mix the coriander, salt and pepper in a small dish and sprinkle it over both sides of the meat.

2. Mince the ginger in a food processor or by hand.

3. Melt 1 tablespoon of butter in a large skillet over medium heat. When it is hot, add the duck. Cook, turning once, until cooked to the desired doneness, either rare or medium. Rare meat will cook in 3 to 3½ minutes, medium in about 5 minutes. If it is cooked beyond medium, the meat will be tough. Remove from the pan to a warm dish, tent with aluminum foil and set aside.

4. Turn the heat to medium-high and add the ginger, wine, stock or broth, lime juice and vinegar. Stir to dissolve any brown bits from the bottom of the pan. Cook until the mixture is reduced to ⅓ cup, about 4 minutes.

5. Pour the sauce through a fine mesh strainer, pushing on the solids to extract as much liquid as possible. Wipe out the pan with a paper towel.

6. Return the strained sauce to the pan and add any juices that have collected around the duck. Place over medium heat. Whisk in the remaining 4 tablespoons of butter, one piece at a time, waiting until each is fully incorporated before adding another. Adjust the seasoning.

7. To serve, cut each breast, on a slight diagonal, into ¼-inch slices. Arrange on plates so each breast is reassembled to its original shape. Nap with sauce and serve immediately.

Note: If your market does not sell boneless duck breasts, a butcher can carve the breasts away from the bone, or you can do this yourself. Duck legs freeze well and can be braised or grilled for another meal.

I developed this recipe for an article on low-calorie cooking, and low calorie it is, tallying in at under 200 calories a serving, a pretty sleek figure by any standards. A low-calorie count is only one of its assets. Equally important to me is that it meets my requirements for great taste, appealing presentation and easy preparation.

Lemon Pepper Turkey "Carpaccio" with Tomato Marmalade

Preparation time: 15 minutes
Baking time: 35 minutes
Yield: 6 servings

1. 15 minutes before baking, place the rack in the center of the oven and preheat oven to 500 degrees.

2. Mince the garlic in the processor or by hand and mix it with the rosemary, sage, salt and pepper. Remove the skin from the turkey and rub the seasoning mixture over the entire surface of the meat.

3. Wrap the turkey in an airtight foil package, leaving a small amount of air space between the meat and foil. Bake until an instant-reading thermometer inserted halfway through the thickest portion registers 160 degrees, about 35 minutes. Don't open the foil when testing the meat; just insert the thermometer through the foil.

4. Cool slightly, then remove the turkey from the foil package and place it in a plastic bag with the pan juices. Add the lemon juice and seal tightly, right against the turkey. Refrigerate until chilled, or up to 2 days.

5. To serve, cut the turkey into paper-thin slices. Divide between 6 plates and top each with about 2 tablespoons chilled Tomato Marmalade.

Note: A boneless veal roast may be substituted for the turkey.

1 *medium boneless turkey breast half (1¾ pounds)*
1 *large garlic clove, peeled*
1 *teaspoon dried rosemary*
1 *teaspoon rubbed sage*
¾ *teaspoon salt*
¾ *teaspoon coarsely cracked black pepper*
2 *teaspoons fresh lemon juice*
1 *recipe Tomato Marmalade (see page 328)*

Here, holiday turkey traditions are rearranged just a bit so it doesn't seem as though they're abandoned altogether. Ease and quick cooking are the key words. A convenient boneless turkey breast half is roasted and sauced with cranberries. Serve it as the new Thanksgiving meal or consider it for entertaining during the winter months. Because old habits are hard to break, I serve this with many of the expected holiday accompaniments—Brussels Sprouts with Mustard Cream (see page 193), Sautéed Sweet Potatoes (see page 206) and Pumpkin Pecan Pie (see page 306), of course.

_____Roast Turkey Breast with Cranberry Port Sauce__

Preparation time: 15 minutes
Cooking time: 45 minutes
Yield: 6 servings

TURKEY:
1 *teaspoon salt*
¼ *teaspoon dried tarragon*
¼ *teaspoon ground coriander*
⅛ *teaspoon ground allspice*
⅛ *teaspoon ground cloves*
⅛ *teaspoon dried marjoram*
  Freshly ground black pepper
1 *medium boneless turkey breast half (1¾ pounds)*
1 *teaspoon safflower oil*

SAUCE:
½ *cup sugar*
6 *tablespoons ruby port*
1½ *cups cranberries*
5 *tablespoons unsalted butter*
3 *to 6 tablespoons pan drippings or water*

1. Fifteen minutes before baking, place the rack in the center of the oven and preheat oven to 450 degrees. Line a shallow roasting pan with aluminum foil.

2. For the turkey, mix the salt, tarragon, coriander, allspice, marjoram and pepper together. Brush the underside of the turkey breast with the oil and season all over with the seasoning mixture. Transfer the breast to the pan, placing it skin side up. Bake until an instant-reading thermometer reads 160 degrees when inserted halfway down into the thickest part of the meat, 40 to 45 minutes. Remove from the oven, tent with foil and let rest for 10 minutes.

3. While the meat is cooking, prepare the sauce. Combine the sugar and port in a small, non-aluminum pan and cook over high heat until the sugar is dissolved, about 4 minutes. Add cranberries and cook just until the skins burst and begin to pop. Set aside, off the heat, until needed. The sauce can also be prepared 2 days in advance to this point and refrigerated.

4. Just before serving, return the sauce to medium heat and cook until hot. Whisk the butter into the sauce, 1 tablespoon at a time, waiting until each is incorporated before adding another. The sauce should be thick, but not jellylike. Thin with meat drippings or water as necessary.

5. To serve, carve the meat on the diagonal into thin slices. Spoon the sauce onto warmed plates and top with turkey. Serve immediately.

Turkey breast meat is a boon to the cook, presenting good dollar value, a low fat and calorie count, quick cooking and delicious flavor. Here it's prepared with a colorful medley of vegetables that cooks in 25 minutes, in 1 pan on top of the stove. Almost no extra fat is added, just 1 tablespoon of oil to brown the meat, yet there is a rich, robust quality that makes you think there is much more.

Turkey Fricassee
with Orange Pepper Marmalade

Preparation time: 20 minutes
Cooking time: 25 minutes
Yield: 8 servings

1. Remove skin from turkey and separate the small fillet from the large piece of meat. Pound the large piece between 2 pieces of plastic wrap until the thickest part is ¾-inch thick.

2. Crush the rosemary with a mortar and pestle or in the palm of your hand and mix with ½ the orange zest, the flour and the salt. Pat half over the rounded side of both pieces.

3. Mince the garlic in a food processor or by hand. Slit the leek lengthwise to within ½ inch of the root end and rinse under cold water, gently fanning out the leaves to get rid of all the grit. Cut the onions and leek into ½-inch slices. Stand the peppers on a board and cut 4 sides from each one. Cut each side crosswise into ½-inch slices.

4. Heat oil in 12-inch non-aluminum sauté pan. When it is very hot, add the meat, seasoned side down, and sprinkle top of each piece with the remaining seasoning mixture. Cook, turning once, until browned on both sides, about 5 minutes total. Set aside on aluminum foil.

5. Add the garlic, onion, leek and 2 tablespoons chicken stock to pan. Cook, stirring occasionally, until soft, about 5 minutes. Add all but ¼ cup of remaining stock, the remaining orange zest, the orange juice and red peppers, and heat to a boil. Recipe can be prepared a day in advance to this point. Wrap turkey in foil and refrigerate. Cover pan with vegetables and refrigerate. Bring contents of pan to a boil before continuing. Remove the turkey from the foil and add it to the pan with the vegetables, cover and cook over medium-high heat, turning both pieces every 5 minutes, until an instant-reading thermometer inserted halfway

1 large boneless turkey breast half (2½ pounds)
¾ teaspoon dried rosemary Zest of 1 orange, removed with a zester or grater
1 tablespoon unbleached all-purpose flour
1 teaspoon salt
2 medium garlic cloves, peeled
1 large leek (8 ounces)
2 small red onions (8 ounces total), peeled
2 medium red bell peppers (12 ounces total)
1 tablespoon light-tasting olive oil
1 to 1¼ cups chicken stock (see page 339) or canned broth
1 cup orange juice
½ cup cilantro leaves for garnish

down into the thickest part of the meat registers 155 degrees, about 10 minutes for the smaller piece, 18 minutes for the larger one. Set meat aside, wrapped again in foil, and let it rest for 20 minutes before slicing. Leave the vegetables in the pan and cover to keep them warm. Thin the vegetables with the remaining stock if it is too thick and reheat if necessary. Adjust the seasoning.

6. Starting on the long side, cut the meat across the grain on the diagonal into ¼-inch slices. Spoon half the vegetables on a platter and arrange the turkey over them. Spoon the rest of the vegetables and their juice over turkey and garnish with cilantro.

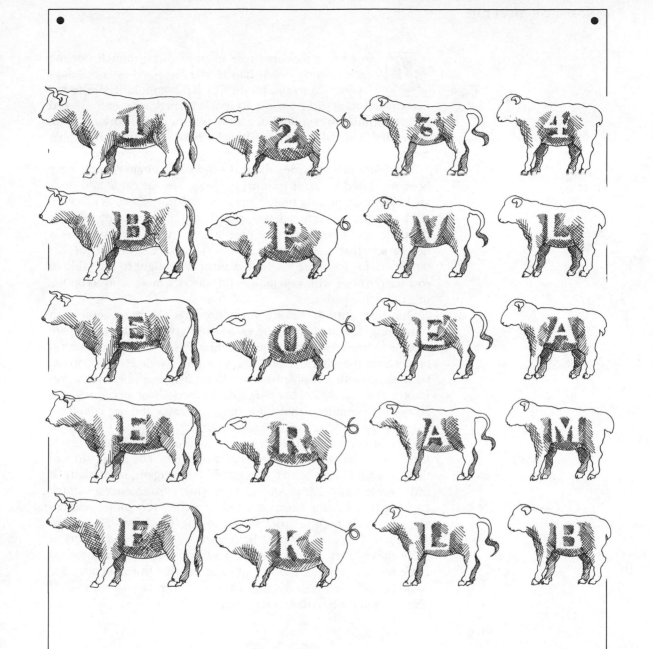

8 · Meats

Meat has a welcome role in most diets, though not the overwhelming one it had in the meat-and-potatoes days of yore. Concerns for health have popularized alternatives to red meat. Still, people have not turned away entirely and meat continues to be popular. Meats, whether beef, pork or lamb, are varied and delicious, forming the basis of many memorable meals.

To some extent, worries about the high fat content of meat have been mitigated by meat producers. Lean, low-fat cattle and pork are being bred, putting these almost in the same league as chicken. With dietary concerns allayed, people are glad to enjoy meat at the table, and consumption is on the upswing once again. This is not to say that some changes haven't occurred. Instead of 12-ounce steaks, it's more likely that meat is brought to the table in smaller portions with vegetables and starches in a strong supporting, or even equal, role.

Our new attitude toward meat presents the busy cook with something of a challenge. The easiest and quickest way to prepare meat is to broil a steak, burger or chop. This is no longer practical on a continuing basis. Other preparations are more appropriate, such as those that supplement smaller portions of meat with vegetables and starches. This chapter addresses those needs with an array of preparations that fill a range of tastes and are adaptable to everyday cooking as well as entertaining.

Certain cuts of meat, such as filet mignon and boneless leg of lamb, are tailor-made for short-order cooking. The high prices of these premium cuts aren't necessarily extravagant, since there is little waste with them. And at times the convenience of quick cooking is worth the extra cost. Other recipes rely on less expensive cuts that require low, slow cooking to show them off to advantage. Properly cooked, the robust, well-developed flavors of these meats offer some of the best eating. The cooking time on these recipes may seem long, but consider that this is unattended cooking and that most dishes of this type can be made ahead of time, frozen if desired, and reheated.

Flank is the beef eaters' meat of choice for those concerned with fat and calories. It tallies in at the low end on both counts and is still juicy and very tasty. Marinating helps to tenderize this cut of meat and also adds extra flavor. Always serve flank steak rare and slice it thinly across the grain on a slight diagonal, so it will be more tender. This marinade is also excellent on pork, chicken and shrimp.

El Paso Flank Steak

Preparation time: 10 minutes
Marinating time: 24 to 36 hours
Grilling time: 10 to 15 minutes
Yield: 6 servings

1. For the marinade, mince the garlic, jalapeño pepper and onion in a food processor or by hand. Mix with the oil, vinegar, tomato paste, cumin, oregano, coriander, salt and pepper.

2. Transfer the marinade to a large plastic food bag and add the meat. Seal tightly, right against the meat. Refrigerate for 24 to 36 hours, turning the bag over several times.

3. Remove the meat from the marinade and season lightly with salt and pepper. Cook over hot coals, preferably a mix of charcoal and 1 cup of soaked mesquite wood chips; or in a preheated broiler, turning once, just until done. Do not overcook; the meat will be most tender when it is still rosy inside. Carve on the diagonal across the grain into very thin slices. Serve hot or at room temperature.

MARINADE:

1 *large garlic clove, peeled*
1 *jalapeño pepper, seeded if desired*
1 *small onion (3 ounces), peeled*
¼ *cup safflower oil*
2 *tablespoons red wine vinegar*
2 *tablespoons tomato paste*
1 *teaspoon ground cumin*
¾ *teaspoon dried oregano*
¾ *teaspoon ground coriander*
½ *teaspoon salt*
Freshly ground black pepper

MEAT:

1 *large flank steak (1¾ pounds)*

For better or worse, meat loaf is one dish that everyone seems to remember from his or her childhood. Everyone except me. Strangely enough, it was absent from my mother's menus. I added it to my own repertoire so I could pass the legacy on to my children, then promptly forgot about it once they left the fold. Here it is again, better than ever. The recipe makes a big meat loaf, but with good reason. I especially love cold leftover meat loaf sandwiches on soft white bread with lettuce and mayonnaise.

—Not Like Mom's Meat Loaf

Preparation time: 20 minutes
Baking time: 1 hour 10 minutes (Microwave: 30 minutes)
Yield: 8 servings

3 large garlic cloves, peeled
2 small onions (5 ounces total), peeled
1 small green bell pepper (4 ounces)
1 large stalk celery (3 ounces)
2 tablespoons unsalted butter
1½ pounds ground chuck or ground round
8 ounces bulk "hot" breakfast sausage
¾ cup soft bread crumbs
2 large eggs
¼ cup catsup, plus ½ cup more for top, if desired
2 tablespoons milk
1½ teaspoons Worcestershire sauce
¾ teaspoon salt
¼ teaspoon cayenne pepper
Freshly ground black pepper

1. 15 minutes before baking, place rack in center of oven and preheat to 375 degrees. Have a 9-inch by 13-inch pan ready.

2. Mince the garlic in a food processor or by hand. Finely chop the onions, green pepper and celery in a processor or by hand.

3. Melt the butter in an 8-inch skillet. Add the vegetables and cook over medium heat, stirring occasionally, until soft, about 6 minutes. Transfer them to a large mixing bowl and cool slightly.

4. Add the ground meat, sausage, bread crumbs, eggs, ¼ cup catsup, milk, Worcestershire sauce, salt, cayenne and black pepper and mix thoroughly.

5. Transfer to pan and shape into a 12-inch by 8-inch oval. Press with your hands to compact the loaf as much as possible. The meat loaf can be prepared a day in advance to this point, covered tightly and refrigerated. Before baking, spread ½ cup catsup over top, if desired.

6. Bake 1 hour and 10 minutes. Serve hot or at room temperature.

MICROWAVE: Increase the bread crumbs to 1 cup. Prepare the vegetables as in step 2. Melt the butter in a 9-inch by 13-inch microwave baking dish. Add the minced vegetables and cook on full power for 4 minutes. Transfer them to a large mixing bowl and wipe out the baking dish with a paper towel. Cool the vegetables slightly, then mix with the remaining ingredients except the catsup for the top. Divide the mixture in half and shape into 2 8-inch by 5-inch ovals. Place them in the pan side by side, leaving

1 inch of space between them. Press the loaves with your hands to compact them as much as possible. Spread ¼ cup catsup over each loaf, if desired. Cook, uncovered, on full power, for 24 minutes, turning them once halfway through cooking. Let rest 5 minutes before serving.

◆

This is one of my favorite meat marinades, pungent, sweet and spicy all at the same time. Here it adds an Asian accent to meaty sirloin steaks. While the steaks are cooking, the drained marinade is used to quickly sauté fresh vegetables to complete the presentation.

The marinade is very versatile and favors shrimp and many kinds of fish as well as chicken and pork. I often make a double batch of the marinade so I have some extra on hand. It lasts in the refrigerator for at least 2 weeks.

Mekong Beef with Vegetables

Preparation time: 15 minutes
Marinating time: 6 hours or up to 2 days
Cooking time: 12 to 15 minutes
Yield: 4 servings

MEAT:
2 sirloin strip steaks (1⅓ pounds total)

MARINADE:
3 large garlic cloves, peeled
3 tablespoons soy sauce
1½ tablespoons honey
4 teaspoons sugar
4 teaspoons Oriental sesame oil
4 teaspoons oyster sauce

VEGETABLES:
2 medium plum tomatoes (6 ounces total)
6 medium green onions (2 ounces total)
¼ cup reserved marinade, from above
1 teaspoon dried mint

1. Trim the steaks and put them in a large plastic bag.
2. For the marinade, mince the garlic in a food processor or by hand, and mix with the soy sauce, honey, sugar, sesame oil and oyster sauce. Add to the meat, seal tightly and marinate at least 6 hours, or up to 2 days, turning bag over several times.
3. For the vegetables, core the tomatoes, cut in half horizontally and squeeze gently to remove the seeds. Cut into ½-inch dice. Cut the green onions, including the tender green ends, into ¼-inch rings. This can be done several hours in advance.
4. To cook the meat, place the broiler rack 8 inches from the heat and preheat the broiler or prepare a hot barbecue grill. Line a broiler pan or jelly roll pan with aluminum foil. Remove the steaks from the marinade and reserve the marinade for the vegetables. Arrange the steaks in the center of the pan. Broil, turning once, until done as desired.
5. Heat ¼ cup of the marinade in an 8-inch skillet over

medium heat. When it is hot, add the tomatoes, green onion and mint. Cook, stirring often, just until heated through, 2 to 3 minutes.

6. To serve, cut the meat across the grain into thin slices. Fan them in a semicircle on each of 4 warmed plates and place a spoonful of vegetables at the point in the center. Serve immediately.

◆

Tenderloin is a costly, special-occasion cut of meat. Here I've added the spark of ethnic interest to its preparation by tapping the cuisine of Peru. A spicy seasoning mixture coats the meat and a vibrant, multicolored vegetable relish tops it off. The meat is seared in a hot cast-iron skillet, much like the "blackened" dishes in Cajun cooking, although some oil is used in the pan. It can be served immediately, but also has the added allure of being equally good at room temperature. Or, do everything, including the searing, ahead of time, and just finish the cooking before serving. Either way, this is ideal for buffet entertaining.

_____Pepper Spiced Tenderloin with Vegetable Relish _

Preparation time: 20 minutes
Cooking time: 30 minutes (Microwave: 12 minutes plus 15 minutes stovetop cooking of meat)
Yield: 6 to 8 servings

RELISH:
 2 medium bell peppers (12 ounces total), preferably 1 red and 1 green
 1 medium red onion (5 ounces), peeled
 1 large garlic clove, peeled
 1 serrano pepper, seeded, if desired
 3 tablespoons peanut oil
 1 medium tomato (6 ounces)

1. For the relish, cut the peppers into ¼-inch strips and the onion into ¼-inch rings, either with the all-purpose (4mm) slicer of a food processor or by hand. Cut the garlic and serrano pepper into paper-thin slices, with the ultra-thin (1mm) slicer of a processor or by hand.

2. Heat 2 tablespoons oil in a 1½-quart pan. When it is hot, add the peppers, onion, garlic and serrano pepper. Cover and cook over medium heat, stirring occasionally, until the vegetables are very soft, about 15 minutes.

3. Core the tomato, cut it in half horizontally and squeeze gently to remove the seeds. With a paring knife, cut out all the inner membrane from the tomato so only the outer shell remains. Cut the tomato into ¼-inch strips. Add to the pan along with the

vinegar, salt and remaining 1 tablespoon oil and remove from the heat. The vegetable relish can be made up to 3 days in advance and refrigerated. Reheat gently before serving.

4. For the meat, stir the cayenne pepper, salt, cumin and black pepper together and rub into the meat.

5. Place a dry cast-iron skillet over high heat. When it is very hot, add the peanut oil and quickly swirl the pan so the oil coats the bottom. Add the meat and sear on all sides. Cook, turning the meat as necessary, until done as desired, 12 to 15 minutes for rare.

6. To serve, carve the meat into thin slices and overlap them on a platter. Top with the vegetable relish. Serve hot or at room temperature.

MICROWAVE: The relish can be made in the microwave oven. Follow step 1 above. Put 2 tablespoons oil, bell peppers, onion, garlic and serrano pepper in a shallow, 10-inch round microwave dish. Cover and cook on high power (100%), stirring once, until peppers are tender, about 12 minutes. Follow steps 3 through 6 above.

Note: The tenderloin can also be made in advance and reheated. Make sure to undercook the meat so it doesn't overcook. Arrange the meat in a shallow casserole, in slightly overlapping rows and cover with the relish. Cover and bake in a preheated 300-degree oven until heated through, 12-15 minutes, or in a microwave oven on medium power (50%) for about 5 minutes.

1 tablespoon red wine
    vinegar
½ teaspoon salt

MEAT:
¾ teaspoon cayenne
    pepper
½ teaspoon salt
½ teaspoon ground cumin
¼ teaspoon freshly
    ground black pepper
1½ pound piece beef
    tenderloin
1 tablespoon peanut oil

I am totally taken in by the charms of earthy, robust stews. The aroma and warmth in the kitchen as they cook are teasing preludes to a meal that never fails to satisfy me and soothe my soul. This one has all the traits that make stews so endearing—it's easy to prepare and bakes without any attention other than to the timer, is hearty and well balanced with meat and vegetables and reheats very well. And like most stews, this one tastes even better reheated. These flavorings are a little different, with Moroccan influences. Serve it with rice, egg noodles or orzo.

Moroccan Beef Stew

Preparation time: 25 minutes
Baking time: 1½ hours
Yield: 6 servings

2 tablespoons unbleached all-purpose flour
2 teaspoons ground cumin
2 teaspoons ground oregano
1¼ teaspoons salt
1 teaspoon ground allspice
⅛ teaspoon cayenne pepper
2 pounds very lean beef or veal stew meat
6 tablespoons light-tasting olive oil
3 large garlic cloves, peeled
1 large onion (8 ounces), peeled
6 medium carrots (1 pound total), peeled
12 small shallots (3 ounces total), peeled
24 small mushrooms (8 ounces total)
1 can (6 ounces) tomato paste
½ cup orange juice
3 tablespoons red wine vinegar
2 tablespoons light brown sugar

1. 15 minutes before baking, place the rack in the center of the oven and preheat oven to 350 degrees.

2. Put the flour, cumin, oregano, salt, allspice and cayenne pepper in a large plastic bag. Add the meat and shake the bag so the meat is evenly coated.

3. Heat 1½ tablespoons oil in a 3-quart stove-to-oven casserole. When it is hot, add a third of the meat and cook over high heat until it is well browned on all sides. Remove meat with a slotted spoon and set aside. Cook the remaining 2 batches of meat the same way, adding oil as necessary, and set aside.

4. Mince the garlic in a food processor or by hand. Quarter the onion lengthwise, then cut crosswise into ¼-inch slices with the all-purpose (4mm) slicer of a processor or by hand. Cut the carrots into ¼-inch slices with the 4mm slicer or by hand.

5. Heat 2 tablespoons oil in the casserole. Add the onion, carrots, whole shallots and mushrooms and cook over high heat, stirring often, for 5 minutes.

6. Combine the tomato paste, orange juice, vinegar and sugar. Add to the casserole along with the meat and mix well. Bring to a boil.

7. Cover the casserole and bake until meat is tender, about 1½ hours. The stew can be made in advance and refrigerated for 3 days, or frozen. To reheat, bring to room temperature. Bake in a preheated 350-degree oven until hot, about 30 minutes. Or, cook on high power (100%) in a microwave oven in a microwave-safe casserole until hot, about 5 minutes.

There are several compelling reasons to use filet mignon, even though it is costly. It is a wonderfully succulent cut of beef, tender and juicy, and yet surprisingly low in fat, especially when compared to a T-bone steak. Because it is so tender, it cooks quickly, always a strong point. And, perhaps because it is so expensive, it automatically adds a festive air to any meal. Here, filets are pounded for even quicker cooking, pan-fried with a full-flavored mushroom coating and lightly sauced with pan juices, cream and a splash of cognac.

Pan-Fried Filets with Mushroom Sauce

Soaking time: 20 minutes
Preparation time: 10 minutes
Cooking time: 8 minutes
Yield: 2 servings

¼	ounce dried mushrooms
1	small shallot (¼ ounce), peeled
2	tablespoons unsalted butter, softened
⅛	teaspoon salt
	Freshly ground black pepper
4	medium fresh mushrooms
2	small beef filets (4 to 5 ounces each)
1½	tablespoons brandy
¼	teaspoon fresh lemon juice
2	tablespoons whipping cream

1. Put the dried mushrooms in a small dish with ¼ cup hot water. Soak until they are soft and pliable, about 20 minutes. Line a fine-mesh strainer with a paper towel and drain the mushrooms, reserving the liquid. Rinse them under running water to remove any grit, and squeeze them dry.

2. Finely mince the shallot and soaked mushrooms in a mini-chopper or by hand. (A standard-size food processor is too large for this small amount.) Mix with the butter, salt and pepper. Trim the stems of the fresh mushrooms and cut the mushrooms into ¼-inch slices.

3. Place each filet between 2 pieces of plastic wrap. Pound with a meat mallet, or other similar object, to a uniform thickness of about ⅜ inch.

4. Spread 1 tablespoon of the dried mushroom mixture over 1 side of each filet. The recipe can be prepared a day in advance to this point. Place the filets on a baking sheet and cover with plastic wrap. Cover the remaining dried mushroom mixture and the soaking liquid and refrigerate. Bring the meat and the butter to room temperature before cooking.

5. Place a large, heavy skillet over medium heat. When it is hot, add the meat, the side with the mushroom paste facing down. Spread the remaining mushroom mixture on the top of each filet. Cook until done as desired, turning once, 4 to 5 minutes altogether for rare. Set meat aside on a warm platter and cover with aluminum foil.

6. Return the pan to medium-high heat. Add the reserved

mushroom liquid and stir up any brown bits from the bottom of the pan so they dissolve. Add the fresh mushrooms, brandy and lemon juice and cook until the liquid is reduced by about half, 1 to 2 minutes. Add the cream and cook until it has thickened slightly, about 1 minute. Adjust the seasoning if necessary. Pour the sauce over the meat and serve immediately.

◆

Beef is once again taking its rightful place on dinner plates across America. Here, brisket, a very tasty cut, is flavored à la Tex-Mex and slow-cooked until it's fork-tender. It's a good idea to cook the meat a day or two in advance so the fat will solidify for easy removal. This also gives the flavors a chance to marry. Don't be daunted by the lengthy cooking. Almost all of it is unattended oven cooking.

Your guests can layer the beef, sauce and favorite taco fixings in a flour tortilla; or serve with mashed potatoes in a big puddle of sauce.

Badlands Brisket of Beef

Preparation time: 10 minutes
Baking time: 4 to 5 hours
Yield: 8 servings

4- to 5-pound lean beef brisket
4 large garlic cloves, peeled
2 tablespoons light brown sugar
1 tablespoon ground cumin
1 teaspoon salt
2 medium onions (10 ounces total), peeled
1 cup chili sauce
2 large canned chipotle peppers (see Note) or 1 jalapeño pepper
¼ cup water

1. 15 minutes before baking, place the rack in the center of the oven and preheat oven to 325 degrees. Have ready a roasting pan just large enough to hold the meat. Cut a piece of heavy-duty aluminum foil large enough to extend 3 inches beyond each side of the pan.

2. Trim all the surface fat from the meat and place it on the foil. Mince the garlic in a food processor or by hand and mix with the brown sugar, cumin and salt. Rub this mixture into the surface of the meat.

3. Slice the onions and put half on the foil. Place the meat on top and strew with the remaining onions. Purée the chili sauce and chipotles or jalapeño pepper in a food processor or blender and spread over the onions and meat.

4. Lift the meat, on the foil, place it in the pan, and fold the

sides of the foil up. Pour the ¼ cup of water around the meat. Cover with another piece of foil and crimp all the edges to seal tightly. Bake 3 hours. Remove the top piece of foil and continue baking until meat is tender, 1 to 2 hours longer. Cover and refrigerate until the fat solidifies, about 6 hours or up to 3 days.

5. Remove any solidified fat from meat and onions. Reserve a small cluster of cooked onions to use as a garnish and transfer the rest to a processor or blender along with the pan juices. Purée until smooth. Cut the meat across the grain into very thin slices —an electric knife works very well—and place in a shallow casserole. Nap with some of the sauce and garnish with onions. Reheat in a 350-degree oven for 30 minutes, basting as necessary. Gently reheat the remaining sauce in a small pan or in the microwave oven.

6. Serve the meat and sauce in warmed flour tortillas with the garnishes of your choice—or, as suggested above, with mashed potatoes and the sauce.

Note: Chipotle peppers are smoked jalapeño peppers, generally sold in cans with adobo sauce. Look for them in Latin American grocery stores and large urban supermarkets.

GARNISHES:
Flour tortillas
Shredded iceberg lettuce
Sliced red onion, avocado,
tomatoes
Cilantro leaves

This is simple and quick to prepare, yet has all the character that long simmering brings to a dish. It's one of my favorite Sunday night suppers, partly because it's a wonderful way to end a weekend and begin the week, but also because it's great to have the leftovers for later in the week. With that in mind, I often double the sauce and use it on shrimp or chicken the second time around.

_____Lamb Curry in a Hurry_____

Preparation time: 20 minutes
Cooking time: 30 minutes
Yield: 6 servings

1½ tablespoons unbleached all-purpose flour
¾ teaspoon salt
Freshly ground black pepper
1½ pounds lamb from the leg, well trimmed, cut in ¾-inch cubes
¼ cup light-tasting olive oil
2 medium onions (6 ounces total), peeled
2 medium carrots (6 ounces total), peeled
4 to 5 teaspoons curry powder, or to taste
2½ cups beef stock (see page 340) or canned broth
½ cup dried currants (3 ounces)
3 tablespoons tomato paste

1. Put the flour, salt and pepper in a large plastic bag and add the lamb. Seal the bag and shake it to coat the lamb with flour.

2. Heat 1½ tablespoons oil in a large skillet over medium-high heat. When hot, add half the lamb and cook until done as desired. Remove lamb with a slotted spoon and set aside. Heat another 1½ tablespoons oil and cook the remaining lamb; set aside. Remove the skillet from the heat.

3. Mince the onions and carrots as fine as possible, either in a food processor or by hand.

4. Heat the remaining oil in the skillet. Add the onions, carrots and curry powder and cook until the onions have softened slightly, about 3 minutes.

5. Add the stock or broth, currants and tomato paste. Simmer, uncovered, for 20 minutes, stirring occasionally. If the sauce gets too thick, thin with up to ¼ cup water.

6. Add the lamb and any accumulated juices to the sauce. Recipe can be prepared in advance to this point. To do so, remove the pan from the heat and refrigerate up to 3 days, or freeze. To finish, bring to room temperature. Reheat on top of the stove or in the microwave oven on medium power (50%) just enough to heat the lamb without cooking it any further. Serve with rice.

Any drawbacks to cuts of meat that require long cooking are more than compensated for by their rich flavor. Lamb shanks, for example, have a robust, meaty succulence that you just won't find in the more tender and costlier cuts. Here, they are simmered with garlic and white wine until the meat is so tender it practically falls off the bone.

Lamb Shanks with Sweet Garlic Sauce

Preparation time: 10 minutes
Cooking time: 1¼ to 1½ hours
Yield: 4 servings

1. Trim all the surface fat from the shanks and season them with salt and pepper. Heat the oil in a sauté pan just large enough to hold the shanks. When it is hot, add the shanks and brown them on all sides. Discard any fat from the pan.

2. Slice the garlic into paper-thin slices. This is most easily done with the ultra-thin (1mm) slicer of a food processor, but it can also be done by hand.

3. Add the garlic to the pan along with the stock or broth, wine and oregano. Cover and bring to a boil. Reduce heat and simmer very gently until the meat is tender, about 1¼ to 1½ hours.

4. Remove the shanks from the cooking liquid and skim the fat. This is easiest to do if the liquid is refrigerated or briefly frozen until the fat solidifies. A gravy strainer works well, too. Serve hot with the sauce. The shanks can be made in advance and refrigerated up to 3 days, or frozen. To reheat, place in a small casserole and cover tightly. Bake in a preheated 350-degree oven or in a microwave oven on high power (100%) until heated through.

4 *medium lamb shanks (about 3 pounds total)*
Salt
Freshly ground black pepper
2 *tablespoons light-tasting olive oil*
8 *large garlic cloves, peeled*
1¼ *cups chicken stock (see page 339) or canned broth*
1 *cup dry white wine*
1 *teaspoon dried oregano*
Orzo with Zucchini and Mint (see page 214)

This simple marinade enhances lamb to perfection. Add to that the slightly smoky taste that comes from grilling it and there's no nicer, tastier or easier way to prepare a leg of lamb. I prefer a boneless butterflied leg of lamb for quick cooking and the ease of slicing and serving it offers.

Grilled Lamb with Rosemary Mustard Marinade

Preparation time: 15 minutes
Marinating time: 12 hours or up to 2 days
Grilling time: 15 minutes
Yield: 8 servings

1 *butterflied whole leg of lamb*
3 *large garlic cloves, peeled*
1 *small onion (2 ounces), peeled*
⅔ *cup light-tasting olive oil*
¼ *cup fresh lemon juice*
4 *tablespoons fresh rosemary or 1 tablespoon dried*
2 *tablespoons Dijon mustard*
2 *teaspoons mustard seeds*
1 *teaspoon salt*
Freshly ground black pepper
1 *lemon*
Fresh rosemary sprigs, for garnish

1. Trim all the surface fat from the lamb. If there are any thin flaps of meat, cut them from the larger segment and reserve. You should have about 3¾ pounds of trimmed meat, including any flaps.

2. For the marinade, mince the garlic and onion in a food processor or by hand. Mix with the oil, lemon juice, rosemary, mustard, mustard seeds, salt and pepper.

3. Transfer the marinade to a jumbo plastic food bag, add all the lamb, including the flaps, and seal tightly, against the meat. Place in another bag and seal again. Turn the bag over several times to distribute the marinade, making sure it seeps into all the folds of the meat. Refrigerate at least 12 hours or up to 2 days, turning the bag over occasionally. Let the meat come to room temperature before cooking.

4. Prepare a medium-hot barbecue grill, preferably with a mix of charcoal and 1 cup of soaked mesquite wood chips; or place broiler rack 8 inches from the heat source and preheat the broiler.

5. Remove the lamb from the marinade and let the excess marinade drip off. Season with salt and pepper if desired. Grill or broil the meat, turning it once. Add the thinner flaps after the meat has cooked for several minutes so they do not get over-cooked. The reading for rare meat is 125 degrees to 130 degrees, which will take 15 to 20 minutes. Medium, 145 degrees to 150 degrees, will take 10 to 15 minutes longer. Cook the meat as desired. To test it, insert an instant-reading thermometer halfway through the thickest portion of the meat. Let the cooked meat rest in a warm spot, covered with foil, for 20 minutes before carving.

6. Score the lemon peel with a citrus stripper or the tines of a fork and cut the lemon into thin slices. Carve the lamb on the diagonal into thin slices. Arrange on a platter and garnish with the sliced lemon and sprigs of rosemary.

◆

Here, sausage and a simple mix of vegetables are combined for a casual main course, full of lusty flavors and rustic charm. Serve this with a green salad, a crusty loaf of bread and a hearty red wine.

Sausage and Pepper Ragout

Preparation time: 15 minutes
Cooking time: 20 minutes
Yield: 4 servings

1. Cut the sausage into 1½-inch pieces. Heat the oil in a large skillet. When it is hot, add the sausage and cook over medium heat, turning occasionally, until pieces are browned, about 12 minutes.

2. While the sausage is cooking, mince the garlic in a food processor or by hand. Cut the onions and peppers into ¼-inch strips.

3. When the sausage is browned, drain off all but 1 tablespoon fat and add the vegetables. Cook over high heat until the onions are lightly browned, about 5 minutes.

4. Carefully pour in the wine and scrape up any browned bits from the bottom of the pan so they dissolve in the sauce. Add the tomato paste, basil, pepper flakes and salt and cook until the flavors are blended, about 3 minutes. Adjust the seasoning and serve hot. The ragout can be refrigerated up to 2 days. Reheat before serving and thin the sauce with a small amount of water if it seems too thick.

1 pound sweet Italian sausage in casing
1 tablespoon light-tasting olive oil
1 medium garlic clove, peeled
2 medium onions (10 ounces total), peeled
1 medium red bell pepper (6 ounces)
1 medium green bell pepper (6 ounces)
¾ cup dry red wine
3 tablespoons tomato paste
1 teaspoon dried basil
¼ teaspoon crushed red pepper flakes
¼ teaspoon salt

The most tender and succulent cut of pork is the tenderloin. Think of it as the filet mignon of pork to get an idea of just how good it is. These filets are, in fact, cut from the same section, respectively, as is the filet mignon. Pork tenderloin has a delicate, mild flavor, so is well suited to cooking in a casserole like a stew, with vegetables to flavor it. And, since pork is commonly used on many of the Caribbean islands, that's where I turned for inspiration.

This recipe relies on an artful blending of flavors. Onions and tomatoes are puréed into a sauce that takes on additional flavor from the meat juices, garlic, herbs and spices. These ingredients are puréed after baking with the meat and enriched with a bit of butter. The Cumin Rice Pilaf (see page 229) is a delicious accompaniment, or try buttered egg noodles.

———Jamaican Pork Tenderloin———

Preparation time: 25 minutes
Baking time: 1½ hours
Yield: 6 servings

2 medium garlic cloves, peeled
2 medium onions (8 ounces total), peeled
3 medium tomatoes (1 pound total)
2 pork tenderloins (about 2 pounds total)
1½ tablespoons unbleached all-purpose flour
1 teaspoon salt
Freshly ground black pepper
2 tablespoons light-tasting olive oil
1½ teaspoons light brown sugar
2 allspice berries
2 whole peppercorns
½ teaspoon dried thyme
¼ teaspoon cinnamon
¼ teaspoon cayenne pepper
Freshly grated nutmeg

1. 15 minutes before cooking, place the rack in the center of the oven and preheat oven to 300 degrees.

2. Mince the garlic in a food processor or by hand and set aside. Cut the onions into very thin slices, either with the thin (2mm) slicer of a processor or by hand. Core the tomatoes, halve crosswise and squeeze gently to remove the seeds. Chop the tomatoes in the processor or by hand.

3. Trim the meat and pat dry. Put the flour, ½ teaspoon salt and the pepper in a plastic bag. Add the meat and shake it to coat all over with flour.

4. Heat the oil in a stove-to-oven casserole that is just large enough to hold the meat. When it is hot, add the meat and cook over high heat until it is browned on all sides. Remove the meat and set aside. Reduce the heat to medium and add the onions and garlic; cook, stirring often, until they are light brown, about 5 minutes.

5. Off the heat, spread the onions in an even layer over the bottom of the pan. Add the sugar, allspice, peppercorns, thyme, cinnamon, cayenne pepper, nutmeg and bay leaf. Place the meat over these ingredients, spoon the tomatoes over the meat and pour the vermouth over all. Cover the pan tightly and bake 1½ hours.

6. Transfer the meat to a platter and tent with aluminum foil. Strain the sauce to separate the solids from the liquid. Purée the solids in a processor or blender. Add about 1 cup of cooking liquid, or enough so that the sauce is loose and flowing. The dish can be prepared in advance to this point and refrigerated for 3 days, or frozen. Bring the meat to room temperature before reheating. To reheat, return the meat and sauce to the casserole. Cover and bake in a 300-degree oven until hot, about 35 minutes. Or place in a microwave casserole, cover and cook on medium power (50%) until hot, about 10 minutes. Set the meat aside.

7. To finish the sauce, cook it in the casserole over high heat for 5 minutes. Whisk in the butter and the remaining ½ teaspoon salt. Adjust the seasoning, adding more cayenne pepper for more of a bite. To serve, cut the meat into thin slices and nap with the sauce.

1 bay leaf
½ cup dry vermouth
1 tablespoon unsalted butter

◆

Veal chops are succulent and flavorful in their own right, requiring little more attention than careful cooking. Here they are brushed with a light mustard glaze that sets them off to perfection. The subtle flavor enhancement that comes from grilling the chops over mesquite or oak chips is special, so grill them outdoors when possible.

Grilled Veal Chops

Preparation time: 5 minutes
Grilling time: About 10 minutes
Yield: 4 servings

1. Prepare a hot grill, preferably with a mix of charcoal and 1 cup soaked mesquite wood or oak chips; or place the broiler rack 8 inches from the heat and preheat the broiler.

2. Mince the garlic and lemon zest in a food processor or by hand. Mix with the oil, mustard, salt and pepper and brush over both sides of the veal chops. Season to taste with salt and pepper.

3. Grill or broil the chops, turning once, until they are cooked as desired. Serve immediately.

1 large garlic clove, peeled
  Zest of 1 lemon, removed with a zester or grater
¼ cup light-tasting olive oil
¼ cup Dijon mustard
½ teaspoon salt
  Freshly ground white pepper
4 veal chops

The robust flavors of Milanese ossobuco, including the distinctive Gremolata sprinkled on at the end, are translated to a stew, with the advantages of quicker cooking and less fat. Traditionally, ossobuco is served with risotto. For the stew, I prefer plain rice or fettuccine tossed with a bit of olive oil.

Veal Stew, Ossobuco Style

Preparation time: 25 minutes
Baking time: 1 hour
Yield: 6 servings

STEW:
- 2 large garlic cloves, peeled
- 1 large onion (7 ounces), peeled
- 6 ounces mushrooms
- 3 tablespoons unbleached all-purpose flour
- 1 teaspoon salt
  Freshly ground black pepper
- 2 pounds lean veal stew, cut in ¾-inch cubes
- 3 tablespoons light-tasting olive oil
- ⅓ cup dry vermouth
- 1 can (16 ounces) whole tomatoes
- ⅓ cup beef stock or broth
- ½ teaspoon dried basil
- ½ teaspoon dried thyme
- 1 bay leaf

GREMOLATA:
- 1 cup parsley leaves
  Zest of 1 lemon, removed with a zester or grater
- 1 large garlic clove, peeled

1. 15 minutes before cooking, place the rack in the center of the oven and preheat the oven to 400 degrees.

2. Mince the garlic and onion in a food processor or by hand. Trim the stems from the mushrooms and cut the mushrooms in half, or in quarters if they are large.

3. Put the flour, salt and pepper in a large plastic bag and add the meat. Seal the bag and shake it to coat the meat all over with flour.

4. Heat 1½ tablespoons oil in a large sauté pan over high heat. When it is hot, add half the meat and brown on all sides. Set aside in a 2-quart casserole and brown the other half in the remaining oil. Add the second batch to the casserole and pour out any fat from the skillet.

5. Put the skillet over low heat and carefully add the vermouth. Stir up any browned bits from the bottom of the skillet and cook until liquid is reduced by about half. Add the garlic and onion and cook over high heat, stirring often, until they are softened, about 4 minutes.

6. Break up the tomatoes with a fork and add them to the skillet along with their juice, the stock or broth, basil, thyme and bay leaf. Bring to a boil, then pour over the meat.

7. Cover the casserole and bake until the meat is tender, about 1 hour. Remove the cover during the last 15 minutes to allow the sauce to thicken. The stew can be made in advance and refrigerated for 4 days, or frozen. Reheat, covered, in a 400-degree oven or in a microwave oven on high power (100%) until hot.

8. For the Gremolata, mince the parsley, lemon zest and garlic in a food processor or by hand. (In a processor they can all

be minced together.) The Gremolata is best made shortly before serving. At serving time, pass the Gremolata separately to sprinkle over the stew.

◆

Much lighter than traditional burritos, these are perfect for any meal between noon and midnight. The filling of pork, spinach, hominy and black beans is baked as a casserole, then served in flour tortillas as burritos. Or, serve the casserole New Mexican style, with fried eggs on top and tortillas on the side. Salsa is the proper condiment. Make one of the recipes (see page 332) from the Basics chapter or buy a good-quality one.

Laredo Beans and Greens Burritos

Preparation time: 20 minutes
Baking time: 35 minutes (Microwave: 20 minutes)
Yield: 4 to 6 servings

1. 15 minutes before baking, place the rack in the center of the oven and preheat oven to 400 degrees. Have a 10-inch oval gratin dish ready.

2. Put the hominy and beans in a colander and rinse under running water. Set aside to drain.

3. Mince the peppers and garlic and chop the onion in a food processor or by hand.

4. Heat the oil in a large skillet. Add the pork, peppers, garlic and onion and cook until the pork is done, about 10 minutes.

5. Add the hominy and beans to the skillet and cook until heated through, about 4 minutes. Add the spinach and cook, stirring gently, just until it wilts. Transfer to the gratin dish.

6. Mince the cheese together with the cilantro in a processor; or shred the cheese with a grater, mince the cilantro and toss them together. Spread in an even layer over the pork and spinach. The dish can be prepared a day in advance to this point and refrigerated. Bring to room temperature before baking.

7. Bake until cheese is melted and very lightly browned,

1 can (16 ounces) hominy
1 can (15 ounces) black beans
2 serrano peppers, seeded if desired
1 large garlic clove, peeled
1 medium red onion (5 ounces), peeled
2 tablespoons safflower oil
6 ounces lean pork loin, cut into ⅜" dice
5 ounces small spinach leaves, stems trimmed
12 ounces Monterey Jack cheese
¾ cup cilantro leaves
6 to 8 flour tortillas
   Red or Green Salsa (see page 332)

about 20 minutes. Stack tortillas and wrap in aluminum foil. Place in oven during the last 10 minutes.

8. To serve, spoon mixture into warm tortillas and roll up. Top with Salsa.

MICROWAVE: Follow steps 2 and 3. Put oil, pork, garlic, peppers and onion in a 2-quart microwave casserole. Cover and cook on high power (100%) until pork is cooked, about 10 minutes. Add hominy, beans and spinach and cook on high power 4 minutes, stirring once halfway through cooking. Follow step 6. Sprinkle cheese and cilantro over top. Cover and cook on medium power (50%) until cheese is melted, about 6 minutes. Stack tortillas and wrap them in dampened paper towels. Add to microwave oven during the last 2 minutes of cooking. See step 8 for serving.

9 · Vegetables—from Artichokes to Sweet Potatoes

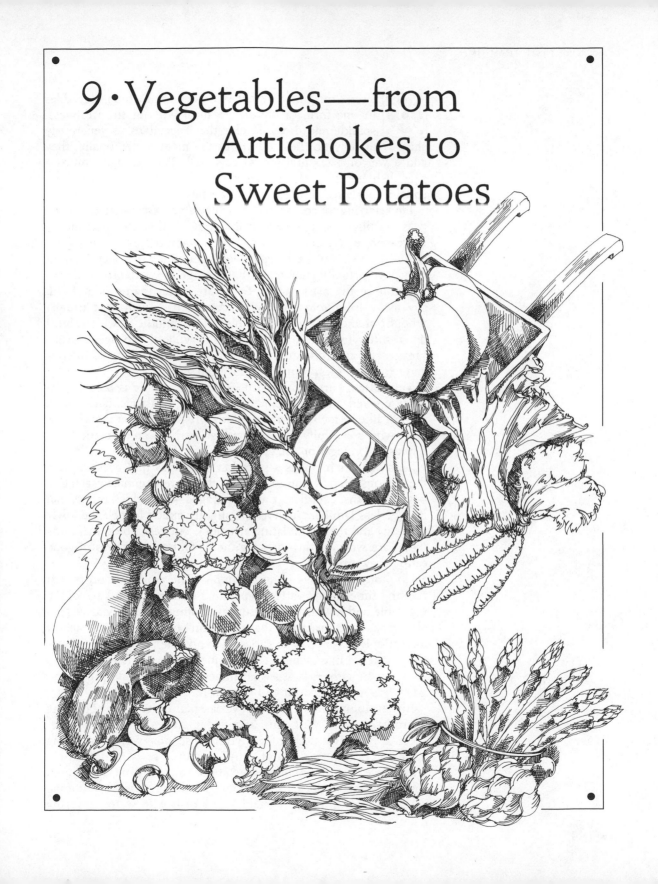

I can't imagine a dinner that does not include vegetables in one form or another, a meal without the freshness, sparkle and dash of color that vegetables so generously share. Not only do they round out the menu nutritionally; they add a welcome textural contrast as well. Their designation as a side dish hardly gives them proper credit. For me, they share equal importance with the main offering.

I'm referring, of course, to fresh vegetables. Occasionally frozen peas or spinach is quite acceptable, but for the most part there's no reason to rely on canned or frozen when there is such a wonderful profusion of fresh vegetables from which to select. Modern transport virtually guarantees that a range of vegetables is always available in the marketplace. Some are better than others. I still shy away from tomatoes (yes, technically a fruit, but usually thought of and used as a vegetable) in the middle of winter, but I don't suffer from a lack of choices. Eggplant, cabbage, carrots, turnips and zucchini are just a few of the choices that add interest and excitement to a winter produce bin.

Very often, particularly with vegetables, simple is best. A perfectly cooked, prime specimen needs little further enhancement. Often I like to focus on a vegetable's pristine character and show it off with a carefully chosen contrast, perhaps an aromatic herb, a splash of vinegar or a flavored butter.

This chapter includes a selection of recipes that goes through the seasons. In addition to some of the more common vegetables —green beans, cauliflower and asparagus—I've added others that may be less familiar, such as the slightly exotic fennel, the lowly rutabaga and the intimidating artichoke. All vegetables, including these, are well worth trying for the newfound pleasures in good eating they provide.

Cooking vegetables is quite simple. The complication is that cooking time always varies, depending on the size and age of the vegetable and how it is cut. I suggest tasting frequently as vegetables cook, good insurance that they won't be cooked too much or too little. Everyone's taste varies as to how he or she likes vegetables cooked. I like them so they are just tender, certainly not hard —or mushy either. That's what the cooking times are predicated on. Adjust them according to your taste.

In developing this chapter, I've learned quite a bit about the microwave oven. With this knowledge comes a whole new respect. If you never used it for anything else, not even for softening butter or reheating a cup of coffee, it would be worth owning a microwave oven for cooking vegetables. I simply can't say enough about how well it does. I started out by following the conventional wisdom of putting the vegetables in a dish with water, covering the dish and cooking until done. Somewhere along the line, I wrapped an ear of corn in plastic, stuck it on a paper plate and cooked it that way. I was hooked! Most vegetables cook quicker and better wrapped in plastic this way, and there's no dish to wash. Many, though not all, microwave instructions are written with the vegetables wrapped. I think you'll be pleased and surprised at how well they cook.

I think of this lusty side dish in the spring, when artichokes are big, abundant and bargain-priced. They're steamed conventionally, or cooked in the microwave oven, then topped with an herb-scented mushroom-and-tomato relish. I'm especially enthusiastic about using the microwave oven here. It does a marvelous job of cooking artichokes in practically no time at all, then goes on to cook the topping effortlessly as well. The artichokes are delicious hot or at room temperature, served alongside grilled lamb or baked chicken.

Artichokes Provençal

Preparation time: 20 minutes
Cooking time: 40 minutes (Microwave: 14 minutes)
Yield: 3 to 4 servings

ARTICHOKES:
- 2 *large artichokes (12 to 14 ounces each)*
- 1 *lemon wedge*

TOPPING:
- 1 *medium garlic clove, peeled*
- 1 *small onion (2 ounces), peeled*
- 1 *small tomato (4 ounces)*
- 3 *medium mushrooms (2 ounces total)*
- 1 *tablespoon light-tasting olive oil*
- ¼ *cup dry vermouth*
- ½ *teaspoon red wine vinegar*
- ¼ *teaspoon dried thyme*
- ¼ *teaspoon salt, or to taste*
- ¼ *teaspoon freshly ground black pepper*

1. For the artichokes, trim the stem so it is flush with the bottom. Discard the dried end of the stem and reserve the rest. Snap off the layers of coarse outer leaves until you reach the lighter yellow ones underneath. Smooth the base with a paring knife or vegetable peeler. Cut about 1½ inches from the top of each artichoke. Rub all the cut surfaces with lemon to keep them from discoloring.

2. Put the artichokes and stems in a steamer over rapidly boiling water. Cover and cook until the base is tender when pierced with the point of a sharp knife, about 25 minutes.

3. When they are cool enough to handle, cut the artichokes in half lengthwise and pull the purple-tipped leaves from the center. Carefully remove the fuzzy choke with a paring knife or grapefruit spoon. Cut each half into 3 wedges and set aside.

4. Prepare the topping while the artichokes are cooking. Mince the garlic and onion in a food processor or by hand and set aside. Quarter the tomato and chop with the mushrooms in the processor or by hand.

5. Heat the oil in a small non-aluminum saucepan. When it is hot, add the garlic and onion and cook over medium heat until they begin to soften, about 2 minutes. Chop the artichoke stems and add them to the pan, along with the tomatoes, mushrooms, vermouth, vinegar, thyme, salt and pepper. Cover and cook over high heat until most of the liquid has boiled away, about 10 minutes.

6. Arrange the artichokes in a dish and spoon the tomato

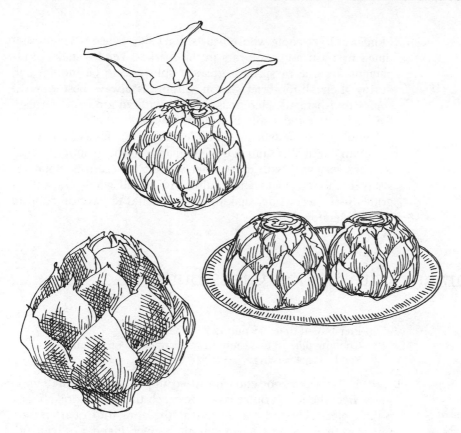

mixture over them. They can be served immediately, or will continue to improve for up to 4 days in the refrigerator. Serve hot or at room temperature.

MICROWAVE: Follow step 1 above. Wrap each artichoke, enclosing the cut stem, in an airtight package of heavy-duty plastic wrap. Stand them on a paper plate and cook on high power (100%) until the bottoms are tender, 5 to 6 minutes. Test by piercing the bottoms with the tip of a knife. Let stand for 5 minutes, then remove the plastic. Follow steps 3 and 4 above. Cook the oil, onion and garlic in a 1-quart microwave casserole on high power for 2 minutes. Chop the artichoke stems and add them along with the tomatoes, mushrooms, ¼ cup of vermouth, the vinegar and thyme. Cook, uncovered, on high power until most of the liquid has cooked away, about 7 minutes. Add the salt and pepper. Serve as in step 6.

I know of few people whose hearts don't skip a beat when spring-time's first asparagus appears in the market. Tender stalks of asparagus are one of spring's greatest splurges, to be indulged in during their all-too-brief season. Simple is always best when it comes to asparagus. Here it is dressed with an aromatic, citrusy-flavored butter and a splash of sushi vinegar.

Lemon grass is a delicious complement to asparagus, well worth searching for at Vietnamese or Thai markets. This compound butter goes very well with most other vegetables—carrots, potatoes, steamed cabbage, peas and cauliflower are all good—as well as grilled fish, so consider making extra batches to have on hand in the refrigerator or freezer.

Asparagus with Lemon Grass Butter

Preparation time: 15 minutes
Cooking time: 8 to 12 minutes (Microwave: 4 to 7 minutes)
Yield: 3 to 4 servings

1   *stalk fresh lemon grass*
3   *tablespoons each,
    unsalted butter, sushi
    vinegar*
½   *teaspoon* nuoc mam
    *(Vietnamese fish sauce)
    (see Note)*
1   *pound fresh asparagus*

1. Trim the root end and dried upper leaves of the lemon grass. Peel the tough outer layers to reach the white core, about a 3-inch piece. Discard the rest. Cut the core into quarters and mince as finely as possible in a mini-chopper, blender or by hand.

2. Transfer the lemon grass to a small pan and add the butter, vinegar and *nuoc mam*. Melt the butter over medium heat, then cook 2 minutes longer.

3. Strain, pressing on the solids to extract as much flavor as possible. The butter can be made in advance and refrigerated up to a week or frozen for 2 months. Melt on the stove or in the microwave oven before using.

4. Trim the tough white ends from the asparagus and peel stalks with a swivel-bladed vegetable peeler so they cook evenly.

5. Bring salted water to a boil in a skillet large enough to hold the asparagus. Cook just until tender—timing will depend on the thickness and age of the asparagus, anywhere from 5 to 9 minutes. Lift the asparagus from the pan with tongs and transfer to a towel and pat dry. Place on a platter and pour butter over. Serve immediately.

MICROWAVE: Follow step 1 above. Transfer the lemon grass to a small microwave-safe bowl and add the butter, vinegar and *nuoc mam.* Cook on high power (100%) for 1 minute. Follow steps 3 and 4. Bunch the asparagus together, wrap in heavy-duty plastic

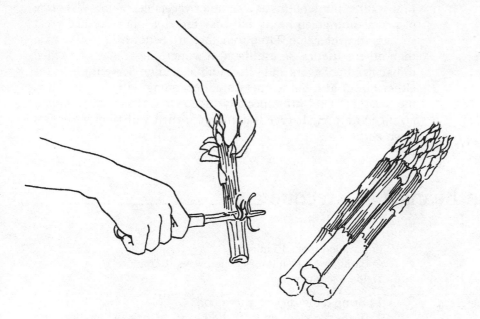

wrap and place on a paper plate. Cook on high power (100%) just until tender 3 to 6 minutes. Test by piercing through the package with a sharp knife. Carefully unwrap, transfer to a platter and pour butter over. Serve immediately.

Note: Sushi vinegar, also called seasoned rice vinegar, is available at oriental markets and some large supermarkets.

I most often think of this as a summer vegetable, taking advantage of pencil-slim green beans and rosy tomatoes, but I've had great success in winter, too. Plum tomatoes are better in the off-season than other varieties, so use them in winter. Sugar may be needed to balance the flavors and offset undue acidity. Serve these beans either hot or at room temperature, depending on your whim and the weather. They are especially nice as a salad in the summer, arranged on a big lettuce leaf and garnished with a sprinkling of fresh herbs.

Green Beans à la Grecque

Preparation time: 15 minutes
Cooking time: 16 minutes (Microwave: 10 minutes)
Yield: 4 servings

1 *pound tender young green beans*
3 *large shallots (2 ounces), peeled*
1 *small garlic clove, peeled*
4 *medium plum tomatoes (8 ounces total)*
3 *tablespoons light-tasting olive oil*
1 *teaspoon dried oregano*
½ *teaspoon salt*
¼ *teaspoon ground cumin*
½ *to 1 teaspoon sugar to taste, if necessary*

1. Bring 6 quarts water to a boil.
2. Trim the stem end off the beans. Mince the shallots and garlic in a food processor or by hand. Core the tomatoes, cut in half crosswise and squeeze gently to remove the seeds. Cut the tomatoes into ⅜-inch dice.
3. Cook the beans in the boiling water until they are tender, 7 to 8 minutes.
4. Drain and refresh under cold water to stop further cooking. Drain again and pat dry. The beans can be cooked up to 2 days in advance and refrigerated. Pat dry again before using.
5. Heat the oil in a large skillet over medium heat. Add the shallots and garlic and cook over medium heat until they are softened, but not brown, about 4 minutes. Add the beans, oregano, salt and cumin and cook, tossing several times, just until the beans are heated through, about 3 minutes. Fold in the tomatoes and cook 1 minute longer. Adjust the seasoning, adding sugar to taste, if necessary. Serve hot or at room temperature.

MICROWAVE: Follow step 2 above. Wrap the trimmed beans in heavy-duty plastic wrap and place on a paper plate. Cook on high power (100%) until they are tender, 4 minutes. Test by piercing through the package with a sharp knife. Carefully unwrap beans and follow step 4. Cook the oil, shallots and garlic, uncovered, in a 2½-quart microwave casserole on high power until they are soft, about 2 minutes. Add the beans, oregano and cumin and cook, uncovered, on high power until the beans are heated through and the flavors blended, about 2 minutes. Gently toss in the tomatoes and cook 30 seconds longer. Add sugar, if necessary, and salt. Serve hot or at room temperature.

◆

Even though it now seems such a natural affiliation, I may never have thought of combining beets and carrots if James Beard hadn't suggested it for a television appearance we did together. As usual, his taste was right on the mark. Here, I've combined them in an immensely satisfying purée. Serve it as a vegetable or go further with it and turn it into a ruby-colored soup with the addition of chicken stock.

Puréed Beets and Carrots

Preparation time: 10 minutes
Cooking time: 25 minutes (Microwave: 14 minutes)
Yield: 6 servings

1. Scrub the beets and carrots and trim the ends. It isn't necessary to peel them. Slice thinly either with the medium (3mm) or all-purpose (4mm) slicer of a food processor or by hand. Thinner slices will cook more quickly.

2. Put the beets and carrots in a pan with water to cover. Bring to a boil and cook until very tender, about 25 minutes. Make sure they are soft enough to purée smoothly. Drain well and pat dry with paper toweling. Transfer to a food processor or blender.

3. Purée the beets and carrots until smooth, about 2 minutes, stopping several times to scrape down the sides of the container. Add the butter, sour cream, vinegar and salt and mix for 30 seconds. Adjust the seasoning if necessary. Serve immediately or refrigerate up to 3 days and reheat gently on the stove or in a microwave oven before serving.

MICROWAVE: Follow step 1 above. Put the beets and carrots in a 2-quart microwave casserole and add ½ cup of water. Cover tightly with plastic wrap and pierce it with the point of a knife so steam can escape. Cook on high power (100%) until they are very soft, about 14 minutes. Drain well and transfer to a food processor. Follow step 3 to finish.

4 *medium beets (1 pound without the greens)*
6 *medium carrots (1 pound total)*
2 *tablespoons unsalted butter*
2 *tablespoons sour cream*
1 *teaspoon cider vinegar*
½ *teaspoon salt*

191 •

Even before broccoli topped the list of "best bet" vegetables, those that are considered the healthiest, it was one of my favorites. Its anti-cancer status and high vitamin and fiber content are bonuses. Here broccoli is glossed over with a light sauce of Oriental ingredients. Ginger is the predominant flavor, and even that is subtle.

_____Broccoli Spears with Ginger_____

Preparation time: 10 minutes
Cooking time: 10 minutes
Yield: 3 to 4 servings

2 *large broccoli spears (1¼*
  pounds total)
2 *tablespoons safflower oil*
2 *tablespoons orange juice*
1 *tablespoon dark soy sauce*
2 *teaspoons Dijon mustard*
½ *teaspoon ground ginger*
½ *teaspoon sugar*

1. Bring 4 quarts salted water to a boil.
2. Peel the broccoli stems with a vegetable peeler. Cut the flowerets 3½ inches from the top of the stems. Split the stems into ½-inch-wide strips.
3. Add the broccoli to boiling water and cook just until tender, about 7 minutes.
4. Drain and hold under cold running water to stop further cooking. Drain well, shaking the colander to remove as much water as possible, then pat dry. The broccoli can be cooked a day in advance and refrigerated. Pat dry again before using.
5. Heat the oil, orange juice, soy sauce, mustard, ginger and sugar in a 8-inch skillet. When mixture is hot, add the broccoli and toss gently so it is well coated with the sauce. Cook just until heated through, 2 to 3 minutes. Serve hot or at room temperature.

Note: In side-by-side cooking, broccoli cooked in boiling water had a better taste, texture and appearance than when cooked in the microwave oven. For these reasons, I have not included microwave instructions here.

While Brussels sprouts are in the market all year long, they are at their best in the fall and winter months, mild and sweet without any trace of bitterness. They're highly touted by the American Cancer Society as being one of the vegetables that may prevent cancer, reason enough to use them often. And besides, they taste delicious, especially in this simple pairing with mustard cream, so how can you miss?

Brussels Sprouts with Mustard Cream

Preparation time: 10 minutes
Cooking time: 15 minutes (Microwave: 13 minutes)
Yield: 6 servings

2 pints Brussels sprouts
(1½ pounds)
1 tablespoon unsalted butter
¼ cup whipping cream
1 tablespoon Dijon mustard
¼ teaspoon ground thyme
¼ teaspoon salt

1. Trim the Brussels sprouts and cut a shallow "X" into the stem of each.
2. Cook the sprouts in a large amount of rapidly boiling water until they are tender, 8 to 9 minutes. Drain immediately and refresh under cold running water to stop further cooking. Cut very large sprouts in half lengthwise. The sprouts can be cooked a day in advance and refrigerated.
3. Melt the butter in a 10-inch skillet. Add the cream, mustard, thyme and salt and cook over high heat, stirring often, until the cream has thickened, about 4 minutes. Add the sprouts and toss lightly to coat them with cream. Cook just until they are heated through. Serve immediately.

MICROWAVE: Follow step 1. Put the sprouts in a 2-quart microwave casserole with ¼ cup of water. Cover and cook on high power (100%) until tender, about 7 minutes, stirring once halfway through. Drain and hold under cold water to stop them from cooking. Cut large ones in half. They can be cooked a day in advance and refrigerated. Melt the butter in the same casserole on high power. Add the cream, mustard and thyme and cook, uncovered, on high power until thickened, about 2½ minutes. Add the sprouts and salt and toss lightly. Cook, uncovered, on high power for 1 to 3 minutes, depending on whether the sprouts are still hot or have been chilled. Serve immediately.

Cabbage is one vegetable that deserves more respect. Finally it seems to be getting its due. Cabbage is more in vogue now than it has been any time in the past decade or so, riding in on the coattails of our preference for earthy and robust foods. The simple ingredients here, anchored by a head of cabbage, have remarkable goodness and finesse. The cabbage itself is not at all strong—in fact, it's quite sweet and mild. Pair it with sautéed sausages for an impromptu version of *choucroute garni* or serve it with roast pork or country-style ribs.

—— Simmered Cabbage and New Potatoes with Tarragon ——

Preparation time: 10 minutes
Cooking time: 20 minutes (Microwave: 19 minutes)
Yield: 5 to 6 servings

2 medium onions (8 ounces total), peeled
5 small red new potatoes 14 ounces total)
½ small head green cabbage (use 1¼ pounds)
2 tablespoons unsalted butter
1½ cups chicken stock (see page 339) or canned broth
3 tablespoons minced fresh parsley
1 teaspoon dried tarragon
¼ teaspoon salt
Freshly ground black pepper

1. Mince the onions in a food processor or by hand. Cut each potato into six wedges. Core the cabbage and cut it into ¼-inch ribbons with the ultra-thick (8mm) slicer of the processor or by hand.

2. Melt the butter in a large sauté pan. When it is hot, add the onions and cook over high heat, stirring occasionally, until they begin to soften, about 2 minutes. Add the potatoes and stock or broth. Cover and cook over medium heat until the potatoes are almost, but not quite, tender, about 10 minutes. Add the cabbage and continue to cook until it is wilted and the potatoes are tender, about 6 minutes longer. The recipe can be prepared up to 2 days in advance to this point. Reheat gently, adding a bit of water if the mixture seems too dry.

3. Just before serving, drain any excess liquid. Add the parsley and tarragon to the pan along with the salt and pepper. Serve immediately.

MICROWAVE: Follow step 1 above. Combine the onions and butter in a 3-quart microwave casserole. Cook on high power (100%) for 2 minutes. Add the potatoes and only ½ cup of stock or broth, cover and cook on high power until vegetables are almost, but not quite, tender, about 8 minutes, stirring once halfway through. Stir in the cabbage, cover and cook on high for 6 minutes. Stir well and cook, uncovered, until the cabbage is tender and most of the liquid has cooked away, about 3 minutes. The recipe can be prepared 2 days in advance to this point and refrigerated. Reheat on high for 4 to 5 minutes. Finish as in step 3.

◆

I can think of few dishes that aren't enhanced by carrots' sunny disposition. Their color favors anything they are served with and their flavor is so pleasant they hardly ever seem out of place. Here, thinly sliced coins of carrots are refreshingly seasoned with lemon and the cool taste of mint. Basil stands in very well for the mint, as does almost any fresh herb.

Carrots with Lemon, Oil and Mint

Preparation time: 10 minutes
Cooking time: 15 minutes (Microwave: 13 minutes)
Yield: 4 servings

1. Cut the carrots into ⅛-inch slices, either with the thin (2mm) slicer of a food processor or by hand.

2. Place them in a large steamer over rapidly boiling water. Cover and cook until they are barely tender, about 4 minutes. Do not overcook. Drain and refresh under cold water to stop further cooking. Drain well and pat dry. The carrots can be cooked up to 2 days in advance and refrigerated.

3. If you wish to serve the carrots hot, heat the lemon juice and oil in a 10-inch skillet. When they are hot, add the carrots and cook over high heat just enough to heat them through, about 2 minutes. Remove from the heat, add the mint, salt and pepper, and serve.

4. They can also be served chilled. To do so, simply toss the cooked carrots with the lemon juice, oil, mint, salt and pepper—do not reheat—and cover and refrigerate until chilled, or up to 2 days.

MICROWAVE: Follow step 1 above. Put the carrots in a 2-quart microwave casserole and add ¼ cup water. Cover tightly with plastic wrap and pierce the plastic so steam can escape. Cook on high power (100%) until they are barely tender, about 10 minutes. Drain well and set aside. Put the lemon juice and oil in the same dish. Heat, uncovered, on high power for 1 minute. Add the carrots, cover tightly and cook on high power for 2 minutes, stirring once halfway through cooking. Add the mint, salt and pepper. Serve hot, if desired, or see step 4.

1¼ *pounds carrots, peeled*
2 *tablespoons fresh lemon juice*
2 *tablespoons extra virgin olive oil*
2 *tablespoons finely snipped fresh mint*
¼ *teaspoon salt*
  Freshly ground black pepper

An old culinary quip, by none other than Mark Twain, asserts that cauliflower is nothing but cabbage with a college education. The vegetables are, in fact, from the same family, which is evident if you look at them side by side in the garden rather than in the supermarket. Like cabbage, cauliflower, if cooked properly, has a mild flavor that is favorably enhanced by members of the onion family. Here, lightly browned bits of leek join the milky-white buds of cauliflower in a mutually beneficial partnership.

Cauliflower and Browned Leeks with Lemon Butter

Preparation time: 10 minutes
Cooking time: 12 to 13 minutes (Microwave: 6 minutes, plus 6 minutes top of stove)
Yield: 3 to 4 servings

1 medium head cauliflower (about 1¾ pounds)
2 medium leeks (8 ounces total)
3 tablespoons unsalted butter
1 tablespoon fresh lemon juice
½ teaspoon salt
Freshly ground white pepper

1. Core the cauliflower and separate into 1-inch flowerets. Cook in a large steamer over boiling water until tender, 6 to 7 minutes. The cooked cauliflower can be refrigerated up to 2 days. Pat dry before using.

2. Prepare the leeks while the cauliflower is cooking. Trim the coarse green ends from the leeks. Slit the leeks lengthwise, almost to, but not through the root end. If the root is left attached, the leeks do not fall apart when they are washed. Rinse them under cold water, fanning the leaves open to rinse away all the dirt. Slit again, lengthwise, almost to the root, then cut off the root. Cut the leeks crosswise into ½-inch slices.

3. Melt the butter in a large skillet, preferably nonstick. Add the leeks and cook over medium-high heat, stirring often, until they soften and some have begun to brown at the edges, about 5 minutes. Do not let the leeks burn. Add the cauliflower, lemon juice, salt and pepper, tossing lightly. Cook just until heated through. Adjust the seasoning and serve immediately.

MICROWAVE: Core the cauliflower, separate into 1-inch flowerets. Wrap them in heavy-duty plastic wrap, making a close-fitting, airtight package. Pierce once with a knife so steam can escape. Cook on high power (100%) until tender, about 6 minutes. Unwrap and set aside. The recipe is finished as in steps 2 and 3 above, since the leeks taste better when browned on the stove.

Chayote, also known as vegetable pear or mirliton, is indigenous to Central America, though it has taken a long, circuitous route before landing on American tables. When it does, it is most likely to be part of a Creole or a Mexican meal. It is similar in taste to zucchini, though sweeter, crisper and more densely textured. Some will describe it as having a taste of cucumber and kohlrabi, which is perhaps true. Here, chayote is prepared in a simple but beguiling manner, flavored with bacon and fresh cilantro. The recipe comes from Rick Bayless, co-author with his wife, Deann, of the wonderful cookbook *Authentic Mexican*. They are also the owners of Frontera Grill in Chicago, one of my favorite haunts. Use zucchini in the recipe if you can't find chayote.

Roasted Chayote with Bacon

Preparation time: 10 minutes
Cooking time: 30 minutes
Yield: 4 to 6 servings

1. 15 minutes before baking, place the rack in the center of the oven and preheat oven to 325 degrees.

2. Cut the bacon into ¼-inch strips. Peel the chayote, remove the pit and cut the flesh into ½-inch cubes. If using zucchini, wash but do not peel, and cut into ½-inch cubes.

3. Brown the bacon in a heavy ovenproof skillet. Discard all but 2 tablespoons of fat. Add the chayote and salt and pepper to taste, stirring so it is well coated with bacon fat. Place the skillet in the oven and bake until the squash is tender-crisp, about 25 minutes. Remove from the oven, add the cilantro and adjust the seasoning if necessary. Serve hot. The recipe can be prepared in advance, if desired. To do so, bake the squash for 15 minutes only, then cool and refrigerate for up to 2 days. To reheat, bake in a preheated 325-degree oven until hot, about 15 minutes. Add cilantro just before serving.

Note: Though it might seem logical, I don't recommend microwave preparation for this recipe. Instead of roasting, as it does in the oven, the chayote "steams" in the microwave oven and becomes too moist.

2 *slices bacon (2 ounces total)*
2 *large chayote squash (1¼ pounds total) or an equal weight of zucchini*
Salt
Freshly ground black pepper
⅓ *cup minced cilantro leaves*

Cucumbers are usually thought of as salad vegetables, but I think they come into their own when they are sautéed in butter. Carefully and quickly cooked, their crunch stays intact while their natural sweetness is intensified. Cucumbers are especially nice served with fish and seafood. A few serving notes: I like to toss in a handful of fresh cilantro just before serving. If your taste preference runs along those lines, try it. This is one of those vegetables that just doesn't reheat well.

Sautéed Cucumbers with Peas and Red Onions

Preparation time: 15 minutes
Cooking time: 10 minutes (Microwave: 8 minutes)
Yield: 3 to 4 servings

1   large English, "gourmet" or "burpless" cucumber (1 pound)
1   small red onion (3 ounces), peeled
3   tablespoons unsalted butter
1   teaspoon fresh lemon juice
½   teaspoon dried dill
½   teaspoon salt
¼   teaspoon dried thyme
    Pinch sugar
½   cup tiny frozen peas, thawed
    Freshly ground black pepper
½   cup minced cilantro, optional

1. Peel the cucumber and cut in half lengthwise. Scoop out the seeds with a melon baller or spoon. Cut each half in half again, then cut crosswise into ¼-inch slices. Cut the onion into ½-inch dice.

2. Melt the butter in a large skillet. Add the onion and cook over medium heat until it begins to soften, about 3 minutes. Add the cucumber, lemon juice, dill, salt, thyme and sugar and continue to cook until the cucumbers are tender, about 5 minutes. Add the peas and pepper and cook just until the peas are heated through. Drain off any liquid. Add the cilantro, if using, adjust the seasoning if necessary, and serve immediately.

MICROWAVE: Follow step 1 above. Cook the onion and butter in a shallow, 10-inch round microwave dish on high power (100%) for 2 minutes. Add the cucumber, lemon juice, dill and thyme. Cook, uncovered, on high power until they are tender, 4 to 5 minutes, stirring once halfway through. Stir in the peas and cook 1 minute longer. Drain off liquid if there is any. Add the cilantro, if using, salt and pepper, and serve immediately.

Eggplant is much more common in cuisines other than our own, so I've taken a cue from the Middle Eastern countries for this preparation. The eggplant is mixed with softly sautéed onions, deeply flavored walnuts and a nice balance of sweet and hot spices. Serve it with simple grilled meat and poultry. Depending on what it accompanies, I sometimes top this off with a spoonful of yogurt and a sprinkling of fresh cilantro.

_____Middle Eastern Spiced Eggplant and Onions _____.

Preparation time: 15 minutes
Draining time: 30 minutes
Cooking time: 27 minutes (Microwave: 17 minutes)
Yield: 6 servings

1. Cut the unpeeled eggplant into ¾-inch cubes. Place in a colander and toss lightly with salt. Let drain for 30 minutes. Proceed with the recipe while the eggplant is draining.

2. Cut the onion into ½-inch dice.

3. Heat the oil in a 3-quart pan. When hot, add the walnuts and cook over medium heat until they are brown and fragrant, about 4 minutes. Remove with a slotted spoon and set aside.

4. Add the onion, sugar, ¾ teaspoon salt, cumin, cinnamon and cayenne pepper to the pan and cook over medium-high heat, stirring occasionally, until the onions are limp, about 15 minutes.

5. Rinse the eggplant under cold water, wrap in a towel and squeeze gently to dry.

6. Stir the eggplant into the onions, cover and cook over medium heat until it is tender, about 8 minutes. Add the walnuts and adjust the seasoning. Serve hot or at room temperature. Can be refrigerated up to 4 days.

1 medium eggplant (1 pound)
Salt
1 large onion (10 ounces), peeled
3 tablespoons light-tasting olive oil
½ cup chopped walnuts (2 ounces)
1 tablespoon light brown sugar
¾ teaspoon ground cumin
½ teaspoon cinnamon
⅛ teaspoon cayenne pepper

MICROWAVE: Follow steps 1 and 2 above. Put the oil in a 3-quart microwave casserole. Cook on high power (100%) for 1 minute. Add the walnuts and cook on high until they are light brown and fragrant, 2 to 3 minutes. Remove with a slotted spoon and set aside. Add the onion, sugar, cumin and cinnamon and cook, uncovered, on high power until the onion is very soft, about 7 minutes. Follow step 5. Add the eggplant to the onion and cook on high power until it is tender, 5 to 6 minutes, stirring once halfway through. Add the walnuts, salt and cayenne pepper. Serve hot or at room temperature.

Fennel, or *finochio,* is one of my favorite vegetables, similar in some ways to celery, but so much more interesting. Its flavor is mild and suggestive of licorice in a very refined and understated way. I often serve it raw in a salad or as a relish. Just as frequently and as successfully I cook it, as here, incorporated into a delicious mix of vegetables.

Sautéed Fennel with Peas and Mushrooms

Preparation time: 15 minutes
Cooking time: 18 minutes
Yield: 6 servings

1 *medium garlic clove, peeled*
1 *medium red onion (5 ounces), peeled*
1 *large fennel bulb (1 pound)*
4 *ounces small mushrooms*
2 *tablespoons light-tasting olive oil*
⅔ *cup tiny frozen peas, thawed*
¼ *teaspoon salt*
⅛ *teaspoon crushed red pepper flakes*
2 *tablespoons minced Parmesan cheese*

1. Mince the garlic and onion in a food processor or by hand. Trim the fennel stalks down to the bulb, trim any brown spots and remove the core. Separate the bulb into layers. If the outer layers are coarse and stringy, peel them with a vegetable peeler. Cut the layers lengthwise into ⅛-inch strips. Halve the mushrooms or quarter them if they are large.

2. Heat the oil in a 12-inch skillet. Add the garlic and onion and cook over medium heat, stirring occasionally, until they are soft but not brown, about 5 minutes. Add the fennel, cover and cook over medium heat until tender, about 8 minutes, stirring occasionally.

3. Add the mushrooms, peas, salt and red pepper flakes. Cover and cook until all the vegetables are tender, about 4 minutes. Remove from the heat and toss in the cheese. Adjust the seasoning and serve immediately.

Note: Cooking time is slightly longer in the microwave oven and the results less satisfactory, so I do not recommend its use here.

As a garnish, mushrooms couldn't possibly be more beautiful than these. A touch of honey and balsamic vinegar cause the mushrooms to turn a rich bronze color, making them look almost as though they've been gilded.

Tawny Mushroom Caps

Preparation time: 5 minutes
Cooking time: 14 minutes
Yield: 3 to 4 servings

1. Brush the mushrooms or wipe them with a dampened paper towel to remove the dirt. Trim the stems flush with the bottom of the caps. Save stems for another use, if desired.

2. Put the oil, vinegar, honey, port and salt in a 10-inch skillet. Cook over high heat until the mixture begins to sizzle, about 3 minutes. Add the mushrooms, rounded side down. Cook, shaking the pan occasionally, until the mushrooms are tender and the liquid has cooked down to a rich syrup that coats them with a thin film. This takes 8 to 10 minutes, depending on the size of the mushrooms.

3. The mushrooms can be made a day in advance. To reheat, cook gently until they are warmed through, about 5 minutes. Or reheat them with their liquid in a microwave oven on high power (100%) for 1½ minutes.

1 *pound large, uniformly sized mushrooms*
3 *tablespoons light-tasting olive oil*
1½ *tablespoons balsamic vinegar*
1½ *teaspoons honey*
2 *tablespoons tawny port*
½ *teaspoon salt*

Mashed potatoes are so deeply ingrained in traditional American cooking that we rarely think about what we're doing as we make them. Add a dab of butter, some milk and seasonings and perfection is reached. José Lampreia, chef of Maison Blanche, a thoroughly modern Parisian *brasserie,* obviously isn't saddled with our stateside culinary habits. He uses olive oil in place of butter and tosses a shower of minced olives over the top. Not a radical change, but a very clever and delicious one. Here is my adaptation.

Mashed Potatoes Niçoise

Preparation time: 15 minutes
Cooking time: 25 minutes (Microwave: 20 minutes)
Yield: 5 to 6 servings

3 *large red potatoes (1¾ pounds total)*
4 *large dry-cured black olives*
¼ *cup extra virgin olive oil*
¼ *cup milk*
½ *teaspoon salt*
 Freshly ground white pepper

1. Peel the potatoes and cut into sixths. Place in a 4-quart pan and cover with cold water. Drain to remove some of the starch and cover with fresh cold water. Bring to a boil, then cook until the potatoes are tender, about 20 minutes.

2. While the potatoes are cooking, pit the olives and cut them into very fine dice, ideally about ¹⁄₁₆-inch.

3. Just before the potatoes are cooked, combine the oil and milk in a small pan and heat gently.

4. Drain the potatoes, shaking them around in the hot pan so they become as dry as possible. Coarsely mash them with a potato masher. A ricer also works well. Add the warm oil and milk along with the salt and pepper and continue to mash until they are smooth and fluffy. Adjust the seasoning if necessary. Spoon into a bowl or onto dinner plates and garnish on top with the diced olives. Serve immediately.

MICROWAVE: Peel potatoes and cut them into sixths. Rinse with cold water to remove some of the starch. Put in a 2-quart microwave casserole and add water to cover. Cover tightly with plastic and cook on high power (100%) until tender, 18 to 20 minutes. Test by piercing through the plastic with a sharp knife. Follow step 2 above. When the potatoes are removed from the microwave oven, combine the oil and milk in a 1-cup microwave dish and cook on high power until hot, about 40 seconds. Follow step 4 above. The potatoes can be reheated in the microwave on high power for 2 to 3 minutes.

Rutabaga is a funny vegetable, one you're not apt to try unless you grew up eating (and liking!) it. A member of the turnip family, it has a distinct flavor that can, at times, be strong. Here, any hint of overassertiveness is tamed with a honey-sweetened orange butter that will endear anyone to this too-often overlooked root.

Rutabaga with Orange Honey Butter

Preparation time: 25 minutes
Cooking time: 15 minutes (Microwave: 13 minutes)
Yield: 4 servings

1. Peel the rutabaga with a sharp paring knife and cut into ⅜-inch-wide by 3-inch-long julienne. It is easiest to do this by double-slicing it with the all-purpose (4mm) slicer of a food processor, but it can also be done by hand. To use the processor, slice while applying firm pressure against the rutabaga in the feed tube. Remove the slices from the bowl and stack them together. Insert them again in the feed tube, this time with the slices placed perpendicular to the slicing blade. Slice again, into juliennes.

2. Cook the rutabaga in a large steamer over rapidly boiling water until just tender, 7 to 8 minutes. Set the rutabaga aside and discard the water from the bottom of the steamer.

3. Melt the butter in the bottom of the steamer. Add the orange juice, honey, mustard, salt, pepper and nutmeg and cook over high heat until the mixture is syrupy, about 4 minutes. Add the rutabaga and toss gently so it is coated with the syrup. Adjust the seasoning and serve immediately. The rutabaga can also be made a day in advance and gently reheated in a large skillet.

MICROWAVE: Follow step 1 above. Wrap the rutabaga in an airtight package of heavy-duty plastic wrap and place on a paper plate. Cook on high power (100%) until tender, 4 to 6 minutes. Test by piercing through the package with a sharp knife. Carefully unwrap the rutabaga and transfer to a serving bowl. Melt the butter in a 2-cup microwave dish. Add the orange juice, honey, mustard and nutmeg. Cook, uncovered, on high power until syrupy, 5 to 6 minutes. Pour over the rutabaga, add salt and pepper and toss gently. Can be made a day in advance and reheated. To reheat, cover and cook on high power until hot.

1 medium rutabaga (1 pound)
3 tablespoons unsalted butter
6 tablespoons orange juice
2 tablespoons honey
2 teaspoons Dijon mustard
¼ teaspoon salt
   Freshly ground black pepper
   Freshly grated nutmeg

This is a straightforward presentation of spinach, one that emphasizes its earthy goodness. Minced shallots and browned butter accentuate the taste without dominating the delicacy of tender, young spinach, while a shower of toasted bread crumbs adds a textural contrast. Avoid the cello packed spinach, if you can, since it has a tendency to be coarse and bitter tasting, traits which this preparation simply will not hide. Choose loosely packed bunches instead.

Brown Butter Spinach

Preparation time: 15 minutes
Cooking time: 7 minutes
Yield: 3 to 4 servings

1 *slice white bread (¾ ounce)*
2 *medium shallots (1 ounce total), peeled*
3 *tablespoons unsalted butter*
1 *pound tender young spinach*
¼ *teaspoon salt*
Freshly ground black pepper
Freshly grated nutmeg

1. Remove the stems from the spinach. Put the spinach in a sink filled with cold water, changing the water once or twice to remove the dirt. Drain and pat dry.

2. Crumb the bread in a food processor, blender or by hand and set aside. Mince the shallots in the processor or by hand.

3. Melt 1 tablespoon of butter in a 12-inch sauté pan. When hot, add the bread crumbs and cook, stirring often, until they are crisp and golden. Transfer to a piece of wax paper.

4. Wipe out the pan with a paper towel and return it to high heat. Add the remaining 2 tablespoons of butter and cook until it is light brown and smells nutty. This will happen almost immediately if the pan is still hot from browning the crumbs. Remove the pan from the heat and stir in the shallots, salt, pepper and nutmeg. When they stop sizzling, return the pan to medium heat and cook, stirring constantly, for 30 seconds. Transfer to a small dish.

5. Add the spinach to the same pan. Cook over high heat, stirring often, just until it wilts, about 2 minutes. Spill off any liquid, then toss with the shallot mixture. Sprinkle with bread crumbs and serve immediately.

Creamed spinach is a favored old classic, irresistibly good and deservedly popular. This version is not dominated by a heavy cream sauce, but just lightly bound. I prefer the texture of leafy spinach. Others like creamed spinach puréed. Either way, it's delicious.

Creamed Spinach

Preparation time: 15 minutes
Cooking time: 22 minutes (Microwave: 15 minutes)
Yield: 6 servings

1. Grind the pancetta or bacon and onion together in a food processor or mince them very finely by hand.

2. Melt the butter in a 10-inch skillet, if you're using pancetta. You won't need it with regular bacon. Add the pancetta or bacon and onion and cook over medium heat until the onion is soft and the fat is rendered from the meat, about 10 minutes. Stir in flour and cook 1 minute. Add the milk, salt, nutmeg and pepper. Heat to a boil, lower heat and continue to cook, stirring often, until thickened, about 3 minutes.

3. Wrap the spinach in a towel and squeeze firmly to remove all the excess moisture. When it is properly dried, you will have about 2 cups of tightly packed spinach.

4. Break the spinach apart with your hands and add it to the skillet. Cook, stirring occasionally, until it is heated through.

5. Return the mixture to the processor and pulse until the spinach is roughly chopped, about 8 pulses. Don't overprocess— you will want to retain some texture. Adjust the seasoning and serve the spinach hot, or refrigerate up to 2 days. To reheat, transfer to a 1-quart casserole, cover and bake in a preheated 350-degree oven until hot, about 25 minutes.

MICROWAVE: Follow step 1 above. Put the butter (if using pancetta—you won't need it for bacon), pancetta or bacon and onion in a 2-quart microwave casserole. Cook, uncovered, on high power (100%) for 4 minutes. Stir in flour and cook on high power for 3 minutes. Add the milk, whisking until smooth. Cook on high power for 6 minutes, stirring after 3 minutes. Follow step 3. Break spinach apart with your hands and add it to the processor along with the sauce mixture, salt, pepper and nutmeg. Pulse 2 to 3 times, so spinach is roughly chopped, but still has much texture.

4 ounces lean pancetta or regular bacon
1 medium onion (5 ounces), peeled
3 tablespoons unsalted butter (if using pancetta)
2 tablespoons unbleached all-purpose flour
1¼ cups milk
½ teaspoon salt
¼ teaspoon freshly grated nutmeg
Freshly ground black pepper
4 boxes (10 ounces each) frozen leaf spinach, thawed (see Note)

If you prefer puréed spinach, process until smooth. Return to casserole and cook on high power just until heated through, about 2 minutes. The spinach can be refrigerated at this point for up to 2 days. To reheat, bring to room temperature. Cover and cook on high power until hot, about 5 minutes.

Note: Two pounds of leaf spinach can be used in place of the frozen, if desired.

◆

As good as these are, I can't understand why this simple preparation isn't more common. It's a quick way to cook sweet potatoes and doesn't rely on lots of sugar as so many recipes for sweet potatoes do. When they're well browned—at the perfect point between cooked and burned—their natural sugar caramelizes into a blissfully crisp crunch. If you want to double the recipe, prepare two pans or keep one batch warm in the oven while you make a second. But don't crowd the pan or the potatoes won't brown properly.

Sautéed Sweet Potatoes

Preparation time: 5 minutes
Cooking time: 13 minutes
Yield: 2 to 3 servings

1 large sweet potato (12 ounces)
2 tablespoons unsalted butter
1 tablespoon safflower oil
¼ teaspoon salt

1. Scrub the potato and trim the ends, but do not peel. Cut into ⅛-inch slices, either with the all-purpose (4mm) slicer of a food processor or by hand.
2. Melt the butter with the oil in a large skillet over high heat. When it is hot, add the potatoes, spreading them as evenly as possible. Cook over high heat, turning occasionally, until they are well browned on both sides, about 12 minutes. For the best flavor, they should be well browned, almost blackened around the edges. Season with salt and serve immediately.

10 · Pasta, Rice and Beans

Pasta needs no preamble or paeans of praise. Americans have an ongoing love affair with it and with good reason. Its convenience, variety, good taste, economy and adaptability make it an enduring favorite. There are myriad shapes and flavors to fill every conceivable need and add a touch of whimsy to the meal. Pasta can stand on its own as a main course or bring balance and interest to meat or fish entrees. Or consider it as an inviting first course. It can be hearty and substantial or pleasantly and refreshingly light—whatever your inclination.

Store-bought pastas are so good that it isn't necessary to spend the time making pasta at home unless you have a passion to do so. Fresh pasta is available in many stores. Often, though not always, it is an excellent product. One advantage to buying fresh pasta is that it cooks very quickly—in just minutes after it is added to boiling water. Although they don't cook as quickly, many dried pastas are excellent as well. In any case, the difference between fresh and dried is neither a matter of convenience nor quality, but of appropriateness. The ultimate choice depends on the preparation. And contrary to what has long been considered to be true, it isn't essential to buy only imported pastas. American manufacturers now offer some of the best. The ultimate test in choosing pasta is your own taste. Pasta is best cooked *al dente,* so it is tender but still a little firm. Sample what is available in your area. Your preferences will become obvious.

I have separated the preparation time for pasta recipes into two parts, one for the topping and another for cooking the pasta, although they will often be cooked simultaneously. The cooking time for pasta begins when the water is at a rolling boil. In some recipes, the pasta can be cooked ahead of time and reheated in the sauce, and I have so indicated. I find that this is enormously helpful in easing the work at mealtime. In those recipes where the cooked pasta is not reheated in the sauce, it can still be cooked ahead of time if you prefer. Drain the cooked pasta and rinse it under cold water. Drain it thoroughly, then put it in a plastic bag with 1 to 2 teaspoons oil to keep it from sticking. It can be refrigerated for up to 2 days. I also find that cooked pasta freezes well, especially spaghetti and linguine. It can then be reheated in a microwave oven on high power (100%) for 1 to 2 minutes, depending on the quantity. Alternately, you can pour boiling water over it if you don't have a microwave. If you are planning to cook pasta ahead, undercook it slightly initially to compensate for reheating.

This chapter is rounded out with Italian Tomato Sauce, a marvelously versatile tomato sauce whose usefulness doesn't end with pasta; and several simple rice and bean recipes that can be used to accompany main courses.

When considering pasta, beans and rice as side dishes, remember that they are delicious in their own right and can be served simply, tossed with butter or olive oil, a handful of herbs and a few grinds of the pepper mill.

This is mild and fresh-tasting, perfect for light summer meals.

_____Pasta Wheels with Primavera Vegetables_____

Preparation time: 15 minutes
Pasta cooking time: About 10 minutes
Other cooking time: 11 minutes (Microwave: 10 minutes)
Yield: 4 to 6 servings as a main course; 8 servings as a side dish

8 ounces dried rotelle pasta (wagon wheels)
½ small jalapeño or serrano pepper
2 large yellow summer squash (12 ounces total)
2 medium zucchini (10 ounces total)
1 medium red bell pepper (6 ounces)
3 tablespoons light-tasting olive oil
⅓ cup chicken stock (see page 339) or canned broth
2½ teaspoons dried dill weed
¾ teaspoon salt
   Freshly ground white pepper
1 cup tiny peas, fresh or frozen
¼ cup whipping cream
1½ tablespoons fresh lemon juice
   Parmesan cheese

1. Cook the pasta in a large pot of boiling water until it is tender to the bite. Drain well. The cooked pasta can be drained, rinsed and tossed with 2 teaspoons oil, then refrigerated for up to 2 days, if desired.

2. While the pasta is cooking, mince the hot pepper in a food processor or by hand. Cut the summer squash, zucchini and red bell pepper into ⅜-inch dice.

3. Heat the oil in a large skillet. When it is hot, add the hot pepper and cook over medium heat for 1 minute. Add the squash, zucchini and sweet red pepper and cook, stirring several times, until they begin to give off liquid, about 5 minutes.

4. Add the stock or broth, dill, salt and white pepper and increase the heat to high and cook until the vegetables are tender-crisp, about 4 minutes. Add the pasta, peas, cream and lemon juice, stirring gently so the pasta doesn't break apart. Cook just until heated through.

5. Adjust the seasoning and serve with a sprinkling of Parmesan cheese.

MICROWAVE: Follow steps 1 and 2 above. Combine hot pepper, summer squash, zucchini, red bell pepper, oil and dill in a 2-quart microwave casserole. Cover tightly with plastic wrap and pierce the plastic with the tip of a sharp knife so steam can escape. Cook on high power (100%) for 6 minutes. Carefully remove the cover and add the stock or broth, cream and lemon juice. Cook, uncovered, on high power until slightly thickened, about 3 minutes. Add the cooked pasta, peas, salt and pepper and cook just until heated through, about 1 minute. Serve as in step 5.

Most people will remember Danny Kaye as a wonderfully gifted actor and comedian. Those fortunate enough to have eaten at his table will also recall being enchanted by his culinary prowess. Chinese cooking was his great specialty though he also had a passion for making his own pasta. One night, when I was his guest, he prepared this simple dish and carried it off with such aplomb that I've tried to recapture the spirit of it. Simple it is, but delicious and satisfying all the same.

Linguine with Garlic, Lemon and Pepper

Preparation time: 10 minutes
Pasta cooking time: About 10 minutes
Other cooking time: 8 minutes (Microwave: 5 minutes)
Yield: 3 to 4 servings as a main course

12 ounces dried linguine
 1 large garlic clove, peeled
 2 ounces Parmesan cheese, preferably imported
⅓ cup extra virgin olive oil
 2 teaspoons fresh lemon juice
¾ teaspoon salt
½ to 1 teaspoon crushed red pepper flakes
 4 wedges lemon

1. Cook the linguine in boiling water until it is just tender to the bite. Take care not to overcook, as the pasta will receive a bit more cooking later on. Drain well. The cooked pasta can be tossed with 2 teaspoons oil and set aside, covered, for a few hours, or refrigerated up to 2 days.

2. Meanwhile, mince the garlic in a food processor or by hand. Grate the cheese as fine as possible in the processor or with the fine side of a grater.

3. Heat the oil in a large skillet. When it is hot, add the garlic and cook over medium heat, stirring often, until softened, about 4 minutes. Mix in the lemon juice, salt and pepper flakes, then toss in the pasta. Cook until heated through.

4. Adjust the seasoning, if necessary, and serve immediately, sprinkled with cheese and each portion garnished with a lemon wedge.

MICROWAVE: Follow steps 1 and 2. Put the oil and garlic in a 2½-quart casserole. Cook, uncovered, on high power (100%) until softened, about 2 minutes. Mix in the lemon juice, salt and pepper flakes, then the pasta. Cook on high power until heated through, about 3 minutes. Serve as in step 4.

Rich and luxurious, this is delightful served as a main course or alongside a simple grilled chicken breast or sautéd veal. The mild flavor of eggplant is enhanced with the rich taste of prosciutto and the natural sweetness of cream. Medium-sized pasta shells are a nice alternate to fettuccine.

_____Fettuccine with Eggplant, Prosciutto and Cream_

Preparation time: 15 minutes
Pasta cooking time: About 10 minutes
Draining time: 30 minutes
Other cooking time: 15 minutes (Microwave: 14 minutes)
Yield: 4 servings as a main course; 6 to 8 servings as a side dish

2 medium eggplants
(2 pounds total)
Salt
3 medium garlic cloves,
peeled
2 large red onions
(1 pound total), peeled
6 tablespoons light-tasting
olive oil
½ cup whipping cream
4 ounces prosciutto, cut in
2-inch by ¼-inch strips
¾ teaspoon freshly grated
nutmeg
Freshly ground black
pepper
8 ounces dried fettuccine
Finely shredded Parmesan
cheese, preferably
imported

1. Cut the unpeeled eggplants into ¾-inch cubes. Put in a colander and toss with ½ teaspoon salt. Let drain for 30 minutes. Rinse under cold water, drain well and wrap in a towel to dry.

2. Mince the garlic in a food processor or by hand and set aside. Cut the onions into small dice.

3. Heat 3 tablespoons of oil in a 12-inch skillet. Add half the garlic and all the onion. Cook over medium-high heat, stirring often, until the onion begins to soften, about 3 minutes. Add the eggplant, cover and cook over medium heat, stirring occasionally, until the eggplant is almost tender, about 8 minutes. Add the cream and cook, uncovered, until the eggplant is tender, 2 minutes. Remove from the heat and add nutmeg and pepper. The recipe can be prepared a day in advance to this point and refrigerated. Reheat gently.

4. Bring a pot of salted water to a boil. Cook fettuccine until al dente. Reserve ½ cup of the water, then drain the pasta well and transfer to a bowl. While it is still hot, toss with the remaining half of the garlic and the remaining 3 tablespoons of oil.

5. To serve, thin the eggplant mixture with ¼ to ½ cup of the hot water from the pasta, as necessary. Add the prosciutto and adjust the seasoning, adding salt, if necessary. Divide pasta among 4 plates and top with a portion of eggplant. Sprinkle generously with cheese and serve immediately.

MICROWAVE: Follow steps 1 and 2 above. Combine half the garlic, all the onions and 3 tablespoons oil in a 2½-quart microwave casserole. Cover tightly with plastic wrap and pierce the plastic with a sharp knife so steam can escape. Cook on high power (100%) until the onions begin to soften, about 4 minutes.

Add the eggplant, cover and cook until it is almost tender, 7 to 8 minutes. Add the cream and cook, uncovered, until eggplant is tender, 2 minutes. Add the nutmeg and pepper. The recipe can be prepared a day in advance to this point and refrigerated. Reheat on high power. Finish as in steps 4 and 5.

◆

Lorenza di Medici of Badia a Coltibuono in Tuscany shared this recipe with me, a simple and wonderful pairing of flavors and textures. Minced anchovies add an underlying strength to the dish, supporting the mild, slightly sweet Swiss chard. The bread crumbs are buttery and crunchy, a welcome contrast to the tender pasta and vegetables. This doesn't reheat well, so cooking is last-minute, but it is very simple and certainly worth the effort. The vegetables can be minced and sliced in advance and the bread crumbs sautéed to ease the last-minute cooking.

Tuscan Penne with Swiss Chard

Preparation time: 15 minutes
Cooking time: 20 minutes
Yield: 6 servings as a side dish

1. Bring 8 quarts water to a boil.
2. Finely crumb the bread in a food processor or blender. Set aside. Mince the garlic in the processor or blender, or by hand. Add the anchovies and red pepper flakes and run the machine several seconds to chop the anchovies.
3. Heat ¼ cup of the oil in an 8-inch skillet. When it is very hot, add the bread crumbs and cook, stirring often, until they are well browned, about 4 minutes. Set aside in a small dish and wipe out the skillet with a paper towel.
4. Heat the remaining ¼ cup of oil in the same skillet. When it is hot, add the garlic mixture and cook over medium heat until it is soft, but not brown, about 3 minutes. Set aside, off the heat.
5. Add the pasta to the boiling water. Cook for about 8 minutes, until it is almost, but not quite, al dente. While it is cooking, prepare the chard.

2 -inch slice dry Italian bread (3 ounces)
3 large garlic cloves, peeled
5 flat anchovies in oil, rinsed and patted dry
½ teaspoon crushed red pepper flakes
½ cup light-tasting olive oil
½ pound dried penne or mostaccioli
1 pound Swiss chard
⅛ teaspoon salt, or to taste
Freshly ground black pepper

6. Wash the chard and cut the leaves and stems into ½-inch slices, either with the ultra-thick (8mm) slicer of a processor or by hand. When the pasta has cooked for 8 minutes, add the chard to the pasta and cook until both are tender, about 4 minutes longer. Drain well, shaking the colander to remove as much water as possible.

7. Transfer the pasta and chard to a shallow bowl and toss with the garlic mixture. Add salt and pepper to taste. Serve with a generous sprinkling of bread crumbs.

◆

This is a simple dish, both in character and execution, whose subtle taste is especially good with lamb or grilled poultry. The pasta and vegetables are cooked in the same pot, though the zucchini is added later so they are both cooked "to the tooth."

Other herbs besides mint are also felicitous here. Fresh oregano and marjoram are especially fragrant and delicious.

Orzo with Zucchini and Mint

Preparation time: 10 minutes
Cooking time: 5 minutes
Yield: 4 servings

3 tablespoons fresh mint or
2 teaspoons dried
1 large zucchini
(12 ounces)
¾ cup dried orzo
2 tablespoons extra virgin
olive oil
½ teaspoon salt

1. Bring 4 quarts water to a boil.

2. Meanwhile, mince the fresh mint, if using. Cut the zucchini into small dice or chop it in a food processor in two batches.

3. Add the orzo to the boiling water and cook until it is almost, but not quite, al dente, about 4 minutes. Add the zucchini and cook until both are just tender, about 45 seconds longer. Drain through a fine-mesh strainer—the holes in most colanders are too large for orzo—and transfer to a warm bowl.

4. Toss with the oil, mint and salt. Can be made in advance and refrigerated for up to 2 days. Reheat gently on the stove or in the microwave oven before serving; or serve at room temperature. Adjust the seasoning at serving time, if necessary.

Mussels are one of the most underrated treasures of the sea, sweet, briny and fresh-tasting, all at a giveaway price. Here, they're tossed into a tangle of fettuccine and glossed with a pungent, peppery butter. The toasted pecans add a crunchy counterpoint as well as a depth of flavor that accents both the mussels and pasta.

__Fettuccine and Mussels in Spicy Cilantro Butter_____

Preparation time: 20 minutes
Soaking time: 30 minutes
Pasta cooking time: About 10 minutes
Other cooking time: 15 minutes (Microwave: 18 minutes)
Yield: 3 to 4 servings as a main course; 6 to 8 servings as a first
    course

1. Scrub the mussels with a wire brush and remove the beards. Discard any that are open and any that are unusually heavy since these will be full of sand. Place in a large pan, cover with cold water and add 1 teaspoon salt. Let soak 30 minutes.

2. Meanwhile, cook the fettuccine in boiling water until it is tender to the bite. Drain well. The pasta can be tossed with several teaspoons oil and refrigerated for up to 2 days.

3. Drain the mussels, rinse out the pan and return the mussels to it. Cover and cook them over high heat, without any added water, just until the shells open. Discard any that do not open. When the mussels are cool enough to handle, remove them from the shells. Cover with foil and set aside. Rinse out the pan.

4. Mince the cilantro, parsley, garlic and jalapeño or serrano pepper in a food processor or by hand; they can all be minced together. Cut each piece of the roasted bell pepper in half lengthwise, then cut crosswise into ½-inch strips. Coarsely chop the pecans, either in the processor or by hand.

5. Put the cilantro, parsley, garlic and hot pepper in the same pan the mussels were cooked in and add the butter and lime juice. Cook over medium heat until the butter is melted. Add the fettuccine and mussels and toss to coat them with butter. Cook, stirring gently, just until heated through, about 6 minutes. Fold in the red bell pepper, pecans and salt to taste and remove from the heat. Serve immediately.

MICROWAVE: Follow steps 1 and 2 above. Put half the mussels in a shallow, 10-inch round microwave dish. Cover with plastic wrap and pierce it once so steam can escape. Cook on high power

32 *small or medium mussels*
   Salt
 6 *ounces dried fettuccine*
½ *cup cilantro leaves*
½ *cup parsley leaves*
 1 *large garlic clove, peeled*
 1 *jalapeño or serrano*
   pepper
 1 *roasted red bell pepper*
   (see page 336)
 1 *cup darkly toasted pecans*
   (see page 338)
 1 *stick unsalted butter*
 1 *teaspoon fresh lime juice*

(100%) until the shells have opened, about 5 minutes. Cook the other half. Remove the shells. Cover with foil and set aside. Rinse and dry the dish. Follow step 4. Put the cilantro, parsley, garlic and hot pepper in the same dish and add the butter and lime juice. Melt the butter on high, about 1 minute. Add the fettuccine and toss to coat. Cook on high until hot, about 3 minutes. Add the mussels and cook on medium power (50%) until they are hot, about 3 minutes. Gently fold in the sweet red pepper, pecans and salt to taste. Serve immediately.

◆

Both the goat and Romano cheese have strong individual tastes but they combine so well that you'll think it is just one perfectly delicious cheese. The oil helps to mute the flavor and smooth out the cheese so it is creamy and light.

I like to serve this as a side dish to grilled meat or by itself, over a pool of Italian Tomato Sauce (see page 226).

Linguine with Goat Cheese

Preparation time: 5 minutes
Pasta cooking time: About 10 minutes
Yield: 2 to 3 servings as a main course; 4 to 6 servings as a first course

8 ounces dried linguine
3 ounces Romano cheese
4½ ounces soft goat cheese, such as Montrachet
¼ cup extra virgin olive oil
1 teaspoon coarsely ground white pepper
Salt to taste

1. Cook the linguine in boiling water until al dente. Drain, reserving 2 tablespoons of the water.

2. Finely mince the Romano in a food processor or blender and put into a bowl large enough to toss the pasta. Crumble the goat cheese and add half of it to the Romano.

3. Add the oil and pepper to the bowl and mix well. Add the hot linguine and 1 tablespoon cooking water and toss the pasta until it is well coated. If the cheese mixture is still too thick, add remaining tablespoon water. Taste and add salt, if necessary. Top with remaining goat cheese and serve immediately.

What speaks of summer more than big, red, vine-ripened tomatoes? Here they are matched with peppers, sweet red onions and a bouquet of fresh basil in a rustic topping for pasta. Other fresh herbs such as oregano and tarragon can also be used. Grilling the red onion and peppers deepens their flavor and lends a subtle, woodsy taste. When grilling is out of the question, broil them indoors. The effect will be less pronounced, though still very good.

Pasta with Tomatoes, Grilled Onions and Peppers

Preparation time: 15 minutes
Pasta cooking time: About 10 minutes
Other cooking time: 15 minutes
Yield: 2 to 3 servings for a main course; 4 to 6 servings for a side dish

1. Prepare a hot grill, preferably with a mix of charcoal and 1 cup of soaked mesquite chips; or place the broiler rack 6 inches from the heat and preheat the broiler.

2. Halve the onion crosswise and lightly brush the cut surface with some of the oil. Stand the peppers on a board and cut 4 flat slices from each. Place peppers, skin side down, and onions,

1   *medium red onion (5 ounces), peeled*
⅓ *cup light-tasting olive oil*
2   *large red bell peppers (1 pound total)*
5   *large tomatoes (2¾ pounds total)*
1   *tablespoon balsamic vinegar*
¾ *cup julienned fresh basil leaves*
1   *teaspoon salt Freshly ground black pepper*
6   *ounces dried pasta shells Fresh basil leaves*

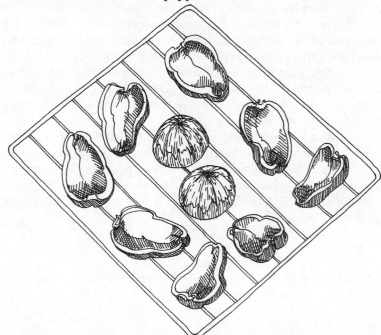

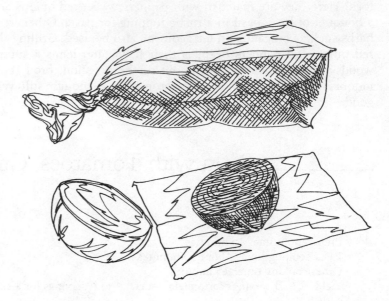

cut side down, on an oiled grill. If broiling, place peppers, skin side up, and onions, cut side up, on a baking sheet lined with aluminum foil. Grill or broil until the onion is soft and charred around the edges and the skin of the peppers is blackened. Wrap the onion in foil. Place the peppers in a paper bag and seal. When the vegetables have cooled, remove the blackened skin from both.

3. Core tomatoes and cut in half crosswise. Remove the seeds and all the membrane from the inside, leaving only the outer shell. Roughly chop the peppers, onion and tomatoes.

4. Toss the vegetables with the remaining oil, vinegar, basil, salt and pepper. This dish can be prepared a day in advance to this point and refrigerated. Bring to room temperature and adjust the seasoning before serving.

5. Bring 6 quarts water to a boil. Add the pasta and cook until it is just tender to the bite. Drain well, shaking the colander to get as much water out of the shells as possible. Transfer to a shallow serving bowl and mound the vegetables in the center. Garnish with fresh basil leaves. Serve hot or at room temperature, tossing at the table.

Certain ingredients share a natural affinity for each other. This is one of those combinations that is simply perfect and perfectly simple. Smoked salmon is also good in place of the prosciutto.

Tortellini with Prosciutto and Peas

Preparation time: 5 minutes
Pasta cooking time: About 12 minutes
Other cooking time: 8 minutes
Yield: 2 to 4 servings as a main course

1. Cook the tortellini in boiling salted water until tender. Drain and set aside. To prepare in advance, toss lightly with oil after cooking and refrigerate overnight.

2. Meanwhile, cook the cream and chicken stock or broth in a large skillet over high heat until liquid has thickened slightly, 4 to 5 minutes.

3. Cut the prosciutto into 2-inch by ¼-inch strips.

4. Add the peas, tortellini, sage, nutmeg and pepper to the cream mixture and cook just until heated through, 2 to 3 minutes. Toss in the prosciutto and remove from the heat. Serve hot, with Parmesan cheese.

8 ounces fresh or frozen cheese- or meat-filled tortellini
½ cup whipping cream
½ cup chicken stock (see page 339) or canned broth
3 ounces prosciutto
1 package (10 ounces) tiny frozen peas, thawed
¼ teaspoon dried rubbed sage
¼ teaspoon freshly grated nutmeg
Freshly ground black pepper
Grated Parmesan cheese, preferably imported

This is pasta with pow, a spicy mixture of stir-fried chicken, fettuccine, and carrots punctuated by peanuts and cilantro. Chili oil is hot stuff, so start out by adding only 2 teaspoons, then see if you want more. Even with the heat, there is a nice balance in the flavors and textures.

Spicy Noodles with Chicken, Carrots and Peanuts

Preparation time: 15 minutes
Pasta cooking time: About 10 minutes
Other cooking time: 8 minutes
Yield: 6 servings

SAUCE:
- ¼ cup oyster sauce
- 2 tablespoons honey
- 1 tablespoon hoisin sauce
- 2 to 3 teaspoons chili oil
- 2 teaspoons nuoc mam (Vietnamese fish sauce)
- 1 large egg yolk

NOODLES:
- 2 whole boneless chicken breasts (1¾ pounds)
- 6 small carrots (12 ounces total), peeled
- 6 medium green onions (4 ounces total)
- 8 ounces fresh or dried fettuccine
- 1¼ cups cilantro leaves
- ¾ cup unsalted dry-roasted peanuts
- 3 tablespoons rice vinegar

1. Bring a large kettle of water to a boil.

2. For the sauce, mix the oyster sauce, honey, hoisin sauce, 2 teaspoons chili oil, *nuoc mam* and egg yolk and transfer to a 10-inch sauté pan.

3. Remove the skin from the chicken and cut the meat into ¾-inch cubes. Cut carrots and green onions into ⅛-inch circles, either with the all-purpose (4mm) slicer of a food processor or by hand. Mince 1 cup of cilantro and the peanuts in the processor or by hand.

4. Heat the sauce over medium-high heat. When it starts to bubble, add the chicken and stir-fry just until the meat is firm but not hard to the touch, about 3 minutes. Set aside, off the heat.

5. When the water is boiling, add the carrots and cook just until tender, about 3 minutes. Remove carrots with a slotted spoon, drain well and add to the chicken. When the water returns to a boil, add the fettuccine and cook until al dente. Drain and add to the chicken along with the carrots, green onions, peanuts, minced cilantro and vinegar. Toss gently. Adjust the seasoning if necessary and add the remaining chili oil, if desired. Serve hot or at room temperature, garnished with the remaining ¼ cup cilantro leaves. Can be refrigerated up to 2 days and served at room temperature or reheated in a microwave oven or on the stove.

This is for anyone who has ever read a recipe for homemade ravioli and filed it away under the category of "sounds great, but too much work." Chinese won ton or egg roll wrappers are the clever, time-saving answer. They imitate homemade pasta dough so well, no one will ever guess your clever improvisation. They're thin, tender and taste almost the same, but come ready to fill—no painstaking mixing and rolling.

Another serving idea is to cook the ravioli as directed, then deep-fry them to serve as appetizers. In place of the Parmesan Cream sauce, try Pesto Mayonnaise (see page 327).

Chicken Ravioli with Parmesan Cream

Preparation time: 25 minutes
Cooking time: 6 minutes
Yield: 2 to 3 servings as a main course; 4 to 6 servings as a first
  course

1. For the ravioli filling, remove the skin and bones from the chicken thighs. Grind the chicken, mozzarella cheese, prosciutto, basil and sage in a food processor or in 2 batches in a blender, until the mixture is finely and uniformly chopped. It should be finely minced rather than puréed.

2. Spoon ½ tablespoon of filling into the center of a won ton wrapper. If you're using the larger egg roll wrappers, put 4 equally spaced half-tablespoon measures on an egg roll wrapper, 2 on the top half and 2 on the bottom. Brush egg yolk on the wrapper, around the filling. Cover with another wrapper. Press from the filling toward the edge to seal together and remove air bubbles. There should be about 20 raviolis.

RAVIOLI:
4 *chicken thighs*
2 *ounces mozzarella cheese*
1 *ounce prosciutto*
2 *tablespoons julienned fresh basil or ½ teaspoon dried*
¼ *teaspoon rubbed sage*
40 *won ton wrappers or 10 egg roll wrappers, preferably fresh*
2 *large egg yolks, beaten*

SAUCE:
½ *cup whipping cream*
1 *large garlic clove, peeled, split in thirds*
2 *tablespoons minced Parmesan cheese, preferably imported Freshly grated nutmeg*
1 *tablespoon minced parsley*

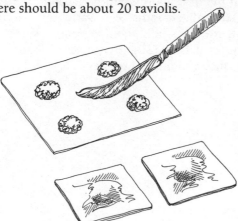

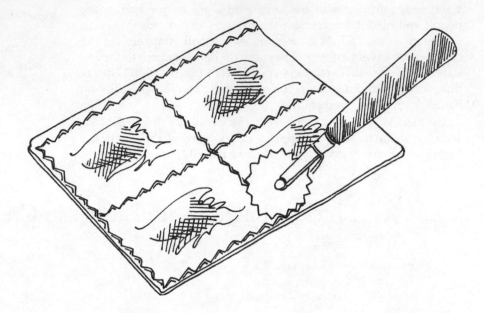

3. To cut the wrapper, use a pastry crimper for a ruffled edge, a pizza cutter or a sharp knife for a straight edge. For won ton wrappers, cut off about ¼ inch of excess dough from each side. For egg roll wrappers, cut into quarters, then trim the edges. Ravioli can be made in advance to this point and refrigerated overnight or frozen for several months. To freeze, arrange on a baking sheet lined with waxed paper. When frozen, double-wrap in airtight bags. It is not necessary to thaw before cooking.

4. Make the sauce. Cook the cream and garlic in a small skillet until the cream has thickened slightly, about 4 minutes. Remove from the heat and discard garlic. Add the Parmesan and nutmeg and stir until smooth. Keep warm until serving time.

5. Cook the ravioli in boiling salted water until tender, about 2 minutes if fresh, slightly longer if frozen; drain. Serve topped with sauce and minced parsley.

This is inspired by one of Joe Decker's recipes, which he created as head chef at Avanzare in Chicago. It's a simple recipe, with a few delicious twists, like little bits of pancetta and cubes of soft, melty mozzarella cheese folded into a rich tomato sauce. Using fresh and canned tomatoes in tandem makes the best of less than perfect winter tomatoes. When vine-ripened tomatoes are available, use 4 cups of these and omit the canned.

Decker uses fresh mozzarella, which he makes himself. Specialty food shops often have imported or domestic fresh mozzarella. If you can't find it, you can substitute commercial mozzarella, although the character of the finished dish will be different.

——————— Corkscrew Pasta with Tomato Sauce, Pancetta and Cheese ———————

Preparation time: 15 minutes
Pasta cooking time: About 10 minutes
Other cooking time: 30 minutes (Microwave: 28 minutes)
Yield: 3 to 4 servings as a main course; 6 to 8 servings as a first course

1. Mince the onion and garlic in a food processor or by hand. Core the tomatoes, cut in half crosswise and squeeze gently to remove the seeds. Coarsely chop in the processor or by hand. Cut the pancetta into ¼-inch dice. Cut the cheese into ½-inch cubes. Drain the tomatoes and coarsely chop them.

2. Heat a 2½-quart pan over medium heat. When it is hot, add 1 teaspoon olive oil and the pancetta. Cook until the pancetta is lightly browned but not completely crisp, about 6 minutes. Add the onion and garlic and continue to cook, stirring several times, until the onion is golden, about 4 minutes.

3. Add the wine or vermouth, stirring up any brown bits from the bottom of the pan. Cook over high heat until the liquid is reduced by about half, about 4 minutes. Add the fresh and canned tomatoes and tomato paste, reduce the heat to medium and cook until thickened, about 15 minutes. The sauce can be prepared several days in advance to this point and refrigerated. Reheat gently before finishing the recipe.

4. Off the heat, stir in the remaining olive oil and salt, pepper and sugar—depending on the natural sweetness of the tomatoes—to taste.

1 small onion (3 ounces), peeled
1 large garlic clove, peeled
3 medium tomatoes (1 pound total)
¼ pound pancetta
¼ pound mozzarella cheese, preferably fresh, at room temperature
1 can (16 ounces) whole tomatoes
¼ cup extra virgin olive oil
1 cup dry white wine or dry vermouth
3 tablespoons tomato paste
¼ teaspoon salt
Freshly ground black pepper
Sugar
½ pound dried fusilli (corkscrew) or rotelle (wagon wheels) pasta

5. While the sauce is cooking, cook the pasta in 6 quarts boiling water until al dente. Drain well and toss with sauce. Divide among 6 warm plates and scatter the mozzarella cheese over the top. Serve immediately.

MICROWAVE: Follow step 1. Put 1 teaspoon of oil and the pancetta in a 2½-quart microwave dish and cook on high power (100%) until lightly browned, 3 minutes. Add the onion and garlic and cook until soft, 2 minutes. Add ⅔ cup wine or vermouth and cook 5 minutes. Add the tomato paste and fresh and canned tomatoes and cook on high power until thickened, about 18 minutes. Finish as in steps 4 and 5.

◆

Where I was raised, cooked cornmeal was called "mush," a name that does little to entice the palate or describe such a delicious dish. Think of it as a traditional and highly esteemed Italian dish and its appeal increases enormously. Here, cooked cormeal is flavored with cheese and a hot pepper for extra added interest. The cheese and herbs can be varied, giving the dish a full range of ethnic personas. This is hearty by nature, so is best slated for fall and winter, paired with grilled meat or fish, topped with Italian Tomato Sauce (see page 226) and sautéed vegetables or served under Chili Non Carne (see page 79).

Baked Polenta

1 jalapeño pepper
6 ounces Monterey Jack cheese
3 cups water
2 tablespoons light-tasting olive oil
1¼ teaspoons salt
1 cup yellow corn grits or cornmeal (4½ ounces)

Preparation time: 10 minutes
Cooking time: 25 minutes (Microwave: 17 minutes, plus cooling time)
Yield: 16 12-inch squares

1. Oil an 8-inch square pan and set aside.
2. Mince the pepper in a food processor or by hand. Shred the cheese in the processor or with a grater.
3. Bring the water, oil and salt to a boil. Reduce the heat to low and slowly add the grits or cornmeal in a thin, steady steam, whisking constantly. Cook gently, stirring often, until it is very thick, 8 to 9 minutes.

4. Add the hot pepper and cheese, stirring until the cheese is melted. Transfer to the prepared pan and smooth the surface with a spatula. Cool completely. The polenta can be prepared to this point up to 3 days in advance, covered and refrigerated.

5. 15 minutes before baking, place rack in center of oven and preheat oven to 425 degrees.

6. Just before serving, uncover the polenta and bake in the preheated oven until hot, 10 to 12 minutes. Cut into 2-inch squares.

MICROWAVE: Follow steps 1 and 2 above, making sure the prepared pan is microwave-safe. Combine water, 2 tablespoons oil, salt and cornmeal in a 3-quart microwave casserole. Cover tightly with plastic wrap and pierce the plastic with a sharp knife so steam can escape. Cook on high power (100%) for 4 minutes. Whisk until smooth, cover and cook until thickened, about 6 minutes more. Follow step 4 above. Just before serving, cook, uncovered, on medium power (50%) until hot, about 7 minutes. Cut into 2-inch squares.

Lusty and full-flavored, this is a multipurpose tomato sauce that's very easy and inexpensive to make. It is based on canned tomatoes so you don't have to wait until summer to make it. Although it cooks for quite a while, most of the cooking time is unattended. Or, follow the microwave oven instructions to cut down on cooking time.

Italian Tomato Sauce

Preparation time: 10 minutes
Cooking time: 65 minutes (Microwave: 31 minutes)
Yield: 3¾ cups

3 medium garlic cloves, peeled
2 medium onions (10 ounces total), peeled
1 medium carrot (4 ounces), peeled
¼ cup light-tasting olive oil
1 cup dry vermouth
1 can (28 ounces) tomatoes
1 teaspoon dried basil
½ teaspoon dried oregano
½ teaspoon salt
¼ teaspoon crushed red pepper flakes

1. Mince the garlic, onions and carrot in a food processor or by hand.

2. Heat the oil in a 2½-quart non-aluminum pan. Add the garlic, onion and carrot and cook over medium heat until they begin to soften, about 4 minutes. Add the vermouth and simmer until most of it is cooked away, about 15 minutes.

3. Coarsely chop the tomatoes and add them to the pan along with their juice, the basil, oregano, salt and red pepper flakes. Cook, uncovered, over low heat, until thickened, about 45 minutes. Serve immediately, or refrigerate for 3 days or freeze. Reheat and adjust the seasoning if necessary before serving.

MICROWAVE: Follow step 1 above. Combine the garlic, onion, carrot and oil in an 8-cup microwave dish. Cook on high power (100%) for 4 minutes. Add the vermouth and cook on high power until it is reduced by about half, about 7 minutes. Chop the tomatoes and add them, along with their juice, and the basil and oregano. Cook, uncovered, on high power until thickened, about 20 minutes, stirring every 5 minutes. Add the salt and pepper and adjust the seasoning.

Simple and colorful, this is a welcome side dish to accompany all manner of foods, from grilled courses to sandwiches.

Black Beans Montenegro

Preparation time: 10 minutes
Cooking time: 12 minutes (Microwave: 7 minutes)
Yield: 3 to 4 servings

1. Cook the bacon in an 8-inch skillet until it is crisp. Drain on paper toweling and crumble into small pieces. Discard all but 1 tablespoon fat from the skillet.

2. Mince the hot pepper and onion in a food processor or by hand.

3. Add the onion, hot pepper, cumin, oregano and salt to the skillet and cook over medium-high heat, stirring often, until softened, about 5 minutes.

4. Rinse the beans under cold water until the water runs clear, then drain well.

5. Add the beans to the skillet along with the corn and bacon and cook just until heated through, about 2 minutes. Serve warm or at room temperature. Can be made in advance and reheated, if desired.

MICROWAVE: Put the bacon in a shallow, 10-inch round microwave casserole and cover it with a paper towel. Cook on high power (100%) until crisp, about 3 minutes. Drain on paper toweling and crumble into small pieces. Discard all but 1 tablespoon fat from the casserole. Follow step 2 above. Add the onion and hot pepper to the casserole and cook, uncovered, on high power until soft, about 2 minutes. Follow step 4. Add the beans, corn and bacon and cook on high power until heated through, about 2 minutes. See step 5.

4 *ounces sliced bacon*
1 *jalapeño or serrano pepper, seeded if desired*
1 *small onion (2 ounces), peeled*
½ *teaspoon ground cumin*
¼ *teaspoon dried oregano*
¼ *teaspoon salt*
1 *can (16 ounces) black beans*
½ *cup cooked corn, fresh or frozen and thawed*

Diced red apple and cucumber add color and crunch to rice cooked in broth, while a subtle blend of spices lends an intriguing flavor and aroma.

Madras Rice

Preparation time: 15 minutes
Cooking time: 25 minutes (Microwave: 19 minutes plus 5 minutes standing time)
Yield: 6 servings

1 medium onion
(4 ounces), peeled
2 tablespoons light-tasting olive oil
1 cup long-grain white rice (6½ ounces)
2⅓ cups chicken stock (see page 339) or canned broth
½ teaspoon ground ginger
½ teaspoon ground coriander
⅛ teaspoon crushed red pepper flakes
⅓ small English, "gourmet" or "burpless" cucumber (3 ounces), peeled
1 small Jonathan or McIntosh apple (5 ounces), unpeeled
⅓ cup dried currants (2 ounces)
Salt

1. Mince the onion in a food processor or by hand.

2. Heat the oil in a 2-quart pan. When it is hot, add the onion and the rice and cook over medium heat, stirring occasionally, until the onion is soft, about 5 minutes.

3. Add the stock or broth, ginger, coriander and red pepper flakes. Cover and bring to a boil. Reduce the heat to low and simmer until the rice is tender and the liquid is absorbed, about 18 minutes.

4. While the rice is cooking, cut the cucumber and apple into ¼-inch dice. Add them to the rice, along with the currants, during the last 3 minutes of cooking.

5. The rice can be made 3 days in advance and refrigerated. To serve, reheat gently and adjust the seasoning.

MICROWAVE: Follow step 1. Combine the oil and onion in a 2-quart microwave casserole. Cook on high power (100%) until onion is soft, about 3 minutes. Add the rice and only 1⅔ cup stock or broth. Cover and cook on high until boiling, about 5 minutes. Reduce to medium power (50%) and cook until most of the liquid is absorbed, 10 minutes. Follow step 4. Add the apple, cucumber, ginger, coriander, salt, red pepper flakes and currants and cook 1 minute on high. Let stand, covered, 5 minutes before serving. See step 5, except reheat on high power until hot.

Pan-toasted cumin seeds lend an exotic fragrance to this pilaf, a well-matched partner to many dishes, including the Baked Shrimp, Greek Style (see page 126), El Paso Flank Steak (see page 165) and the Chicken and Vegetable Brochettes (see page 149). To give it extra style, pack the rice into timbale molds and invert them into serving plates. No timbale molds? Clever on-hand improvisations include little demitasse cups or small paper cups.

The microwave oven does an admirable job of cooking rice, not in less time than on the stove, but with perfect results and less cleanup.

Cumin Rice Pilaf

Preparation time: 10 minutes
Cooking time: 24 minutes (Microwave: 21 minutes plus 5 minutes
  standing)
Yield: 6 servings

1. Mince the onion and garlic in a food processor or by hand.

2. Put the cumin seeds in a 2-quart pan. Cook over medium heat until they are lightly toasted and smell fragrant, 3 to 4 minutes. Add the oil, onion and garlic and cook, stirring occasionally, until the onion is softened, about 4 minutes.

3. Add the stock or broth and water and bring to a boil. Add the rice, cover and cook over low heat until the liquid is absorbed, 15 to 18 minutes. Add salt and pepper to taste.

4. Serve immediately or cover tightly and refrigerate for up to 3 days. Reheat gently before serving.

MICROWAVE: Follow step 1 above. Put the cumin and oil in a 2-quart microwave casserole. Cook on high power (100%) until seeds are fragrant, 1 minute. Add the garlic and onion and cook on high power until they are soft, about 2 minutes. Add the stock or broth, rice and only ½ cup of water. Cover with heavy-duty plastic wrap, leaving a 1-inch opening on one side for ventilation. Cook on high power until the liquid is boiling. Reduce the heat to medium power (50%) and cook until the rice is tender and most of the liquid is absorbed, 11 to 12 minutes. Let stand, covered, for 5 minutes before serving. Add salt and pepper to taste. To reheat, cook on high power until hot.

1   *small onion (3 ounces),*
    peeled
1   *medium garlic clove,*
    peeled
¾   *teaspoon cumin seeds*
1½ *tablespoons safflower oil*
1¼ *cups chicken stock (see*
    page 339) or canned
    broth
1   *cup water*
1   *cup long-grained white*
    rice (6½ ounces)
    Salt
    Freshly ground pepper

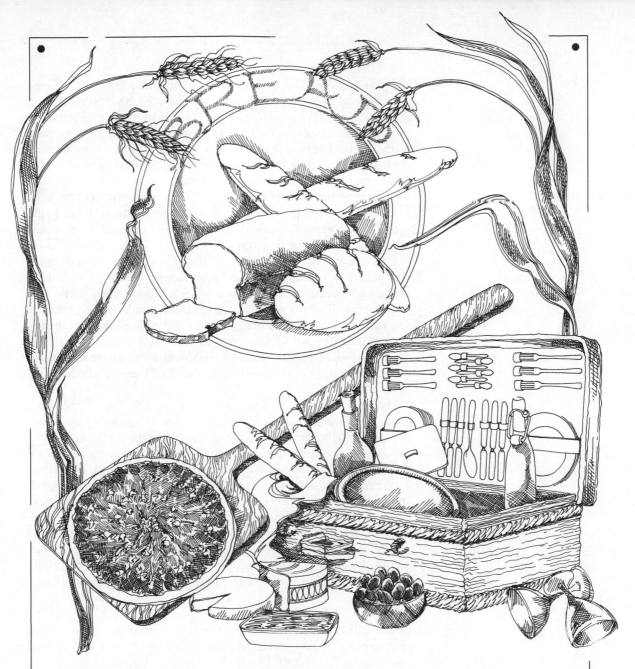

11 · Breads, Pizzas and Sandwiches

Making yeast breads is one of my very favorite culinary endeavors, one that goes beyond cooking. For me, it is a pleasant and always satisfying pastime. I make breads purely for the pleasure they bring, both to my peace of mind and to the table. There was a time when making bread at home was almost a necessity. Until fairly recently it was not easy to find a good loaf of bread in the stores, and that is precisely what got me started as an inveterate bread baker. That, of course, has changed. Many bakeries sell excellent breads, as do supermarkets, but I still get such enormous pleasure and satisfaction from homemade bread that I still bake it as often as I can.

Considering the nature of this book, it may seem odd, even contradictory, to have such a lengthy chapter dealing with home-made breads. Of course, I have included more than just yeast breads here. There are sandwiches, savory quick breads, muffins and pizza, which is itself really just an embellished form of bread, as well. And I'm not suggesting that you make bread every single day. I do hope, though, that you'll consider the merits of home-made bread and decide to give it a try when time and inclination allow.

My own bread-making is predicated on the use of the food processor. I personally can't imagine kneading dough by hand anymore, spending at least 10 minutes versus 1 minute in the processor. The processor does as good a job kneading dough as the old-fashioned, arduous method of doing it by hand. As for the argument that food processor kneading is too mechanical and not at all creative, I say, "To each his own." Certainly, shaping loaves, tailoring them and baking them provide sensual pleasures. And the aroma of the bread as it bakes just may be the most satisfying part of the experience. Because I feel so strongly about this, I have included only food processor instructions for kneading dough. Other methods are neither timesaving nor otherwise practical for busy cooks.

I've devised many shortcuts and tips, so making bread will be as streamlined as possible. Most bread doughs require two risings of roughly one hour each. Several here only require one rising, specifically the Italian Flat Bread Dough and the Pizza Crust Dough. Those that have two risings can often be interrupted at certain stages, breaking the process up into a two-part, partially do-ahead job. I've indicated this wherever it applies. Some people will find two-stage operations helpful while others will find it more advantageous to work from start to finish on the same day.

Bread dough that is allowed to rise slowly in a warm, controlled environment will produce the best results. When the kitchen is cool or drafty, the dough can be placed in the oven for rising. If you have a gas oven, the pilot produces about the right amount of heat for rising. If you have an electric oven, preheat it for 2 minutes—any temperature is okay—then turn it off and add the bread dough. Remove the dough from the oven when it is almost, but not quite doubled so you can preheat the oven for baking the bread dough.

Most recipes direct you to place bread dough in a large, oiled bowl for the first rising. In all of the recipes in this chapter, I suggest placing the dough in a large plastic food bag first and then placing the bag in a glass or ceramic bowl. The bowl keeps the dough from spreading all over and cushions it from the warm, metal oven rack if you use the oven for rising. The bag, in turn, keeps the bowl clean.

The freezer is an integral part of my bread-baking routine. Without preservatives, homemade breads stale quickly. Unless the bread is earmarked for entertaining, it probably won't all get eaten before it dries out. As soon as the bread is cool, I freeze it as described on page 236. If it is thawed while still wrapped, it will be as fresh and inviting as the day it was baked. Always keep bread wrapped while it is thawing.

Since they are based on bread, sandwiches and pizzas are included here as well. If at one time they seemed trite and predictable, they have re-emerged with new vigor and excitement. The toppings and fillings are imaginative and colorful, tasting every bit as good as they look. Pizza and sandwiches, accompanied by salads, are suited to informal, unpretentious meals any time of the day.

This is a basic bread recipe, the one I turn to most often. Lionel Poîlane, the well-known owner of several *boulangeries* in Paris, and I worked it out together, adapting his great technique to American ingredients and the food processor. It is a moist dough that, when baked, has a gorgeous, crisp, bronze crust and a soft, nicely chewy interior.

This bread stales quickly, so plan on baking it shortly before serving. Or freeze it and reheat it at serving time. However, don't think that means you can't have fresh-baked bread when your schedule is tight. There are two options at the end of the recipe that make it possible to have fresh-baked bread in practically no time.

French Bread

Preparation time: 15 minutes
Rising time: 2 hours
Baking time: 28 minutes
Yield: 2 12-inch loaves

1 package active dry yeast
1 teaspoon sugar
1 cup plus 2 tablespoons
 warm water (105 to 115
 degrees)
2 cups bread flour
 (10 ounces)
1 teaspoon salt

GLAZE:
1 large egg
1 cup unbleached all-
 purpose flour (5 ounces)
½ teaspoon salt

1. Stir the yeast and sugar into the warm water and let stand until foamy, about 10 minutes.

2. Put the flour and salt in a food processor and turn it on. Slowly pour the yeast mixture through the feed tube and process until the dough cleans the sides of the work bowl but is still moist. If it is too sticky, add a little more flour; if too dry, add a little more water. When the dough is the right consistency—moist but not so wet that it sticks to your fingers or to the sides of the work bowl—process it until it is uniformly kneaded, 40 seconds. It should be supple and elastic.

3. Transfer the dough to a large plastic bag and squeeze out the air. Seal tightly at the top of the bag, leaving enough room inside for the dough to expand. Place the bag in a bowl and let rise in a warm place until the dough has doubled, about 1 hour.

4. Oil a double French loaf pan and sprinkle it with cornmeal. Punch the dough down. Turn it onto a floured board and divide it in half with a sharp knife. Shape each half into a 10-inch oblong to fit the pan. Cover with oiled plastic wrap.

5. Let the shaped dough rise in a warm spot until it has doubled, 45 minutes to 1 hour.

6. 15 minutes before baking, place the rack in the center of the oven and preheat oven to 425 degrees.

7. For the glaze, mix the egg and salt. Lightly brush the top of the dough with the glaze, then make 3 diagonal slashes, about ¼-inch deep, on each loaf. Unused glaze can be refrigerated for up to 1 week.

8. Bake the loaves until they are golden and sound hollow when rapped on the bottom, about 28 minutes. Immediately remove them from the pan and cool on a wire rack.

Note: There are 2 different points at which the bread-making process can be interrupted and finished at a later time. The first one allows you to keep the dough in the refrigerator for up to 5 days, at which time it will have developed a slight tang, similar to sourdough. The second option is to shape the risen dough and refrigerate it up to 24 hours before baking it. Baked, this bread has a porous texture and a crisp crust. Use one of the following options:

1. Prepare the bread through step 3. Punch the dough down. Squeeze all the air from the bag and seal it tightly at the top. Refrigerate up to 5 days. Follow steps 4 through 8 to finish the bread, except note that the second rising (step 5) will take up to 2 hours because the dough has been refrigerated.

2. Prepare the bread through step 4. Make 3 diagonal slashes across each loaf. Cover loaves loosely, but completely, with oiled

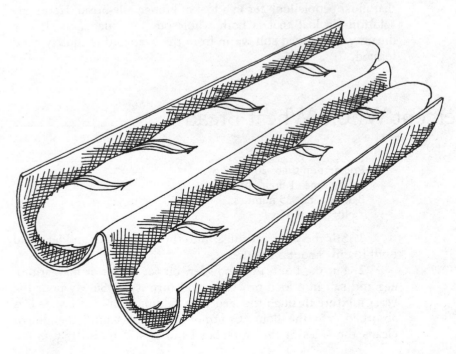

plastic wrap, making sure the ends are covered so the dough doesn't dry out. Refrigerate up to 24 hours. To bake, mix the egg and salt for the glaze and brush over the chilled dough. Put the loaves into a cold oven and turn it to 425 degrees. Bake until they are golden and sound hollow when rapped on the bottom, about 32 minutes.

Freezing: To freeze baked breads, cool completely, then place them in the freezer, unwrapped, just until they are frozen. Remove them from the freezer and double wrap them in airtight plastic bags as described on page 16. Return them to the freezer for up to 6 months.

◆

One of the most frequent requests I get about bread baking is for a recipe that uses all whole-wheat flour yet isn't as heavy as lead. It took some doing. Whole-wheat flour has less gluten than white flour so it doesn't rise as much or have the springy, light texture that most people look for in a loaf of homemade bread. Here's my solution—a loaf that is both wholesome and delicious. It is a dream when served still warm from the oven and is equally good toasted.

_____100 Percent Whole-Wheat Bread_____

Preparation time: 20 minutes
Rising time: 1 hour, 40 minutes
Baking time: 35 minutes
Yield: 1 round loaf

*1 package active dry
    yeast
3 tablespoons dark brown
    sugar
¾ cup warm water
    (105 to 115 degrees)*

1. Stir the yeast and sugar into the warm water and let stand until foamy, about 5 minutes.
2. Put the flour, milk powder, oil (or butter or margarine), egg and salt in a food processor and turn it on. Slowly pour the yeast mixture through the feed tube, adding it only as fast as it is absorbed into the flour. Continue to process until the dough cleans the sides of the work bowl but is still moist. If it is too

sticky, add a little more flour; if too dry, a little more water. When the dough is the right consistency—moist but not so wet that it sticks to your fingers or to the sides of the work bowl—process it until it is uniformly kneaded, about 60 seconds. It should be supple and elastic.

3. Transfer the dough to a large plastic bag, squeeze out all the air and seal tightly at the top of the bag, leaving enough room inside for the dough to expand. Set the bag in a bowl and let the dough rise in a warm spot until it has doubled, about 1 hour.

4. Oil a baking sheet. Punch the dough down. Flour your hands and shape the dough into a smooth ball. Place on the baking sheet and cover with oiled plastic wrap.

5. Let the dough rise in a warm spot until it has doubled, about 40 to 50 minutes.

6. 15 minutes before baking, place the rack in the center of the oven and preheat oven to 375 degrees.

7. When the dough has doubled, dust the top lightly with flour and make a decorative slash across the top. Bake until the bread is well browned and sounds hollow when it is rapped on the bottom, 30 to 35 minutes. Immediately remove from the pan and cool on a wire rack.

Note: You can omit the egg and increase the water to ¾ cup plus 2 tablespoons. The bread will not be quite so soft and springy.

2¾ cups whole-wheat flour (13¾ ounces)
3 tablespoons instant nonfat dry milk powder
3 tablespoons safflower oil, or melted butter or margarine
1 large egg (see Note)
1 teaspoon salt

This is the type of bread that epitomizes homemade. If your grandmother made bread, chances are it was just like this. It's a big, soft loaf with a beautiful golden crust and nice crumb. It slices well for sandwiches and makes delicious toast.

Home-Style White Bread

Preparation time: 15 minutes
Rising time: 2½ hours
Baking time: 35 minutes
Yield: 1 9-inch loaf

1 *package active dry yeast*
1 *teaspoon sugar*
1 *cup plus 2 tablespoons warm water (105 degrees to 115 degrees)*
3 *cups bread flour or unbleached all-purpose flour (15 ounces)*
¼ *cup instant nonfat dry milk powder*
2 *tablespoons unsalted butter or margarine, softened*
1 *teaspoon salt*
Melted butter, optional

1. Stir the yeast and sugar into the warm water and let it stand until foamy, about 5 minutes.

2. Put the flour, milk powder, butter or margarine and salt in a food processor and turn it on. Slowly pour the yeast mixture through the feed tube and process until the dough cleans sides of work bowl, but is still moist. If it is too sticky, add a little more flour; if too dry, a little more water. When the dough is the right consistency—moist but not so wet that it sticks to your fingers or to the sides of the work bowl—process it until it is uniformly kneaded, about 40 seconds. It should be supple and elastic.

3. Transfer the dough to a large plastic bag, squeeze out the air and seal at the top, leaving enough room inside for the dough to expand. Place the bag in a bowl and let it rise in a warm spot until doubled, about 1 hour and 30 minutes.

4. Oil an 8-cup loaf pan. Punch dough down and shape to fit pan. Cover with oiled plastic wrap.

5. Let the dough rise in a warm spot until doubled, about 1 hour.

6. 15 minutes before baking, place the rack in the center of the oven and preheat oven to 375 degrees.

7. When dough has doubled, brush the top with melted butter, if desired. Bake until loaf is golden and sounds hollow when rapped on the bottom, about 35 minutes. Immediately remove from pan and cool on a wire rack.

I've used hot peppers at one time or another in every course except dessert. Here, they pep up soft, oversized corn rolls that are perfect to serve with soup or stew for fall or winter meals. Try these rolls warm—they're really best that way. Leftover rolls make great croutons or melba toast. Or slice the rolls and use them for grilled sandwiches.

Jalapeño Cornmeal Bubble Rolls

Preparation time: 15 minutes
Rising time: 1 hour, 55 minutes
Baking time: 35 minutes
Yield: 8 large rolls

1. Stir the yeast and 1 teaspoon sugar into the warm water and let stand until foamy, about 5 minutes.

2. Mince the peppers in a food processor. Transfer 1½ teaspoons to a small dish and leave the rest in the work bowl.

3. Add the flour, cornmeal, 1 teaspoon salt, 3 tablespoons butter, the egg and the remaining sugar to the work bowl and turn on the processor. Slowly pour the yeast mixture and milk through the feed tube and process until the dough cleans the sides of the work bowl, but is still moist. If it is too sticky, add a little more flour; if too dry, a little more water. When the dough is the right consistency—moist but not so wet that it sticks to your fingers or to the sides of the work bowl—process it until it is kneaded, about 40 seconds. It should be uniformly supple and elastic.

4. Transfer the dough to a large plastic bag and squeeze out the air. Seal the bag tightly at the top, leaving enough room inside for the dough to expand. Place the bag in a bowl and let the dough rise in a warm spot until it has doubled, about 1½ hours.

5. Butter an 8-inch round cake pan. Punch the dough down and divide it into 8 pieces. Roll each piece into a smooth ball. Arrange them in pan, starting from the center and placing them so they touch each other lightly. Cover with oiled plastic wrap.

6. Let rise in a warm spot until doubled, about 1 hour.

7. 15 minutes before baking, place the rack in the center of the oven and preheat oven to 375 degrees.

8. Melt the remaining 3 tablespoons butter and brush half of it over the top of the risen dough.

9. Bake until rolls are golden and sound hollow when rapped on the bottom, about 35 minutes. Remove from the pan

1 package active dry yeast
3 tablespoons sugar
3 tablespoons warm water (105 to 115 degrees)
2 jalapeño peppers, seeded, if desired
2½ cups bread flour or unbleached all-purpose flour (12½ ounces)
½ cup yellow cornmeal (2¼ ounces)
1⅛ teaspoons salt
6 tablespoons unsalted butter, softened
1 large egg
½ cup milk

and place on a wire rack. Stir the reserved jalapeño peppers and the remaining ⅛ teaspoon salt into the rest of the melted butter. Brush over the top of the rolls while they are still hot. Serve warm or at room temperature.

◆

This versatile bread has just about everything going for it—a yeast bread that's fast and easy to make, rises only once, tastes fabulous, adapts to almost any style meal from fun to formal, and can be made in advance. If you've shied away from making yeast breads, this recipe may be the perfect invitation. Variations on the theme follow.

Basic Italian Flat Bread Dough (Focaccia)

Preparation time: 20 minutes
Rising time: 1 hour
Baking time: 17 minutes
Yield: 2 10-inch by 12-inch flat breads

1   package active dry yeast
1   teaspoon honey
1¼ cups warm water
     (105 to 115 degrees)
2¾ cups bread flour
     (13¾ ounces)
½   cup rye flour
     (2½ ounces)
3   tablespoons light-tasting
     olive oil
1   teaspoon salt
     Topping of your choice
     (recipes follow)

1. Stir the yeast and honey into the warm water and let stand until foamy, about 5 minutes.

2. Combine both flours, 1 tablespoon oil and the salt in a food processor. Turn on the machine and slowly pour the yeast mixture through the feed tube. Process until the dough cleans the inside of the work bowl but is still moist. If it is too sticky, add a little more flour; if too dry, a little more water. Once the dough is the right consistency—moist but not so wet that it sticks to your fingers or to the sides of the work bowl—process it until it is uniformly kneaded, about 40 seconds. It should be supple and elastic.

3. Transfer the dough to a large plastic food bag, squeeze out the air and seal at the top, leaving enough room for the dough to expand. Place the bag in a bowl and let it rise in a warm spot until doubled, about 1 hour. Punch dough down and use immediately or refrigerate overnight.

4. 15 minutes before baking, place the rack in the center of the oven and preheat oven to 450 degrees. Oil 2 large baking sheets, preferably black steel and sprinkle with cornmeal.

5. Divide dough in half with a sharp knife. With floured

hands, gently stretch each piece to a free-form shape, about 10 inches by 12 inches, and transfer to prepared baking sheets. Prick all over with a fork. Spread with topping of your choice.

6. Bake until golden, about 15 to 17 minutes. Brush with remaining oil, especially the edges of the crust. Cut into squares and serve hot. The bread can be baked in advance and frozen. Cool completely, then wrap airtight and freeze. To reheat, place frozen bread on a baking sheet. Place in a cold oven and turn up to 300 degrees. Bake until hot, about 12 minutes.

◆

This is the simplest of the toppings, loaded with character nonetheless. Bring it to the table to round out a light meal of soup and salad or a hearty winter casserole.

Spicy Onion and Poppy Seed Flat Bread

Preparation time: 5 minutes
Yield: Topping for 2 flat breads

1. Cut the onions into paper-thin slices either with the thin (2mm) slicer of a food processor or by hand, and set aside.

2. Mince the garlic either with the processor or by hand. Mix with the oil, poppy seeds and crushed red peppers. Use immediately or cover and refrigerate for up to a week. If you refrigerate the oil mixture, do not add the red pepper flakes until just before using, as they will get even hotter while mixture is stored.

3. To assemble, distribute onions evenly over rolled Italian Flat Bread Dough, then brush with the oil mixture. Season to taste with salt and pepper. Refer to Italian Flat Bread Dough recipe for baking instructions.

2 *small onions (3 ounces total), peeled*
2 *large garlic cloves, peeled*
6 *tablespoons extra virgin olive oil*
2 *teaspoons poppy seeds*
1 *teaspoon crushed red pepper flakes*
 Basic Italian Flat Bread Dough (see page 240)
½ *teaspoon salt*
¼ *teaspoon coarsely ground black pepper*

Wild mushrooms are nice to add, but admittedly something of a luxury. Omit them if you wish and increase the amount of cultivated mushrooms. On the other hand, you can be much more generous with the chanterelles. Either way, this is a delicious interpretation.

Flat Bread with Forest Mushrooms, Prosciutto and Cheese

Preparation time: 10 minutes
Cooking time: 7 minutes
Yield: Topping for 2 flat breads

5 large shallots (3 ounces total), peeled
6 tablespoons light-tasting olive oil
¼ teaspoon dried rosemary
6 ounces domestic mushrooms, small, if possible
2 to 3 ounces fresh chanterelles or other wild mushrooms
4-ounce piece prosciutto, cut in ¼-inch dice
Salt
Freshly ground black pepper
4 ounces mozzarella cheese
1 ounce Parmesan cheese, preferably imported
Basic Italian Flat Bread Dough (see page 240)

1. Mince the shallots in a food processor or by hand.
2. Heat the oil in a 10-inch skillet and add the shallots. Crush the rosemary in a mortar and pestle or between your fingers and add it to the pan. Cook gently until the shallots are soft, about 3 minutes.
3. Cut any large mushrooms, both domestic and wild, in half. Add them to the skillet with salt and pepper to taste. Cook just until the mushrooms are soft, but not limp, about 3 minutes. Remove the pan from the heat and add the prosciutto. The topping can be used immediately or refrigerated overnight.
4. Shred the cheeses separately in a processor or with a grater. Keep them separate.
5. To assemble, sprinkle mozzarella evenly over the rolled Italian Flat Bread Dough, then distribute the mushroom mixture and finish with the Parmesan cheese. Refer to Italian Flat Bread Dough recipe for baking instructions.

Little flecks of dried tomatoes bolster and intensify the flavor of fresh tomatoes. In the winter, use plum tomatoes, as they have more flavor and better texture than other winter tomatoes.

Two-Tomato Flat Bread

Preparation time: 10 minutes
Cooking time: 7 minutes
Yield: Topping for 2 flat breads

1. Put the sun-dried tomatoes in a small dish, cover with hot water and soak until softened, 10 to 15 minutes. Drain and cut them into small dice. Mince the garlic in a food processor or by hand.

2. Heat the oil in an 8-inch skillet. Add the dried tomatoes, garlic, basil, salt and pepper and cook gently until the garlic is soft, about 5 minutes.

3. Core the fresh tomatoes and cut in half crosswise. Remove the seeds and all the membrane from the inside, leaving only the outer shell. Cut the shell into ½-inch dice. Toss into skillet with the dried tomato mixture and cook just until heated through, about 1 minute. Adjust the seasoning.

4. Shred the cheese in the processor or with a grater.

5. Divide tomato mixture evenly and spread over the rolled Italian Flat Bread Dough and sprinkle with cheese. See Italian Flat Bread Dough recipe for baking instructions.

6 *dry-packed sun-dried tomatoes*
2 *large garlic cloves, peeled*
6 *tablespoons light-tasting olive oil*
1 *teaspoon dried basil*
¾ *teaspoon salt*
  Freshly ground black pepper
2 *medium tomatoes (or 4 to 5 plum tomatoes) (12 ounces total)*
1 *ounce Parmesan cheese, preferably imported Basic Italian Flat Bread Dough (see page 240)*

My affection for homemade pizza knows no limits. I like them thick, thin or paper-thin; baked, grilled, plain and simple, or over-loaded. This dough covers all the possibilities, providing a crust that is crisp, chewy and tender. And recipes for toppings follow.

Basic Pizza Crust Dough

Preparation time: 15 minutes
Rising time: 1 hour
Yield: 5 8-inch or 2 14-inch pizzas

1 package active dry yeast
1 teaspoon sugar
1 cup warm water (105 to 115 degrees)
3 cups unbleached all-purpose flour (15 ounces)
2 tablespoons light-tasting olive oil
1 teaspoon salt

1. Stir the yeast and sugar into the water and let it stand until foamy, about 5 minutes.

2. Put the flour, oil and salt in a food processor and turn the machine on. Slowly pour the yeast mixture through the feed tube and process until the dough cleans the sides of the work bowl but is still moist. If it is too sticky, add a little more flour; if too dry, a little more water. When dough is the right consistency—moist but not so wet that it sticks to your fingers or the sides of the work bowl—process it until it is kneaded, about 40 seconds. It should be supple and elastic.

3. Transfer the dough to a large plastic food bag, squeeze out the air and seal at the top, leaving enough room inside for the dough to expand. Place the bag in a bowl and let it rise in a warm spot until it has doubled, about 1 hour. Dough can be used now or refrigerated for up to 5 days. To refrigerate, open the bag and punch the dough down. Reseal the bag and refrigerate.

4. Divide the dough into portions, depending on how large a pizza you are making. Roll each piece on a floured board to make a circle. Stack between oiled sheets of wax paper. Dough can be rolled in advance and refrigerated for several hours or frozen. See pizza recipes that follow for toppings and cooking instructions.

Pizza just doesn't get any better than this! The slightly smoky taste of a mesquite fire infuses the chewy dough with the flavor of the great outdoors. A dazzling summer-fresh topping of vine-ripened tomatoes and garden herbs, covered with melting cheese is sensational. Best bet for easy entertaining—put bowls of different toppings out and let guests construct their own made-to-order pizza.

Grilled Garden Tomato and Herb Pizza

Preparation time: 20 minutes
Grilling time: About 10 minutes
Yield: 2 8-inch pizzas

1. Roll each portion of the dough on a floured board to an 8-inch circle. Stack between oiled sheets of wax paper. Dough can be rolled in advance and refrigerated for several hours or frozen. If frozen, thaw in the refrigerator before using.

2. To make the herb oil, mince the herbs and garlic in a food processor or by hand. Mix with the oil and salt. The oil can be made a day in advance and refrigerated.

3. For the topping, seed the tomato and cut it into ¼-inch dice. Toss with 2 teaspoons herb oil and set aside. Cut the onion into paper-thin slices.

4. To cook the pizzas, grill the circles of dough over the hot barbecue grill with the cover on until they are browned on the underside, 2 to 4 minutes. Remove from the grill and put them on a piece of foil with the grilled side facing up. Stir herb oil and spoon 1 tablespoon onto each circle of dough, then brush evenly over the surface. Divide the remaining ingredients and arrange evenly over dough in this order: onions, mozzarella, tomatoes, Parmesan.

5. Transfer from the foil to the grill, cover and cook just until bottoms are browned and cheese is melted, 4 to 5 minutes. Brush surfaces, and especially the edges, with remaining herbed oil and snip fresh basil over the top. Slice and serve immediately.

2 5-ounce pieces Basic Pizza Crust Dough (see page 244)

HERB OIL:
5 large fresh basil leaves
3 fresh sage leaves
2 tablespoons fresh oregano leaves
1 medium garlic clove
¼ cup light-tasting olive oil
¼ teaspoon salt

TOPPING:
1 medium tomato (7 ounces)
1 small onion (2 ounces)
4 ounces thinly sliced mozzarella cheese
1 ounce shredded Parmesan cheese, preferably imported
Julienned fresh basil leaves, for garnish

Even though pizza is traditionally thought of as Italian, it needn't be limited to ingredients that fit that description. Here, pizza takes a Southwestern route. The ever-so-slightly hot Anaheim peppers accentuate the natural sweetness of red bell peppers with a peppery bite. Both are accented by a mix of cheeses that marries mellow Monterey Jack with a tangier Italian cheese.

Pizza with Sweet and Spicy Peppers

Preparation time: 20 minutes
Baking time: 14 minutes
Yield: 1 14-inch pizza

2 medium red onions (10 ounces total), peeled
2 large red bell peppers (1 pound total)
2 Anaheim peppers (see Note)
2 large garlic cloves, peeled
3 tablespoons light-tasting olive oil
¼ to ½ teaspoon salt
¼ teaspoon crushed red pepper flakes
5 ounces Monterey Jack cheese
5 ounces Fontinella cheese
½ recipe Basic Pizza Crust Dough (see page 244)
½ cup pizza sauce or tomato purée
3 tablespoons minced cilantro leaves

1. 15 minutes before baking, place the rack in the center of the oven and preheat oven to 450 degrees. Line the oven rack with unglazed quarry tiles or a pizza stone if you have them. Oil a 14-inch round pizza pan, preferably black steel.

2. Cut the onions in half lengthwise and lay them on their cut side. Slice crosswise into ⅜-inch slices. Cut the sweet and Anaheim peppers into 2-inch by ½-inch strips. Mince the garlic in a food processor or by hand.

3. Heat the oil in a 10-inch skillet. Add the garlic and onion and cook until the onions are translucent, about 5 minutes. Add the peppers, salt and red pepper flakes and continue to cook until all the vegetables are soft, about 7 minutes longer.

4. Shred both cheeses, either with a processor or with a grater and toss them together.

5. Roll the dough on a floured board to a 14-inch circle. Carefully transfer to the prepared pan and press into place. Spread Pizza Sauce over the crust, leaving a ½-inch border. Spread the vegetable mixture over the sauce, then sprinkle with the cheeses.

6. Bake until the bottom of the crust is light brown, about 14 minutes. Slide the pizza from the pan onto a wire rack and let it rest for 5 minutes before serving. Add the cilantro just before serving.

Note: If Anaheim peppers are not available, use one small green bell pepper and one seeded jalapeño or serrano pepper instead.

These fluffy, light corn muffins are slightly sweet and fragrant. Consider serving them with hearty soups or stews, or at breakfast for a nice homey touch.

Spiced Masa Muffins

Preparation time: 15 minutes
Baking time: 25 minutes
Yield: 8 muffins

1. 15 minutes before baking, place the rack in the center of the oven and preheat oven to 375 degrees. Line 8 muffin cups with paper liners or grease the cups.

2. To make in a food processor, process the flour, masa or cornmeal, baking powder, pepper flakes, baking soda, salt, sugar, sour cream, oil and eggs for 3 seconds. Run a spatula around the sides of the work bowl and process again just until mixed, 1 to 2 seconds.

3. To make by hand, put the flour, masa or cornmeal, baking powder, pepper flakes, baking soda, salt and sugar in a mixing bowl and stir to combine. Break up the eggs with a fork and add to the dry ingredients along with the sour cream and oil. Mix just enough to combine.

4. Divide the batter among 8 muffin cups. Bake until light brown, about 25 minutes. Let muffins cool in the cups for 5 minutes, then turn out onto a rack. Serve warm.

Note: Masa harina is very finely ground parched corn that has been treated with lime. Most often, it is used for making corn tortillas, so it is a staple in many large supermarkets and Latin American markets.

1 *cup unbleached all-purpose flour (5 ounces)*
½ *cup masa harina (see Note) or finely ground yellow cornmeal (2¼ ounces)*
2 *teaspoons baking powder*
1 *teaspoon crushed red pepper flakes*
½ *teaspoon baking soda*
½ *teaspoon salt*
¼ *cup sugar (1¾ ounces)*
¾ *cup sour cream*
½ *cup safflower oil*
2 *large eggs*

Biscuits have a timeless appeal, and, to my taste, none are better than these. Light, flaky and slightly sweet, they're fine accompaniments to soups and stews. They are also good split open and made into small sandwiches or, at breakfast time, served warm with a dab of butter and some honey.

———— Butterflake Biscuits ————————————————.

Preparation time: 15 minutes
Baking time: 15 minutes
Yield: 10 2-inch biscuits

2   cups unbleached all-
    purpose flour
    (10 ounces)
2   tablespoons sugar
4   teaspoons baking powder
½   teaspoon cream of tartar
¼   teaspoon salt
1   stick unsalted butter or
    margarine, chilled
⅔   cup plain yogurt or sour
    cream

1. 15 minutes before baking, place the rack in the center of the oven and preheat oven to 425 degrees. Butter a baking sheet.

2. Combine the flour, sugar, baking powder, cream of tartar and salt in a food processor or medium-size mixing bowl. Cut the butter or margarine into 8 pieces. Work it into the dry ingredients either with the metal blade of a processor or with a pastry blender until it resembles a coarse meal.

3. Drain any liquid from the yogurt or sour cream. Add the yogurt or sour cream to the bowl and process or stir just until the ingredients clump together, before they begin to form a ball.

4. Transfer the dough to a large plastic bag. Working through the bag, shape the dough into a neat ball, then flatten the ball to a circle ½-inch thick. Rip the bag open so the top of the dough is uncovered but the dough is still on the plastic. Cut with a 2-inch round biscuit cutter.

5. Transfer the biscuits from the plastic bag to the baking sheet, leaving at least 1 inch of space between each one. Bake until they are golden, about 15 minutes. Serve immediately.

Popovers are among those old-time treats that never seem dated. Their short list of ingredients produces a most unexpected result. The steam from a very hot oven puffs them up to unbelievable heights and hollows them out. The end result is a crisp outer crust encasing a light, eggy center that, in a manner of speaking, is full of hot air. Here there's a bit of pesto sauce in the batter for an added touch of flavor and a lovely pale green tint.

If you don't have pesto on hand, you can make these popovers plain by using 2 tablespoons of melted butter instead. Or spice up this plain version with ½ teaspoon each of curry powder and ginger. Whichever you choose, the batter can be made the day before and refrigerated.

Pesto Popovers

Preparation time: 10 minutes
Baking time: 40 minutes
Yield: 6 to 10 popovers

1. 15 minutes before baking, place the rack in the center of the oven and preheat oven to 450 degrees. Have a popover pan or muffin tin ready.

2. Combine the flour, eggs, milk, Pesto Sauce and salt in a food processor or blender. Mix until smooth. Use the batter now or refrigerate overnight. If refrigerated, stir well before using.

3. Place the pan in the oven and preheat it for 3 minutes. Remove it from the oven and brush the inside of 6 popover cups or 10 muffin cups with the melted butter.

4. Pour the batter into the cups. Bake at 450 degrees for 25 minutes. Reduce the temperature to 375 degrees and continue to bake until the popovers are well browned, about 10 minutes longer. Loosen from the sides of the cups, if necessary, with a small flexible metal spatula, and transfer immediately to a basket. Serve immediately.

1 *cup unbleached all-purpose flour (5 ounces)*
4 *large eggs*
1½ *cups milk*
5 *tablespoons Pesto Sauce (see page 330)*
1 *teaspoon salt*
1 *tablespoon unsalted butter, melted*

Here is a wonderfully wholesome loaf made from all whole-wheat flour and oatmeal. It has a country style and flavor as evidenced by its rustic round shape, dense, crumbly texture and nutlike taste. It's delicious served warm with butter and jam, or as a tableside companion to hearty soups and stews.

Irish Oat Bread

Preparation time: 10 minutes
Baking time: 40 to 45 minutes
Yield: 1 round loaf

2 cups whole-wheat flour
(10 ounces)
1 cup rolled oats
(3 ounces)
⅓ cup firmly packed light
brown sugar
(2⅓ ounces)
1 large egg
4 tablespoons unsalted
butter or margarine,
melted
1½ teaspoons baking
powder
¾ teaspoon salt
½ teaspoon baking soda
¾ cup buttermilk
1 cup dried currants or
raisins (6 ounces)

1. 15 minutes before baking, place the rack in the center of the oven and preheat oven to 350 degrees. Grease a baking sheet.

2. To make in a food processor, put the flour, oats, sugar, egg, butter, baking powder, salt and baking soda in the work bowl and turn on the machine. Pour the buttermilk through the feed tube and process 30 seconds. The dough will be moist and sticky. Stop the machine and add the currants or raisins. Pulse several seconds, just until they are mixed in.

3. To make by hand, mix the flour, currants or raisins, oats, sugar, baking powder, salt and baking soda in a large bowl. Make a well in the center and add the buttermilk, egg and butter. Gradually stir the flour mixture into the buttermilk mixture until they are completely blended. Stir vigorously with a wooden spoon for 1 minute more.

4. Transfer dough to the baking sheet. Flour your hands and shape the dough into a ball. Slash a "T" across the top with a sharp knife. Bake until golden, 40 to 45 minutes. Do not let loaf become too brown. Transfer to a wire rack. Serve warm or at room temperature.

This is a sublime sandwich whose total is far greater than the sum of its parts. Crunchy vegetables contrast with tender pieces of chicken breast and a slightly sweet mayonnaise dressing. Cooked pork and turkey are delicious alternatives to the chicken.

Oriental Chicken Sandwich

Preparation time: 10 minutes
Yield: 2 sandwiches

1. Combine the mayonnaise and hoisin sauce in a small dish. Spread 1 tablespoon over each slice of bread.

2. Remove the skin from the chicken and cut across the grain into thin slices. Cut the cucumber and lettuce into thin slices. Shred the carrot.

3. Divide the chicken, lettuce and carrot between 2 pieces of bread and add cilantro. Top each with another slice of bread and serve immediately.

¼ cup mayonnaise (see page 327), or store-bought
2 teaspoons hoisin sauce
4 slices whole-wheat bread
1 whole cooked chicken breast, split
⅓ English, "gourmet" or "burpless" cucumber (3 ounces)
1 small wedge iceberg lettuce
½ small carrot (1 ounce), peeled
⅓ cup cilantro leaves

Here's another combination that has jumped from the salad bowl to the sandwich board. This idea comes from Joyce Goldstein, owner and chef of Square One and Caffe Quadro in San Francisco. It's delightful in summertime, when the lightness of a salad is in order. In winter, pair it with a bowl of steaming hot soup.

Greek Salad Sandwich

Preparation time: 15 minutes
Yield: 4 sandwiches

1 small garlic clove, peeled
½ cup extra virgin olive oil
2 tablespoons red wine vinegar
2 teaspoons toasted dried oregano (see Note)
⅛ teaspoon salt
½ English, "gourmet" or "burpless" cucumber (5 ounces), unpeeled
1 small onion (1½ ounces), peeled
1 small green bell pepper (3 ounces), cored
2 small plum tomatoes (5 ounces total)
4 large romaine lettuce leaves
8 oil-cured pitted black olives
8 slices good-quality bread
3 ounces crumbled feta cheese

1. To make the dressing, mince the garlic in a food processor or by hand. Mix with the oil, vinegar, toasted oregano and salt. Set aside.

2. Score the cucumber with a stripper or the tines of a fork, if desired, so it has a decorative edge. Cut the cucumber, onion and green pepper into very thin slices. It's best to do this with the thin (2mm) slicer of a processor so all the slices will be even. Cut the tomato into somewhat thicker slices, either with the all-pur-

pose (4mm) slicer or by hand. Remove the ribs from the lettuce, split the leaves lengthwise and cut into 2-inch ribbons.

3. Assemble the sandwiches as follows: spread each slice of bread with 1 tablespoon of the dressing. Divide the lettuce among 4 of the slices, then layer the remaining ingredients in this order: cucumber, onion, tomato, green pepper, olives and cheese. Top with the remaining 4 slices. Cut each sandwich in half and serve immediately

Note: To toast dried oregano, spread it on a baking sheet and bake in a preheated oven until fragrant, 5 to 6 minutes.

◆

This scrumptious sandwich not only uses up leftover turkey, it helps put a dent in your supply of cranberry relish, too. I'm absolutely crazy for it broiled, but it can be served at room temperature as well. Sourdough bread is my first choice. Its tangy flavor is just right with the filling.

___Grilled Turkey and Smoked Gouda Sandwich___

Preparation time: 10 minutes
Yield: 2 large sandwiches

1. Spread both sides of 2 slices of bread with butter and set aside. Spread 1 side of each of the other 2 slices with butter and divide mustard between these 2 slices.

2. Cut cucumber into paper-thin slices.

3. Spread cranberry relish over the slices with the mustard, then layer with cucumbers, turkey and cheese.

4. Arrange all 4 slices face up on a baking sheet lined with aluminum foil. Broil 8 inches from the heat until cheese is bubbly. Turn the buttered slices over once halfway through cooking. Close sandwiches, cut in half and serve immediately.

4 large slices good-quality bread, preferably sourdough
2 tablespoons unsalted butter, softened
1 tablespoon Dijon mustard
⅓ English, "gourmet" or "burpless" cucumber (3 ounces)
2 to 3 tablespoons cranberry relish or cranberry sauce
5 ounces thinly sliced turkey breast meat
3 ounces thinly sliced smoked Gouda cheese

This is an Italian update of the ever-popular ham and cheese sandwich. Tissue-thin slices of prosciutto and smoky flavored provolone cheese are accented with the robust flavor of roasted sweet red peppers and a boldly flavored dressing of fresh basil and Parmesan cheese. It's an unbeatable combination.

Prosciutto, Provolone and Roasted Red Pepper Sandwich

Preparation time: 15 minutes
Yield: 4 servings

1 medium garlic clove, peeled
1 ounce piece Parmesan cheese, preferably imported
½ cup fresh basil leaves
¼ teaspoon salt
6 tablespoons extra virgin olive oil
1 tablespoon red wine vinegar
1 loaf (16 inches) French or Italian bread
8 ounces lean prosciutto, thinly sliced
5 ounces provolone cheese, preferably imported, thinly sliced
1 large red bell pepper (8 ounces), roasted (see page 336)

1. To make a dressing, combine the garlic, cheese, basil and salt in a food processor or blender and mix until everything is finely minced. Add the oil and vinegar and mix well. Set aside.

2. Slice the bread in half lengthwise and remove the soft bread from the inside, leaving a 1-inch shell of bread inside the crust. Brush the dressing on both halves. Layer the bottom with prosciutto, then cheese.

3. Arrange the red pepper over the cheese. Replace the top of the bread and press together lightly. The sandwich can be assembled 2 hours in advance, wrapped in plastic wrap and refrigerated. Bring to room temperature before serving. To serve, cut into 1½-inch slices and arrange, cut side up, on a platter.

Inspiration for this sandwich comes from Greens Restaurant in San Francisco, the most celebrated and innovative vegetarian restaurant in the country. Since I don't get out there often enough to become satiated with their cooking, I'm thrilled that they have a cookbook, *The Greens Cookbook*, by Deborah Madison. The book is a gem—so, too, is this sandwich.

Sausalito Cheese Sandwich

Preparation time: 10 minutes
Cooking time: 5 minutes
Yield: 4 sandwiches

1. Cut the onion into paper-thin slices and the tomato into ⅜-inch slices.

2. Mix the mayonnaise and adobo sauce and spread on one side of each slice of bread. Top 4 slices with onion, cheese, tomato, cilantro and, last, another slice of bread.

3. Melt butter on a large griddle or skillet. Add the sandwiches, cover and cook until golden brown on the bottom. Turn the sandwiches and finish cooking, uncovered, until the bread is browned and the cheese is melted. Serve immediately.

Note: Chipotle peppers are jalapeño peppers that have been smoked. Sold in cans, they are most often packed in a red adobo sauce. Look for them at Latin American grocery stores and some large supermarkets. For this recipe, you can use the sauce, or purée the peppers and use those.

1 *small red onion*
  (1½ ounces), peeled
1 *large tomato (8 ounces)*
¼ *cup mayonnaise (see page 327 or store-bought)*
¼ *cup adobo sauce from chipotle chiles (see Note)*
8 *slices good-quality whole wheat bread*
6 *ounces Monterey Jack or Herkimer cheese, cut in 6 slices*
¾ *cup cilantro leaves*
2 *tablespoons unsalted butter*

255 •

This is a between-bread counterpart of the Cobb Salad, made famous by the Brown Derby Restaurant in California. Why it's famous is no mystery—it's a delicious combination of tastes and textures. The same ingredients do just as well tucked into pita pockets as they do in a bowl. For some, one half of a pita sandwich will satisfy. Others will want two halves.

Cobb Salad Sandwich

Preparation time: 15 minutes
Yield: 6 pita halves

1 small red onion
  (1½ ounces)
2 plum tomatoes
  (5 ounces total)
4 large leaves romaine
  lettuce
2 whole chicken breasts,
  cooked
1 ripe dark-skinned
  avocado
1½ ounces blue cheese
⅓ cup mayonnaise (see
  page 327 or store-
  bought)
3 pita breads, cut in half
6 slices bacon, cooked
  until crisp

1. Cut the onion into paper-thin slices and the tomatoes into slightly thicker slices. Cut the lettuce into 2-inch ribbons. Remove the skin and fat from the chicken and cut into thin slices.

2. Purée the avocado in a food processor or blender, or mash it with a fork.

3. Crumble the blue cheese and stir it into the mayonnaise.

4. Assemble the sandwiches as follows: Spread mayonnaise mixture in each pita half, followed by the avocado. Add, in this order, chicken, onions, tomato, bacon and lettuce. Serve immediately.

No demure tearoom chicken sandwiches here. This is a lively rendition that taps into Southwestern influences. Big chunks of chicken breast in a creamy mayonnaise sauce are spiced with 3 different types of hot peppers. If you've got cooked chicken on hand in the refrigerator or freezer, preparing the sandwiches is quick. If not, it's easy to poach the uncooked breasts in chicken broth. The salad needn't be reserved just for sandwiches. I also serve it on lettuce leaves or in avocado halves with a garnish of cilantro leaves and slices of mango, papaya or peach.

Chili Chicken Sandwich

Preparation time: 25 minutes
Yield: 6 servings

1. Mince the jalapeño and chipotle peppers in a food processor or by hand and transfer to a medium-size mixing bowl.

2. Cut the poblano pepper into ¼-inch dice. Add to the bowl along with Mayonnaise, sour cream, lime juice and salt. Gently fold in the chicken. This salad can be made a day in advance, covered tightly and refrigerated. Adjust seasoning.

3. Cut the rolls open and remove the soft inside from the top half, leaving a ½-inch shell. Brush the insides of the top and bottom with melted butter and toast lightly.

4. Cut the onion into paper-thin slices and the tomato into ¼-inch slices.

5. Assemble the sandwiches as follows: layer lettuce, onion and tomato on the bottom of each roll. Put about ½ cup chicken salad in hollowed-out tops and add cilantro. Close sandwiches and secure with toothpicks. The components of the sandwiches can be prepared several hours in advance, but it is best to assemble them just before serving.

Note: Chipotle peppers are smoked jalapeño peppers. In most areas they are sold in cans, packed in red adobo sauce. If they aren't available, omit them and add a dash of liquid smoke, if desired.

1 *jalapeño pepper, seeded if desired*
2 *large canned chipotle peppers (see Note)*
1 *large poblano pepper (4 ounces), roasted (see page 336)*
½ *cup mayonnaise (see page 327 or store-bought)*
2 *tablespoons sour cream*
1½ *teaspoons lime juice*
½ *teaspoon salt*
2¼ *cups cooked, coarsely shredded chicken breast*
6 *good-quality soft rolls*
2 *tablespoons unsalted butter, melted*
1 *small red onion (1½ ounces)*
1 *medium tomato (6 ounces)*
6 *Boston lettuce leaves*
½ *cup cilantro leaves, optional*

I remember how much I loved egg salad sandwiches as a child, and I feel the same about them to this day. With a concerned eye on the amount of cholesterol in egg yolks, I've doubled up on high protein whites with wonderful results. It all adds up to great taste, so good, in fact, you're not likely to notice the missing yolks. I recommend using reduced-calorie, light mayonnaise here on the premise that you really can't taste the difference.

The Good-Egg Egg Salad Sandwich

Preparation time: 25 minutes
Yield: 4 sandwiches

2　large green onions
　　(2 ounces total)
1　medium stalk celery
　　(2 ounces)
8　large hard-cooked egg
　　whites
3　large hard-cooked egg
　　yolks
⅓　cup reduced-calorie
　　mayonnaise
1　teaspoon Dijon mustard
½　teaspoon dried tarragon
　　Freshly ground pepper
8　slices whole-wheat or rye
　　bread
4　large leaf lettuce leaves

1. Cut the green onions into thin rings. Split the celery lengthwise into quarters, and cut it crosswise into a ¼-inch dice.

2. Coarsely mash the egg whites and yolks with a fork. Add the mayonnaise, mustard, tarragon and pepper and mix well. Use immediately or refrigerate overnight.

3. Make 4 sandwiches, adding a lettuce leaf to each one.

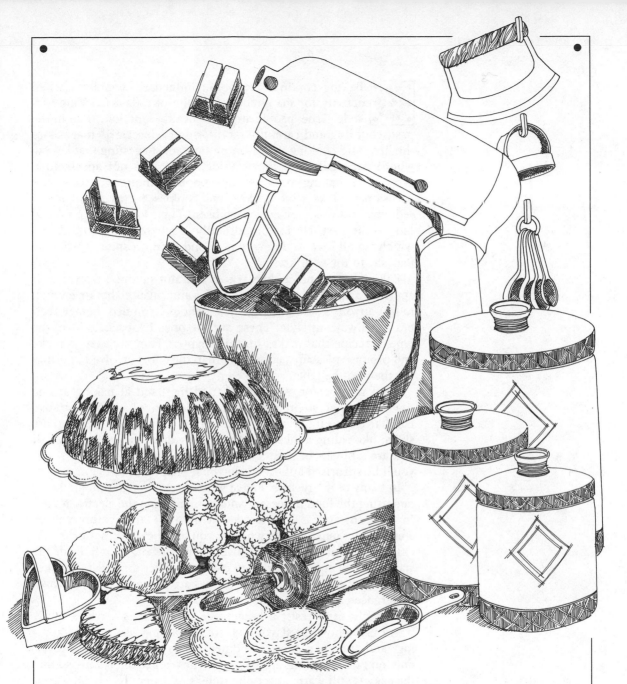

12 · Cakes and Cookies

Baking continues to be an immensely popular kitchen activity for many cooks in spite of today's cooking lifestyle. True, people are more health-conscious than in the past, counting and carefully monitoring every calorie that passes the lips. And cooking time is more limited, suggesting that baking would have fallen by the wayside, since it is not an essential activity. Yet baking continues to be popular among avid cooks and occasional cooks alike. Cakes and cookies are as popular and seductive now as they ever have been. Their legacy is a powerful link to the past. No less importantly, they are a way to indulge, which we all love to do every now and then, in spite of what we may say to the contrary.

Baking cakes and cookies is easy and not as time-involved as it appears to be. While there are cookies and cakes elaborate enough to test anyone's skill and patience, the old-fashioned, homey recipes are always in style. These are the ones I especially love, the type of recipe that makes up this chapter. They are easy to make and promise pleasures far greater than the effort involved in bringing them to the table.

It's a rare person who hasn't tried his hand at baking at one time or another, so preparing cakes and cookies has a comfortable, familiar feel to it. Creaming and folding, mixing and beating, are skills, like riding a bike that, once learned, are never forgotten. If you are a novice or suspect your baking skills have gotten rusty, you'll be surprised at how easily you'll pick them up.

In many of the recipes, I have written two preparation methods, one using the food processor and another using the electric mixer. In these instances, be assured that the taste and texture will be comparable, regardless of whether you use the processor or mixer. Often, I find it preferable to use the processor, if only from the standpoint of speed and ease of cleanup. Other than that, it makes no difference which way these recipes are prepared. Let your own preference choose the course.

I simply can't resist a homemade cake that is served slightly warm. Somehow the flavor, texture and aroma seem more haunting, and the suggestion of homemade is undeniable. However, only on rare occasions am I able to synchronize the baking so that the cake is still warm at serving time, so I generally rely on warming the cake just before serving. With brief, gentle reheating, a day-old cake can be as good as one freshly baked. Many of these cakes are finished with a glaze, rather than a frosting, which allows them to be reheated most satisfactorily. If they are frosted, do not try to reheat them. I have indicated in the recipes which ones are best served warm.

The microwave oven provides a great way to gently reheat a

cake, either by the serving or as a whole. Pieces of the cake can be reheated on medium power (50%) until warm throughout—not hot—about 30 to 40 seconds. Whole cakes are also reheated on medium power and will take from 4 to 5 minutes. Some cakes, like the Peaches and Cream Cake, will still be in the pan while being reheated. In any case, make sure the pan or dish is safe to use in the microwave oven.

To reheat cakes in the conventional oven, place the whole cake on a foil-lined baking sheet. Place in a cold oven, then turn the temperature up to 325 degrees. Bake until the cake is warm, about 15 minutes. Individual pieces of cake will dry out in the oven, so I don't recommend reheating a cake this way.

Most cakes and cookies freeze well. To freeze cakes, cool them completely, then place them on a baking sheet lined with wax paper. Place in the freezer until frozen solid. Wrap the cake in a plastic bag, seal tightly, then wrap it in another bag and seal it. Return to the freezer for up to 4 months. Thaw while still wrapped in the plastic. Double-bagging may seem like a lot of bother, but it effectively removes the possibility of freezer burn or off flavors.

To freeze cookies, cool completely, then layer them between pieces of wax paper in an airtight tin. Freeze for up to 4 months.

I'm crazy about fresh banana cakes, especially one like this—rich, softly textured and fragrant. Adding to its charm is an old-fashioned cooked Brown Sugar Glaze that would make an old shoe taste good. The cake can be made either in a food processor or with a mixer. Either way, it's quite easy to put together. In this particular cake, I prefer to use margarine since it results in a more softly textured cake without affecting the flavor of it.

Anna Banana Cake

Preparation time: 20 minutes
Baking time: 38 minutes
Yield: 1 Bundt cake

3 medium very ripe bananas (1¼ pounds total)
3 large eggs
2¼ cups sugar (15¾ ounces)
2¼ sticks unsalted butter or margarine, softened
6 tablespoons plain yogurt
1 tablespoon pure vanilla extract
1 tablespoon dark rum
2 cups plus 2 tablespoons cake flour (8½ ounces)
1½ teaspoons baking soda
¼ teaspoon salt
Brown Sugar Glaze (recipe follows)

1. 15 minutes before baking, place the rack in the center of the oven and preheat oven to 350 degrees. Butter a 12-cup Bundt pan, dust the inside with flour and tap the pan to remove any excess.

2. Mash the bananas in a food processor or with a fork until they are pulpy, but not entirely smooth. There should be some small bits of banana left. You should have 1½ cups.

3. If you're using a processor, put the eggs and sugar in the same work bowl—it is not necessary to wash it—and process until light and fluffy, about 1 minute, stopping once to scrape down the sides of the work bowl. Add butter or margarine and process 1 minute, stopping once to scrape down the sides of the work bowl. Add the yogurt, vanilla and rum and mix 5 seconds to combine. Transfer batter to a large bowl. Skip to step 5.

4. If you're using a mixer, cream the sugar and margarine or butter on high speed until light and fluffy. Add the eggs, yogurt, vanilla and rum on low speed, then increase to medium and mix until combined.

5. Stir the flour, baking soda and salt together in a plastic bag or small bowl, then gently fold it into the batter along with the mashed banana. Transfer to prepared pan.

6. Bake until a toothpick inserted in the center comes out clean, about 38 minutes. Let cool in the pan for 5 minutes, then turn onto a wire rack and cool completely. Place the rack over a piece of wax paper and spoon the glaze over the top of the cake, letting it drip down the sides.

Brown Sugar Glaze

Preparation time: 5 minutes
Cooking time: 5 minutes (Microwave: 3½ minutes)

1. Melt the butter or margarine in a small pan. Add the brown sugar and cook until the sugar is dissolved and the mixture is bubbling. Cook over medium-high heat, stirring constantly, for 2 minutes. Add the milk and cook 1 more minute.

2. Off the heat, sift in the confectioners' sugar. Whisk until smooth, then add the vanilla. Cool before using.

MICROWAVE: Melt the butter or margarine on high power (100%) in a 4-cup glass measuring cup. Stir in the brown sugar and cook on high power for 1 minute. Stir well, then cook 1 minute longer. Add the milk and cook 45 seconds. Finish as in step 2.

4 tablespoons unsalted butter or margarine
½ cup firmly packed light brown sugar (4 ounces)
2 tablespoons milk
½ cup confectioners' sugar (2 ounces)
1 teaspoon pure vanilla extract

"Had I but one penny in the world, thou shouldst have it for gingerbread."—William Shakespeare

I didn't always agree with the bard on that point, finding gingerbread too heavy in taste and texture for my liking. Yet there is something about the comfort of warm-from-the-oven gingerbread that I find very appealing. With that in mind, I've lightened the texture and added a sparkle of freshness with fresh ginger and lemon.

Spiced Fresh Gingerbread

Preparation time: 15 minutes
Baking time: 30 to 35 minutes
Yield: 1 8-inch cake

*Zest of 1 lemon,
removed with a zester or
grater*
1 *piece fresh ginger,
peeled (¾-inch cube)*
½ *cup firmly packed dark
brown sugar
(4 ounces)*
1 *large egg*
1 *stick unsalted butter,
softened*
½ *cup cold coffee*
¼ *cup molasses*
¼ *cup light corn syrup*
1¼ *cups cake flour
(5 ounces)*
1 *teaspoon baking soda*
½ *teaspoon cinnamon*
¼ *teaspoon salt*
⅛ *teaspoon freshly ground
black pepper
Confectioners' sugar
Sweetened whipped
cream or vanilla ice
cream, if desired*

1. 15 minutes before baking, place the rack in the center of the oven and preheat oven to 350 degrees. Butter an 8-inch square pan.

2. Mince the lemon zest and ginger together in a food processor or blender. Add the sugar and run the machine 1 minute to mince the zest as fine as possible. If you're using a processor, leave the mixture in the work bowl (skip to step 4 if you're not using a processor).

3. Add the egg and butter and process until smooth, about 1 minute. With motor running, add coffee, molasses and corn syrup through feed tube and process 10 seconds. Remove the cover and add the flour, baking soda, cinnamon, salt and pepper. Pulse the machine on and off just until ingredients are combined, 2 to 3 times.

4. To make with a mixer, cream sugar mixture and butter on high speed until fluffy. Mix in egg on low speed, then slowly pour in the coffee, molasses and corn syrup. Add the flour, baking soda, cinnamon, salt and pepper and mix until combined.

5. Transfer to the prepared pan. Bake until a toothpick inserted in the center comes out clean, 30 to 35 minutes. The cake is best served warm. Sift confectioners' sugar over the whole cake and serve topped with whipped cream or ice cream, if desired.

This old-fashioned cake is a real sensation for several reasons. Out of over 100 entries, this one was the winner in a blue ribbon chocolate cake contest that *The Chicago Tribune* ran in my Weekend Cook® newspaper column. It's dark, dense and wonderfully fudgey—chocolate at its very best. It has another winning trait: the cake is simplicity itself to make. All the ingredients are mixed together in one easy step.

_____ One in a Hundred Fudge Cake _____

Preparation time: 20 minutes
Baking time: 40 minutes
Yield: 1 9-inch by 13-inch cake

1. 15 minutes before baking, place the rack in the center of the oven and preheat oven to 350 degrees. Butter a 13-inch by 9-inch cake pan, dust lightly with flour and tap to remove any excess.

2. Sift the flour, cocoa, baking soda and salt into a large mixer or mixing bowl and stir in the sugar.

3. Mix in the sour cream, butter or margarine, eggs and vanilla with an electric mixer on low speed. Increase to medium and mix for 3 minutes.

4. Transfer to the prepared pan and bake until a toothpick inserted in the center comes out clean, about 40 minutes. Cool completely, then frost with Satin Fudge Frosting.

1¾ *cups cake flour*
   (7 ounces)
¾ *cup unsweetened cocoa*
   powder (2¼ ounces)
1½ *teaspoons baking soda*
½ *teaspoon salt*
1¾ *cups sugar*
   (12¼ ounces)
2 *cups sour cream*
1 *stick plus 3 tablespoons*
   unsalted butter or
   margarine, softened
2 *large eggs*
1 *teaspoon pure vanilla*
   extract
   Satin Fudge Frosting
   (recipe follows)

This is my favorite chocolate frosting, the best I've ever tasted. It's creamy, thick and gorgeous and stays that way, even after several days on a cake.

Satin Fudge Frosting

Preparation time: 5 minutes
Cooking time: 10 minutes (Microwave: 8 minutes)

1½ cups sugar
     (10½ ounces)
  1 cup whipping cream
  6 ounces unsweetened
     chocolate, cut in small
     pieces
  1 stick unsalted butter,
     softened
  1 tablespoon pure vanilla
     extract

1. Combine the sugar and cream in a heavy 3-quart pan, stirring to dissolve sugar. Bring to a boil, then reduce the heat and simmer gently for 6 minutes from the time it comes to a boil.

2. Remove from the heat and immediately add the chocolate and butter. Stir until smooth, then add the vanilla.

3. Refrigerate until the frosting is well chilled, and has set partially, but is not quite solid. Process it in a food processor or beat with a wooden spoon until it is smooth, light and fluffy. (The processor works best.)

MICROWAVE: Combine the sugar and cream in a 4-cup glass measuring cup and cook, uncovered, on high power (100%) for 8 minutes, stirring once halfway through. Finish as in steps 2 and 3.

◆

One of the first desserts I made as a new bride was a soft, lightly spiced cake baked over a layer of sliced peaches. I lost the recipe and asked everyone even remotely connected with that part of my life if they had it. Coming up blank, I've relied on my sensory memory to devise a close facsimile. Years and changing tastes haven't altered my fondness for the cake. It's still wonderful.

Georgia Peaches and Cream Cake

Preparation time: 20 minutes
Baking time: 28 minutes
Yield: 8-inch square cake

1. 15 minutes before baking, place the rack in the center of the oven and preheat oven to 375 degrees. Butter an 8-inch square baking pan, preferably Pyrex.

2. Cut the peaches into ½-inch slices. Put in a pan with sugar, lemon juice, tapioca and nutmeg and toss gently. Cook over high heat until syrup begins to bubble, about 4 minutes. Set aside.

3. For the topping, work the flour into the sugar, butter and cinnamon until the butter is the size of small peas. This can be done with a food processor or pastry blender. Set aside.

4. Stir the sour cream and baking soda together and let stand while you begin the cake.

5. Cream the egg, sugar and butter in the processor or with a mixer until it is light and fluffy. Add the vanilla and sour cream and mix well. Gently fold in the flour, baking powder and salt. In the processor, do this by pulsing the machine on and off several times.

6. Spread the warm peaches and their juice in the bottom of the baking pan. Spoon the batter over the peaches and spread in a thin, even layer with a rubber spatula. It's okay if the peaches are not completely covered. Sprinkle the topping over the batter. Bake until a toothpick inserted into the center of the cake—not the fruit—comes out clean, 25 to 28 minutes. The cake is best served warm, with ice cream, if desired.

Note: If the peaches have fuzzy skins, wipe them with a cloth to remove the fuzz.

FRUIT:
- 2 *pounds ripe peaches, unpeeled (see Note)*
- ⅓ *cup sugar (2⅓ ounces)*
- 2 *tablespoons fresh lemon juice*
- 1 *tablespoon quick-cooking tapioca*
- ¼ *teaspoon freshly grated nutmeg*

CRUMB TOPPING:
- ½ *cup unbleached all-purpose flour (2½ ounces)*
- 6 *tablespoons light brown sugar*
- 4 *tablespoons unsalted butter, chilled*
- ¼ *teaspoon cinnamon*

CAKE:
- 6 *tablespoons sour cream*
- ¼ *teaspoon baking soda*
- 1 *large egg*
- ⅓ *cup sugar*
- 4 *tablespoons unsalted butter, softened*
- 1½ *teaspoons pure vanilla extract*
- ¾ *cup unbleached all-purpose flour (3¾ ounces)*
- ½ *teaspoon baking powder*
- ¼ *teaspoon salt*
  Vanilla ice cream, if desired

This cake epitomizes what I've always thought a pound cake should be. It tastes very buttery and rich and has a fine, light crumb and properly dense texture without being heavy. It stays fresh for about a week if it's tightly wrapped in plastic wrap. By itself, a pound cake makes a wonderfully plain dessert, loaded with simple charms. It dresses up very well, too, with citrus curd, sweet sauces, fresh fruit or ice cream.

Deluxe Pound Cake

Preparation time: 15 minutes
Baking time: 90 to 95 minutes
Yield: 1 8-inch loaf

2 *sticks unsalted butter, softened*
1½ *cups confectioners' sugar (6 ounces)*
4 *large eggs*
1 *tablespoon pure vanilla extract*
1¼ *cups plus 2 tablespoons cake flour (5½ ounces)*
¼ *teaspoon salt*

1. Butter a 6-cup loaf pan, dust the inside with flour and tap it to remove the excess. Do not preheat the oven.

2. Mix the butter and sugar on high speed in an electric mixer until very light and fluffy, about 2 minutes. (Do not use a food processor.) Turn the speed to medium and add the eggs, one at a time, beating well after each addition. Add the vanilla. Turn again to high and beat for 2 minutes. Turn off the mixer and add the flour and salt. Beat on low speed until mixed. Transfer to the prepared pan and smooth the surface with a rubber spatula.

3. Place the pan on the center rack of a cold oven. Turn the oven to 325 degrees and bake the cake until well browned and the center appears dry, 90 to 95 minutes. Using a toothpick to test the cake is not useful here since the toothpick will come out clean before the cake is properly baked. Let cool in pan for 10 minutes, then turn onto a wire rack and cool completely before serving.

Here's the ultimate chocolate sensation, a dense, fudgey layer cake that's a cross between cake and candy. It's a roaring success when I make it in class and is almost magical in its ability to disappear, despite the fact that it's richer than sin.

Fudge Truffle Cake

Preparation time: 20 minutes
Baking time: 50 minutes
Yield: 1 8-inch round layer cake

1. 15 minutes before baking, place the rack in the center of the oven and preheat oven to 300 degrees. Line the bottom and sides of 2 round pans, 8 inches wide by 3 inches deep, with a piece of aluminum foil, smoothing out as many wrinkles in the foil as possible. Butter the foil and dust lightly with flour. Tap out the excess flour.

2. To make the cake in a food processor (for an electric mixer, skip to step 3), melt the butter or margarine and keep it very hot, but don't let it brown. Process the chocolate with the sugar, cocoa and salt with the metal blade until the chocolate is as fine as the sugar. With the machine running, pour the hot butter or margarine through the feed tube and mix until chocolate is smooth and melted, stopping once to scrape down sides of bowl. Add egg yolks and bourbon and mix for 1 minute. Add flour and fold in with 2 to 3 pulses. Transfer to a large mixing bowl and skip to step 4.

3. To make with a mixer, melt the chocolate with butter, sugar and cocoa in the top of a double boiler or in the microwave on high power (100%) for 2½ minutes, stirring once after 1 minute. Transfer to a mixing bowl and cool slightly. Mix egg yolks, sugar and bourbon with an electric mixer on high speed for 2 minutes. Mix in chocolate mixture on low speed, then the flour.

4. Whip the egg whites and cream of tartar with a mixer until they hold soft peaks. Thoroughly mix ¼ of egg whites into the chocolate mixture, then gently fold in the remaining whites.

5. Divide the batter between the 2 pans. Bake until a toothpick inserted in center comes out with moist, but not wet, crumbs, about 35 minutes. Do not overbake. Cool 1 hour in pans, then invert onto a rack and remove foil. Cool completely before frosting.

6. Place 1 layer upside down on a cake plate. Work four strips of wax paper under edges of cake to keep plate clean as you

2¼ sticks unsalted butter or margarine
6 ounces semisweet chocolate
1½ cups sugar (10½ ounces)
¼ cup unsweetened cocoa powder (¾ ounce)
Pinch of salt
8 large eggs, separated
¼ cup bourbon whiskey (see Note)
½ cup cake flour (2 ounces)
½ teaspoon cream of tartar
Chocolate Truffle Frosting (recipe follows)

work. Spread a layer of Chocolate Truffle Frosting over cake, and place second layer of the cake upside down over the first so the top is smooth. Trim edges, if necessary, to even the sides and brush away crumbs. Spread remaining frosting over top and sides, smoothing it with a long icing knife. Cake can be served immediately or held up to 2 days at a cool room temperature.

Note: 1 tablespoon pure vanilla extract and 3 tablespoons water can be used in place of bourbon.

◆

Chocolate Truffle Frosting

Preparation time: 5 minutes
Cooking time: 5 minutes (Microwave: 2 minutes)
Chilling time: 20 to 30 minutes

1½ *sticks unsalted butter*
6 *ounces semisweet chocolate, broken in pieces*
1 *teaspoon pure vanilla extract*

1. Melt the butter with the chocolate in the top of a double boiler over gently simmering water, stirring often, until smooth. Remove from the heat and add the vanilla.

2. Refrigerate the glaze just until it has thickened to a spreadable consistency but has not hardened, 20 to 30 minutes.

MICROWAVE: Cut the butter into 6 pieces. Put in a 1-quart microwave dish with the chocolate. Cook, uncovered, on high power (100%) until smooth, about 2 minutes, stirring once after 1 minute. Add the vanilla and stir until smooth. Finish as in step 2.

The tart, fresh flavor of lemon adds a lively note to this pecan-studded cake. Instead of a sweet, heavy frosting, it is finished with a fresh lemon syrup that soaks through the top of the cake.

Lemon Pecan Tea Cake

Preparation time: 20 minutes
Baking time: 45 minutes
Yield: 1 Bundt cake

1. 15 minutes before baking, place the rack in the center of the oven and preheat oven to 350 degrees. Butter a 12-cup Bundt pan and dust the inside with flour.

2. To make the cake in a food processor (for a mixer, skip to step 4), process the egg whites with the metal blade until foamy, about 8 seconds. With the machine running, pour the lemon juice through the feed tube and process until egg whites are stiff and hold their shape, about 2 minutes. Transfer to a bowl.

3. Process the zest with the sugar until the zest is as fine as the sugar. Add the egg yolks and butter or margarine and process for 2 minutes, stopping once to scrape down the sides of the work bowl. Add sour cream, Cointreau, vanilla and lemon extract and process for 10 seconds. Spoon the flour, pecans, baking powder, baking soda and salt in a ring onto batter and pulse 5 to 6 times. Run a spatula around the sides of the work bowl, then pulse 1 to 2 more times, until nuts are coarsely chopped. It's okay if all the flour isn't quite mixed in. Transfer batter to a large bowl. Skip to step 6.

4. To make the cake in a mixer, mince the zest with a small amount of the sugar so the zest is as fine as possible. Transfer to a large bowl and add the rest of the sugar and the butter or margarine. Beat on high speed until light and fluffy, about 2 minutes. Add the egg yolks, one at a time, beating well after each addition. Add the sour cream, lemon juice, Cointreau and vanilla and lemon extracts and mix in on low speed. Mince the nuts and fold them into the batter along with the flour, baking powder, baking soda and salt.

5. Wash and dry the beaters. Put the egg whites in a medium bowl. Beat until they hold soft peaks.

6. Thoroughly mix ¼ of the egg whites into the batter, then gently fold in the balance.

7. Transfer to prepared pan and bake until a toothpick in-

CAKE:
- 3 large eggs, separated
- 2 teaspoons fresh lemon juice
  Zest of 1 lemon, removed with a zester or grater
- 1⅔ cups sugar (12⅔ ounces)
- 2½ sticks unsalted butter or margarine, softened, cut in 12 pieces
- 1 cup sour cream
- 2 tablespoons Cointreau
- 2 teaspoons pure vanilla extract
- 1 teaspoon lemon extract
- 2½ cups cake flour (10 ounces)
- 1 cup toasted pecans (see page 338)
- 1 tablespoon baking powder
- ¾ teaspoon baking soda
- ¼ teaspoon salt

SYRUP:
- ½ cup confectioners' sugar (2 ounces)
- 3 tablespoons fresh lemon juice
- 2 tablespoons Cointreau
- 2 tablespoons confectioners' sugar, for top of cake

serted in the center comes out clean, about 45 minutes. Let cool in pan for 10 minutes. Make the syrup while cake is cooling.

8. For the syrup, cook the confectioners' sugar and lemon juice in a small pan over high heat until smooth and syrupy, 1 to 2 minutes; or combine in a 1-cup glass measuring cup and cook on high power (100%) for 1 minute. Add the Cointreau.

9. Invert the cake onto a wire rack placed over a piece of wax paper. Brush the syrup over the cake while both are still hot. The cake is best served while still slightly warm. Just before serving, sift confectioners' sugar over the top.

An angel food cake is one of the wonders of cooking. A big froth of egg whites swells the cake to great heights, giving a marvelously light and airy texture. They have always been a favorite of mine but never more so than when I tasted this cocoa-flavored version from Campton Place Hotel in San Francisco. Executive chef Brad Ogden quickly sent me the recipe, proving that he, too, is an angel.

Don't get all wrapped up in the usual caveats about making an angel food cake. It's really not difficult and, to carry the pun a bit further, the rewards are heavenly.

Chocolate Angel Food Cake

Preparation time: 20 minutes
Baking time: 30 to 35 minutes
Yield: One 10-inch cake

1½ cups superfine sugar (10½ ounces)
¾ cup cake flour (3 ounces)
¼ cup cocoa, preferably Dutch process
2 cups egg whites (about 16 large)
1½ teaspoons cream of tartar
1 teaspoon pure vanilla extract
¼ teaspoon salt
Chocolate Glaze (recipe follows)

1. 15 minutes before baking, place the rack in the center of the oven and preheat oven to 375 degrees. Have an ungreased 10-inch tube pan ready.

2. Divide the sugar in half. Sift one half 3 times. Set aside. Sift the other half of the sugar with the flour and cocoa 3 times. Set aside.

3. Put the egg whites in a 4-quart grease-free bowl and beat on low speed with a mixer until they are foamy. Add the cream of tartar, vanilla and salt and gradually increase the speed to medium. Add the ¾ cup of sugar, one tablespoon at a time, beating well after each addition, then continue to beat on medium speed until the whites have increased in volume about fivefold and hold their shape but are still shiny and moist. Gently but thoroughly fold in the flour mixture, by thirds.

4. Transfer to the baking pan. Smooth the surface with a rubber spatula and cut through the batter in 5 or 6 places to break any large air pockets. Bake until a toothpick inserted in the center comes out clean, 30 to 35 minutes. Invert over a narrow-necked bottle and cool completely.

5. When cake is completely cool, loosen it from the sides of the pan with a knife and invert onto a rack. Frost with Chocolate Glaze. This cake should not be reheated.

Chocolate Glaze 1

Preparation time: 5 minutes
Cooking time: 5 minutes (Microwave: 3 minutes)

8 ounces semisweet
  chocolate, broken in
  pieces
1 stick unsalted butter
¼ cup water

1. Cook the chocolate, butter and water in the top of a double boiler over gently simmering water, stirring often, until smooth. *Or,* to make the glaze in the food processor, melt the butter with the water and keep boiling hot; process the chocolate with the metal blade until it is as fine as possible. Pour the hot butter and water through the feed tube and process until chocolate is melted and smooth.

2. Let the glaze stand at room temperature until it is cool and slightly thickened.

MICROWAVE: Combine the chocolate, butter and water in a medium microwave-safe bowl. Cook, uncovered, on high power (100%) until smooth, 2 to 3 minutes, stirring once a minute.

CAKES AND COOKIES •

Some cakes are just too tempting, too irresistible for me to have in my kitchen. This is one of them—fragrant, moist, rich and very good-tasting. And if this wasn't enough, the glaze absolutely unravels me. My resistance crumbles and one bite always leads to another. So I make it when there are guests coming for dinner, and I make sure they carry away any leftovers.

___Spiced Applesauce Cake with Caramel Glaze___

Preparation time: 20 minutes
Baking time: 50 minutes
Yield: 1 9-inch cake

1. 15 minutes before baking, place the rack in the center of the oven and preheat oven to 350 degrees. Butter a 9-inch springform pan, dust lightly with flour and tap it to remove the excess.

2. To make the cake in a food processor, process both sugars and eggs until light, about 1 minute, stopping once to scrape down the sides of the work bowl. Cut the butter or margarine into tablespoon-size pieces and add them to the work bowl. Process 1 minute, stopping once to scrape down the sides of the work bowl. Add the applesauce and sour cream and process 5 seconds. Add the flour, cinnamon, baking soda, allspice, cloves, salt, walnuts and currants. Pulse twice. Run a spatula around sides of the work bowl, then pulse 1 to 2 more times, just until combined. Do not overprocess.

3. To make with a mixer, cream both sugars and butter or margarine on high speed until fluffy. Add the eggs, one at a time, and mix for 1 minute. Mix in applesauce and sour cream on medium speed. Mince the walnuts and add them along with the currants. Stir the flour, cinnamon, baking soda, allspice, cloves and salt together and mix into batter.

4. Transfer batter to prepared pan. Place the springform pan on a baking sheet. Bake until a toothpick inserted in center comes out clean, about 50 minutes. While cake is baking, prepare the Broiled Caramel Glaze.

5. When the cake is baked, place the springform pan, still on the baking sheet, on a wire rack. Let the cake cool for 5 minutes. Spread glaze over the surface, letting it drip down between the cake and the sides of the pan. Broil the cake for 4 to 8 minutes, watching closely and rotating the cake as necessary until the entire surface is bubbly. Let rest on a wire rack for 10 minutes,

1 cup sugar (7 ounces)
½ cup firmly packed dark brown sugar (4 ounces)
2 large eggs
1½ sticks unsalted butter or margarine, softened
1¼ cups unsweetened applesauce
½ cup sour cream
2 cups cake flour (8 ounces)
2 teaspoons cinnamon
1½ teaspoons baking soda
1 teaspoon ground allspice
½ teaspoon ground cloves
½ teaspoon salt
¾ cup toasted walnuts (see page 338)
¾ cup dried currants (3¾ ounces)
Broiled Caramel Glaze (recipe follows)

then remove the sides from the pan. If any glaze drips onto the baking sheet, spread it over the sides of the cake. The cake is best served slightly warm.

Broiled Caramel Glaze

Preparation time: 5 minutes
Cooking time: 5 minutes (Microwave: 4 minutes)

5 tablespoons unsalted butter or margarine
5 tablespoons whipping cream
½ cup firmly packed dark brown sugar (4 ounces)

Cook the butter or margarine, cream and sugar in a small pan until mixture is no longer grainy, about 5 minutes.

MICROWAVE: Combine the butter or margarine, cream and sugar in a 4-cup microwave measuring cup and cook, uncovered, on high power (100%) until mixture is slightly thickened, 4 minutes, stirring once halfway through.

This cake reminds me of a chocolate chip cookie lusciously transformed into a big, soft cake. The list of ingredients is long, but they are easy to assemble and the cake isn't at all hard to make. It transports very easily so it's ideal for picnics and beach parties, potluck and housewarming occasions.

Chocolate Chip Cookie Cake

Preparation time: 15 minutes
Baking time: 40 minutes
Yield: 1 9-inch square cake

1. 15 minutes before baking, place the rack in the center of the oven and preheat oven to 350 degrees. Butter a 9-inch square pan.

2. For the streusel, work the butter into the sugar and flour until the butter is in small pieces. This can be done in a food processor or with a pastry blender.

3. For the cake, stir the sour cream and baking soda together and set aside.

4. To make the cake in a processor, process the butter, sugar and eggs 2 minutes, stopping once to scrape down the sides of the work bowl. Add the sour cream, Kahlua and vanilla and process 10 seconds. Remove the cover and scrape down the sides of the work bowl. Add, in this order, the flour, baking powder, salt, semisweet morsels and pecans in a ring onto batter. Pulse 3 times. Run a spatula around the sides of the work bowl and pulse 3 to 4 times, just until the flour disappears.

5. To make in a mixer, cream the butter and sugar on high speed until light. Add the eggs, one at a time, and mix well. Mix in the sour cream, Kahlua and vanilla on medium speed. Fold the flour, baking powder and salt into the batter. Chop the pecans and add them to the batter along with the semisweet morsels.

6. Spread batter evenly in the prepared pan and sprinkle the streusel evenly over the top. Bake until a toothpick inserted in the center comes out clean, about 40 minutes. Serve warm or at room temperature.

Note: The liqueur can be omitted, if desired.

STREUSEL:
- 2 tablespoons unsalted butter or margarine, chilled, cut in 3 pieces
- ¼ cup sugar
- 2½ tablespoons unbleached all-purpose flour

CAKE:
- 1¼ cups sour cream
- 1 teaspoon baking soda
- 10½ tablespoons unsalted butter or margarine, softened, cut in 5 pieces
- 1 cup sugar (7 ounces)
- 2 large eggs
- 1 tablespoon Kahlua or other coffee-flavored liqueur (see Note)
- 2 teaspoons pure vanilla extract
- 2 cups unbleached all-purpose flour (10 ounces)
- 1½ teaspoons baking powder
- ½ teaspoon salt
- 1 cup semisweet chocolate morsels (6 ounces)
- ¾ cup pecans (3 ounces)

These are the cookies I remember most fondly from my childhood days. Nothing pleased me more than to come home from school and find a plate of these crisp little squares and a glass of milk awaiting me. After looking in every recipe book and file box, I finally found my mother's recipe for them, adapted from a pamphlet published by, of all things, the Massachusetts Gas Company.

Brown Sugar Butterscotch Bars

Preparation time: 15 minutes
Baking time: 18 minutes plus 10 minutes resting time
Yield: 54 2-inch squares

1 large egg, separated
1 cup firmly packed light brown sugar (8 ounces)
2 sticks unsalted butter, softened
⅛ teaspoon salt
2 cups unbleached all-purpose flour (10 ounces)
1 cup minced pecans (4 ounces)

1. 15 minutes before baking, place the rack in the center of the oven and preheat oven to 350 degrees. Have an ungreased 12-inch by 18-inch pan ready.

2. To make the cookies in a food processor, process the egg white for 5 seconds, until foamy. Set aside in a small dish. In the same work bowl—it is not necessary to wash it—process the sugar, butter, salt and egg yolk until smooth, about 1 minute, stopping once to scrape down the sides of the work bowl. Spoon the flour evenly over the batter and pulse the machine on and off just until combined, about 4 to 5 times. Do not overprocess. Skip to step 4.

3. To make the cookies with a mixer, stir the egg white with a fork until foamy. Set aside. Cream the sugar and butter on high speed until smooth. Mix in the egg yolk and salt, then the flour.

4. Spoon the dough into the pan. Working through a piece of plastic—a small food bag is ideal—press the dough into a thin, even layer. Brush with egg white and sprinkle with pecans.

5. Bake until the dough is set in the center, about 18 minutes. Remove from the oven and cut into 2-inch squares, in the pan, while still hot. Turn off the oven and return the pan to the oven to allow the squares to dry for 10 minutes. Remove from the oven and cool completely before removing from the pan.

These are just plain good old-fashioned cookie-jar cookies, nicely flavored with just the right blend of spices.

Buttery Gingersnaps

Preparation time: 20 minutes
Baking time: 12 minutes per batch
Yield: 36 2½-inch cookies

1. 15 minutes before baking, place the rack in the center of the oven and preheat oven to 350 degrees. Have ungreased cookie sheet(s) ready.

2. To make the cookies in a food processor, mince the ginger by turning on the machine and dropping it through the feed tube. Add the sugar and process for 30 seconds so the ginger is as fine as possible. Add the butter, egg white, molasses, cinnamon, cloves, ginger and salt and process for 1 minute, stopping once to scrape down the sides of the bowl. Stop the machine and add the flour and baking soda. Pulse 3 to 4 times, just until the flour is mixed in. Do not overprocess.

3. To make the cookies with a mixer, mince the ginger and set it aside. Cream the sugar and butter on high speed until fluffy. Reduce to low speed and add the egg white and molasses and mix well, then add the flour, baking soda, cinnamon, cloves, ginger and salt.

4. Measure 1 level tablespoon of dough for each cookie and shape into balls. Roll in sugar and place on the baking sheet, leaving a 2-inch space between each one. Dip the bottom of a glass in sugar and press each ball to a 2½-inch round.

5. Bake until set, about 12 minutes. Cool on the baking sheet for 1 minute, then transfer cookies to a wire rack and cool completely. The cookies can be stored in an airtight container and held at room temperature for up to a week, or they can be frozen.

1 small piece fresh ginger (½-inch cube)
½ cup plus 2 tablespoons sugar (4 ounces)
1½ sticks unsalted butter, softened
1 large egg white
2 tablespoons molasses
1¼ teaspoons cinnamon
1¼ teaspoons ground cloves
1¼ teaspoons ground ginger
¼ teaspoon salt
1¾ cups plus 2 tablespoons unbleached all-purpose flour (9½ ounces)
1 teaspoon baking soda
Sugar, for rolling

Cooking is always challenging—but easy? Not always. It took me two full months working with dogged determination to develop a recipe that would turn my dream of a lemon cookie into an irresistible reality. Here it is, a thin, crisp, sugar-coated cookie, full of sunny, fresh lemon flavor. These are delicious as a light dessert, either by themselves or with fresh fruit or sherbet.

Lemon Sparkle Cookies

Preparation time: 20 minutes
Baking time: 7 minutes per batch
Yield: About 2 dozen 3-inch cookies

LEMON SUGAR:
2/3 *cup sugar (4 2/3 ounces)*
    Zest of 1 lemon, removed
    with a vegetable peeler
    (see Note)

COOKIES:
2/3 *cup blanched almonds (3*
    ounces)
1/2 *cup plus 2 tablespoons*
    unbleached all-purpose
    flour (3 ounces)
 1 *teaspoon cream of tartar*
1/2 *teaspoon baking soda*
1/8 *teaspoon salt*
    Zest of 2 lemons,
    removed with a
    vegetable peeler
1/3 *cup sugar (2 1/3 ounces)*
 1 *stick unsalted butter,*
    softened

1. 15 minutes before baking, place the rack in the center of the oven and preheat to 350 degrees. Have ungreased baking sheet(s) ready.

2. For the lemon sugar, mix the 2/3 cup sugar and zest of 1 lemon in a food processor or blender until the zest is almost as fine as the sugar. Set aside.

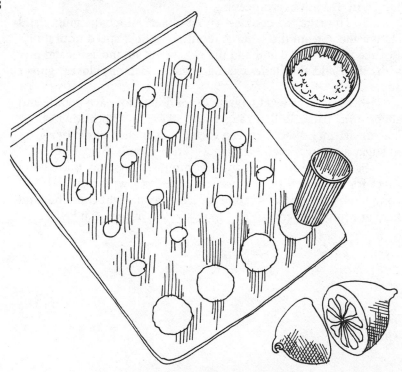

3. For the cookies, combine the almonds, flour, cream of tartar, baking soda and salt in the processor or blender and pulverize the nuts. Set aside.

4. Put the zest of the 2 lemons and the ⅓ cup sugar in the processor or blender and run the machine until the zest is almost as fine as the sugar.

5. If you're using a processor, leave the zest-sugar mixture in the work bowl and add the butter. Process until smooth, 1 minute, stopping once to scrape down the sides of the work bowl. Add the flour-nut mixture and process just until combined.

6. To finish cookies with a mixer, cream the sugar and butter until smooth. Mix in the flour-nut mixture.

7. Using a measuring spoon, measure 2 level teaspoons of dough for each cookie and roll into a ball. Place on baking sheet(s), spacing them 2½ inches apart. Flatten to a 2-inch circle with the bottom of a glass dipped in the lemon sugar. Sprinkle tops with additional lemon sugar so they are well coated.

8. Bake until cookies are golden around the edges, about 7 minutes. Let cool on baking sheet 1 minute, then carefully transfer cookies to a wire rack to cool completely. The cookies can be stored in an airtight container for up to a week.

Note: Use a vegetable peeler to remove all the zest (colored part) from the lemons. A zester or grater will not remove enough of the zest to give the cookies a tart/puckery flavor.

How do you decide which brownie to make from the thousands of recipes there are for them? If you love dense, rich, moist and fudgey brownies, your search is over. This is the recipe for you.

Double Fudge Brownies

Preparation time: 15 minutes
Baking time: 50 minutes
Yield: 36 1½-inch squares

8 ounces semisweet chocolate, broken in pieces
¾ cup sugar (5¼ ounces)
1½ sticks unsalted butter or margarine, softened
2 large eggs
1 tablespoon pure vanilla extract
¾ cup pecan or walnut halves (3 ounces)
¼ cup unbleached all-purpose flour (1¼ ounces)
¼ teaspoon baking powder
¼ teaspoon salt
¾ cup semisweet chocolate morsels (4½ ounces)

1. 15 minutes before baking, place the rack in the center of the oven and preheat oven to 325 degrees. Butter a 9-inch square pan.

2. To make in a food processor, process the chocolate and sugar until the chocolate is as fine as the sugar. Add the butter, eggs and vanilla and process for 1 minute, stopping once to scrape down the sides of the work bowl. Add, in this order, the nuts, flour, baking powder, salt and semisweet morsels. Pulse the machine on and off just until the ingredients are combined, 2 to 3 times. Skip to step 5.

3. To make by hand, melt the chocolate in a double boiler over gently simmering water or in a microwave oven on medium power (50%), stirring several times until smooth. Cool slightly. Mince the nuts.

4. Beat the sugar, eggs, butter and vanilla with a mixer until smooth. Mix in the melted chocolate, then the semisweet morsels, the nuts, flour, baking powder and salt.

5. Transfer batter to prepared pan and smooth the surface with a spatula. Bake until set in center, but still moist, about 50 minutes. Cool completely before cutting. Store in an airtight container for several days, or freeze.

"Irresistible," "delicate" and "rich" are the best words to describe these little morsels. Buttery, crumbly shortbread tartlets are punctuated with a jot of raspberry preserves and covered with a shower of confectioners' sugar.

Viennese Crumb Cakes

Preparation time: 20 minutes
Baking time: 22 minutes
Yield: 24 1-inch cakes

1. Place the rack in the center of the oven and preheat oven to 350 degrees. Have ready 2 miniature muffin pans (for muffins 1 inch by 1½ inches). If you have only 1 pan, bake in 2 batches.

2. Chop the chilled butter and the sugar in a food processor or with a pastry blender until the butter is the size of small peas. Add the sour cream, vanilla and salt and mix just enough to moisten the dough. Sprinkle the flour over the top and mix until the dough is uniformly granular. It will still be crumbly.

3. Spoon a generous 1½ tablespoons crumbs into each muffin cup and press with your fingers to lightly compress the dough and neaten the edges.

4. Bake until the cakes just begin to turn gold around the edges, 20 to 22 minutes.

5. While they are still hot, make a small, round indentation —about the diameter of a pencil—in the center of each cake. You can wrap the eraser end of a pencil in foil for this. Fill with about ¼ teaspoon preserves. Let cakes cool in the pan(s) for 10 minutes, then carefully transfer them to a wire rack, loosening them with a small knife, if necessary. Cool completely. When cool, they can be held at room temperature in an airtight container for several days, or frozen.

6. Shortly before serving, sift confectioners' sugar over top.

1½ *sticks unsalted butter, chilled, cut in 12 pieces*
¼ *cup sugar (1¾ ounces)*
1 *tablespoon sour cream*
1 *teaspoon pure vanilla extract*
¼ *teaspoon salt*
1½ *cups unbleached all-purpose flour (7½ ounces)*
2 *tablespoons raspberry preserves*
2 *tablespoons confectioners' sugar*

Offer me a candy bar or a cookie and I'm stuck with a moment of delicious indecision. I want both. Here's my solution—a great cross between an irresistible cookie and a gooey, rich candy bar. The filling, nested in a buttery shortbread base, is an unspeakably rich mixture of brown sugar, maple syrup and lots of pecans.

Caramel Pecan Candy Bar Cookies

Preparation time: 20 minutes
Baking time: 70 minutes total, plus 20 minutes cooling
Yield: 36 1½ inch squares

CRUST:
1½ sticks unsalted butter, chilled
1½ cups unbleached all-purpose flour (10 ounces)
¼ cup sugar (1¾ ounces)
¼ teaspoon salt

FILLING:
1¼ cups firmly packed light brown sugar (10 ounces)
⅔ cup pure maple syrup
2 large eggs
4 tablespoons unsalted butter, melted
2 teaspoons bourbon or pure vanilla extract
¼ teaspoon salt
2 cups pecans (8 ounces)

1. 15 minutes before baking, place the rack in the center of the oven and preheat oven to 350 degrees. Have an ungreased 9-inch square pan ready.

2. For the crust, cut the butter into tablespoon-size pieces. Work it into the flour, sugar and salt in a food processor or with a pastry blender until the butter is the size of small peas. It should still be crumbly.

3. Pat the crumbs into the bottom of the pan and ½ inch up the sides. Bake until crust begins to color, about 20 minutes. Cool for 20 minutes before filling.

4. For the filling, mix the brown sugar, maple syrup, eggs, butter, bourbon or vanilla and salt in a processor or with a mixer until smooth. Mix in the pecans.

5. Pour the filling into the crust. Bake until set, 45 to 50 minutes. Cool completely, then refrigerate until they are firm enough to cut. Cut into 1½-inch squares. Can be made in advance and refrigerated in an airtight container for up to 4 days, or frozen for 3 months.

These little cookies are so tender and light they almost melt in your mouth. They're delicately spiced with cardamom, a typical Scandinavian flavoring in baking. Its taste and aroma are distinctive and delicious, and so, too, are these cookies.

Swedish Snowballs

Preparation time: 15 minutes
Baking time: 12 minutes per batch
Yield: 3½ to 4 dozen

1. 15 minutes before baking, place the rack in the center of the oven and preheat oven to 350 degrees. Have ungreased cookie sheet(s) ready.

2. Mix the sugar, egg yolk, butter, vanilla, cardamom and salt until light and fluffy in a food processor or with a mixer.

3. Add the flour and mix just until combined. If you're using a processor, do this by pulsing it on and off. Do not overmix the dough once the flour has been added.

4. Roll dough into balls, using about 2 measuring teaspoons of dough for each. Place on cookie sheet(s), spacing balls 1½ inches apart.

5. Bake until the cookies are set but not yet colored, about 12 minutes. Transfer cookies to a wire rack and cool for 10 minutes.

6. Place the wire rack, with the cookies on it, over a piece of wax paper. Sift a heavy coating of confectioners' sugar evenly over them. Cool completely, then store in airtight containers for up to 4 days or freeze up to 3 months. You may wish to sift confectioners' sugar over them a second time, just before serving.

¾ cup firmly packed dark brown sugar (6 ounces)
1 large egg yolk
2 sticks unsalted butter, softened, each stick cut into 4 pieces
1 teaspoon pure vanilla extract
½ teaspoon ground cardamom
⅛ teaspoon salt
2 cups unbleached all-purpose flour (10 ounces)
1 cup confectioners' sugar (4 ounces)

Jim Dodge, pastry chef at the Stanford Court Hotel in San Francisco, and author of *The American Baker*, stole my heart with this recipe. Luscious morsels of dense, dark, rich chocolate almond cake are cut into whimsical little heart shapes (or any other shape, for that matter) and glazed with high-gloss chocolate. A scoop of ice cream, a puddle of raspberry sauce or a big dollop of whipped cream are delicious embellishments, though heaven knows they don't need anything to make them richer or more sumptuous.

To personalize the hearts, melt white chocolate and pipe messages or decorations on them when the chocolate glaze has hardened.

Chocolate Sweethearts

Preparation time: 20 minutes
Baking time: 20 minutes
Yield: 8 2½-inch hearts

8 ounces almond paste, preferably Blue Diamond or Odense brand
2 sticks unsalted butter, softened
¾ cup Dutch process cocoa (2¼ ounces)
¼ cup confectioners' sugar (1 ounce)
3 large eggs
Chocolate Glaze 2 (recipe follows)

1. 15 minutes before baking, place the rack in the center of the oven and preheat oven to 350 degrees. Butter a 9-inch round cake pan. Fit the bottom with a circle of parchment paper. Butter and flour the paper and tap out the excess flour.

2. Mix the almond paste, butter, cocoa and sugar until completely smooth, either in a food processor for 2 minutes or with a mixer for 3 minutes.

3. With the processor or mixer on, add the eggs, one at a time, and mix thoroughly.

4. Transfer to the prepared pan and smooth the top with a spatula. Bake until set in the center and just beginning to pull away from the sides of the pan, about 20 minutes. Cool completely, then carefully loosen from sides of pan with a small knife. Invert onto a piece of plastic, wrap and refrigerate overnight.

5. The next day, remove cake from refrigerator. Cut a 2½-inch heart shape from heavy paper or cardboard to use as a template. Place over the cake and use it to cut 8 hearts with a sharp paring knife. Or use a cookie cutter that is just the outline of a heart shape without a top. (See Note for a way to use the trimmings.) Press in any crumbs and neaten the shapes. Transfer to a wire rack placed over a sheet of wax paper.

6. Make the glaze. Pour it over hearts while it is still warm, letting it run down the sides. Tap the rack on the counter several times to smooth glaze. Let the glaze set before serving.

Note: Make the trimmings into Brownie Truffles as follows: Put the scraps in a food processor with 2 tablespoons whipping cream, ⅓ cup confectioners' sugar and 1 teaspoon pure vanilla extract or brandy, and process until smooth. Transfer to a small dish and refrigerate until the mixture is firm and no longer sticky. Roll into bite-size balls, then coat with unsweetened cocoa powder or confectioners' sugar. Refrigerate or freeze until serving time.

Chocolate Glaze 2

Preparation time: 5 minutes
Cooking time: 5 minutes (Microwave: 2 minutes)

8 ounces bittersweet or
semisweet chocolate,
broken in pieces
1 stick unsalted butter

Melt the chocolate with the butter in the top of a double boiler over gently simmering water, stirring often. Pour onto the Chocolate Sweethearts while the glaze is still warm.

MICROWAVE: Put the chocolate and butter in a microwave dish. Cook on high power (100%) until smooth, about 2 minutes, stirring once after 1 minute.

Toasted coconut filling tops off crisp brown sugar bar cookies that are as enticing from the cookie tin as they are from the freezer.

Chewy Coconut Bars

Preparation time: 20 minutes
Baking time: 50 minutes
Yield: About 16 2-inch bars

1. 15 minutes before baking, place the rack in the center of the oven and preheat oven to 325 degrees. Have a 9-inch square baking pan ready.

2. Spread the coconut on a jelly roll pan and bake in the preheated oven until most of it is lightly browned, about 7 minutes, stirring several times. Watch carefully so it does not burn. *Or*, to make in a microwave oven, spread coconut on a paper plate and cook on high power (100%) for 2 minutes. Stir well, then cook 1½ minutes longer, stirring every 20 seconds.

3. For the crust, mix the flour, brown sugar and butter in a food processor or with a pastry blender until crumbly. Lightly pat into the pan. Bake until lightly browned, about 30 minutes.

4. Make the filling while the crust is baking. Mix the brown sugar, flour, eggs, vanilla, baking powder and salt. If using a processor, use the same bowl the crust was mixed in.

5. Pour the filling on the crust, then sprinkle with the coconut. Bake until golden, about 20 minutes. Cool completely, then cut in 2-inch squares. Can be made in advance and held at room temperature in an airtight container for 4 days, or frozen.

1½ cups sweetened, flaked coconut

CRUST:
1 cup unbleached all-purpose flour (5 ounces)
¼ cup firmly packed light brown sugar (2 ounces)
1 stick unsalted butter, chilled

FILLING:
¾ cup firmly packed light brown sugar (6 ounces)
2 tablespoons unbleached all-purpose flour
2 large eggs
1 teaspoon pure vanilla extract
½ teaspoon baking powder
⅛ teaspoon salt

13 · Desserts and Pies

Calories don't always count, even in these days of dietary prudence. Consider desserts, the most enduringly popular part of a meal. Celebratory meals are often finished with the flourish of a special homemade dessert. Even at less important meals, the need to indulge calls for something delicious and sinful, two good reasons why a cook's repertoire can never include too many desserts. While my own sweet tooth doesn't run rampantly, it does surface on occasion, and I have no qualms about sating it in an appropriate fashion. As for entertaining, even on the most modest or casual scale, it seems less than gracious not to end the meal with some sort of a dessert.

Fresh fruit is a very popular dessert choice, and with good reason. It matches the desire for fresh, light foods with the unquenchable yen for a sweet ending to the meal. Taking my cues from the season, I often offer a bowl of mixed berries, poached oranges or pineapple in a simple syrup. A sauce dresses these up, as does a bowl of softly whipped cream, lightly sweetened and flavored with vanilla or liqueur. At other times, I can't resist the urge to make a more elaborate dessert. Such a dessert is undeniably festive and conveys that same spirit to one's guests.

The recipes I have included are not difficult to reproduce, nor do they require a great expenditure of time in the kitchen. This is a collection of some of my favorites, recipes I turn to as the need or the notion arises. They are homey and comfortable desserts, and guests adore them.

Even something as sybaritic as dessert can be practical, and I have sought to focus on that aspect whenever possible. With some rare (and worthy!) exceptions like hot soufflés, I am presenting a collection of dessert recipes that don't require lots of last-minute attention. Saucing and serving the dessert attractively is usually all that needs to be tended to at the last minute.

A homey, old-fashioned and downright delicious dessert, served warm with a big scoop of ice cream and Caramel Butter Sauce.

Granny Apple Crisp

Preparation time: 20 minutes
Baking time: 40 to 50 minutes
Yield: 8 servings

1. 15 minutes before baking, place the rack in the center of the oven and preheat oven to 375 degrees. Have a 6-cup ceramic, glass or terra-cotta pie plate ready.

2. For the topping, cut the butter into 8 pieces. Work it into the flour, ¼ cup granulated sugar, all the brown sugar, oats, ¾ teaspoon cinnamon and a pinch of salt until the butter is the size of small peas. This can be done in a food processor or with a pastry blender. Stir in the hazelnuts.

3. Peel the apples, halve lengthwise and remove the cores with a melon baller. Cut into ¼-inch slices, either with the all-purpose (4mm) slicer of a processor or by hand. Toss with the remaining ¼ to ½ cup of sugar and the remaining ¼ teaspoon cinnamon. The amount of sugar depends on how tart the apples are; the filling shouldn't be too sweet.

4. Transfer the apples to the baking dish, mounding them in the center. Spoon the topping over and pat into place. Bake until the apples are tender, but not soft, and the top is golden brown, 40 to 50 minutes. Test by piercing the apples with a paring knife. Serve warm with a scoop of ice cream and warm Caramel Butter Sauce. The crisp can be baked in advance and refrigerated for 2 days. To reheat, place in a cold oven and turn up to 325 degrees. Bake until heated through, about 20 minutes.

1 stick unsalted butter, chilled
½ cup unbleached all-purpose flour (5 ounces)
½ to ¾ cup granulated sugar (3½ to 5¼ ounces)
¼ cup light brown sugar (2 ounces)
¼ cup rolled oats (¾ ounce)
1 teaspoon cinnamon
Pinch of salt
¾ cup toasted, minced hazelnuts (see page 338)
6 large tart apples, (2¼ pounds total) such as Granny Smith, Jonathan, Cortland or McIntosh
Vanilla ice cream
Caramel Butter Sauce (see page 315)

Clafouti, a rustic, peasant-style French dessert, is traditionally made with cherries suspended in a light, crêpe-like batter. I've added plums and an optional handful of raspberries for an especially delicious rendition. It's meant to be served warm, but leftovers can be served from the refrigerator or reheated.

The microwave oven does an admirable job at cooking the Clafouti in a scant fraction of the time, yielding a softer, more custardlike center than when it is baked in the conventional oven.

Red Fruit Clafouti

FRUIT:
- 12 ounces Bing cherries
- 5 red plums (12 ounces total)
- Zest of 1 orange, removed with a grater
- ⅓ cup sugar (2⅓ ounces)
- 2½ tablespoons kirsch
- 1 tablespoon balsamic vinegar
- ½ cup raspberries, optional

BATTER:
- Milk (fruit liquid from above plus milk to equal 1 cup)
- ½ cup unbleached all-purpose flour (2½ ounces)
- ¼ to ⅓ cup sugar, depending on the sweetness of the plums (1¾ to 2⅓ ounces)
- 3 large eggs
- 2 tablespoons pure vanilla extract
- Pinch of salt
- ¼ teaspoon cinnamon
- Confectioners' sugar

Preparation time: 20 minutes
Marinating time: 1 hour
Baking time: 50 to 55 minutes (Microwave: 16 minutes)
Yield: 6 servings

1. To prepare the fruit, halve and pit the cherries and plums, then quarter the plums. Put both in a bowl with the sugar, orange zest, kirsch and vinegar. Toss gently and marinate for 1 hour. Drain the fruit in a strainer placed over a measuring cup and reserve the liquid.

2. 15 minutes before baking, place the rack in the center of the oven and preheat oven to 325 degrees. Butter a shallow, round 6- to 8-cup baking dish, preferably ceramic.

3. Add milk to the fruit liquid to measure 1 cup. Mix with the flour, sugar, eggs, vanilla and salt in a food processor or blender until smooth.

4. Arrange the plums and cherries, cut side down, in the baking dish. Slowly pour in the batter. Scatter the raspberries over the top, if using, and sift cinnamon over all.

5. Bake until set in center, 50 to 55 minutes. Serve warm or at room temperature with confectioners' sugar sifted over the top. Can be reheated in a preheated 325-degree oven for 10 minutes.

MICROWAVE: Butter a 6-cup microwave-safe ring mold. Follow steps 1, 3 and 4 above, but omit the raspberries, which do not do well in the microwave adaptation. Cook, uncovered, on medium power (50%) until set, about 16 minutes. It is okay if there are a few moist spots on top—they will set as it cools. This is best served the day it is made. Serve warm or at room temperature. To reheat, cook, uncovered, on medium power for 5 minutes.

Here, bread and butter pudding takes on a holiday air. The flavors of the best holiday beverage—brandy, vanilla and lots of freshly grated nutmeg—are used to flavor the rich custard. Another seasonal enhancement, Cranberry Maple Sauce (see page 314), shimmers over the top.

Eggnog Bread Pudding

Preparation time: 15 minutes
Baking time: 60 minutes (Microwave: 12 minutes)
Yield: 6 to 8 servings

1. 15 minutes before baking, place the rack in the center of the oven and preheat to 350 degrees. Butter a 6-cup soufflé dish. Have a kettle of boiling water ready and a baking pan large enough to hold the soufflé dish.

2. Whisk the eggs, egg yolk and sugar until light. Mix in the butter, the half-and-half, brandy, vanilla, nutmeg and salt.

3. Place the bread in the soufflé dish and pour the custard over it. Press the bread into the custard so it gets well-soaked.

4. Put the soufflé dish in the baking pan and place on the oven rack. Pour boiling water into the baking pan so it comes halfway up the sides of the soufflé dish. Bake until the custard is softly set in the center, about 1 hour. Remove from the water bath.

5. Serve warm or at room temperature with Cranberry Maple Sauce. Once cooled, the pudding can be refrigerated for up to 3 days. To reheat, cover with aluminum foil with several slits in it. Bake in a preheated 350-degree oven for 20 minutes.

MICROWAVE: Skip steps 1 through 5. Put the half-and-half and butter in a 4-cup glass measuring cup and cook on high power (100%) until hot, 2 minutes. Whisk the eggs, egg yolk, sugar, nutmeg and salt until light. Slowly pour in the hot half-and-half, whisking as you do. Return to the measuring cup and cook on medium power (50%) until slightly thickened, about 2 minutes. Stir in the brandy and vanilla. Put the bread in a 6-cup microwave soufflé dish and pour the custard over. Press the bread into the custard so it gets well-soaked. Cover with wax paper and cook on medium power until it is almost set in the center, about 8 minutes. Let rest at least 10 minutes before serving. Broil, if desired, to

3 large eggs
1 large egg yolk
¾ cup sugar (5¼ ounces)
4 tablespoons unsalted butter, melted
1¾ cups half-and-half
3 tablespoons brandy
2 tablespoons pure vanilla extract
¾ teaspoon freshly grated nutmeg
⅛ teaspoon salt
6 slices dry cinnamon raisin bread (5 ounces total), quartered
Cranberry Maple Sauce (see page 314)

brown the top. Or sift cinnamon over the top. Serve warm or at room temperature with Cranberry Maple Sauce. To reheat, cover with wax paper and cook on medium power for about 4 minutes.

◆

A luscious mix of citrus-scented fresh and dried fruits is wrapped in multiple layers of flaky phyllo dough. Even the uninitiated will find phyllo dough surprisingly easy to work with, and the results very satisfying. Fresh phyllo dough is your best bet, but hard to find. Frozen is excellent, too. The strudel is large, so you may want to cut it in half and freeze part. It's nice to have it on hand for another time.

——— Winter Fruit Strudel ———

Preparation time: 20 minutes
Baking time: 30 minutes
Yield: 1 16-inch or 2 8-inch strudels

½ cup pitted prunes (3 ounces)

½ cup dried apricots (3 ounces)

¼ cup orange juice

¼ cup strongly brewed orange-spiced tea

3 tablespoons sugar

2 -inch piece vanilla bean

2 small tart apples (8 ounces total)

¼ cup dried currants (1½ ounces)

¼ teaspoon freshly grated nutmeg

4 sheets phyllo dough, thawed if frozen

5 tablespoons unsalted butter, melted

½ cup graham cracker crumbs (3 crackers)

1. 15 minutes before baking, place the rack in the center of the oven and preheat oven to 350 degrees. Butter a jelly roll pan.

2. Cut the prunes and apricots into ⅓-inch dice. Cook over medium-low heat in a small, non-aluminum pan with the orange juice, tea, sugar and vanilla bean until no liquid remains, about 10 minutes. Or use a microwave oven: Combine the ingredients in a 3-cup microwave-safe dish. Cook on high power (100%) until no liquid remains, about 6½ minutes. Remove the vanilla bean.

3. While the prunes and apricots are cooking, peel, core and quarter the apples. Cut into ⅛-inch slices, either with the thin (2mm) slicer of a food processor or by hand.

4. Combine the hot cooked fruit with the apples, currants, and nutmeg.

5. Lay a sheet of plastic wrap that is 4 inches longer than the phyllo on the work surface. Lay 1 sheet of phyllo on the plastic and cover the remaining sheets with a damp towel so they don't dry out. Brush the sheet of phyllo with butter, then sprinkle with 2 tablespoons graham cracker crumbs. Cover with another sheet of phyllo, brush with butter, sprinkle with crumbs, and continue layering in that order, ending with crumbs.

6. Spoon the fruit mixture in a 2-inch wide row down the long side of the phyllo. Using the plastic wrap to help you, make one turn of the phyllo so the fruit is covered. Tuck fruit in and neaten roll, then finish rolling into a compact roll. Cut in half, if desired, and brush with melted butter. The strudel can be baked immediately or frozen for several months. To freeze, place on a baking sheet in freezer until solid. Double bag as explained on page 16 and return to freezer. Do not thaw before baking.

7. Bake until golden, about 30 minutes or slightly longer if frozen. Transfer to a wire rack. Slice with a serrated knife and serve warm or at room temperature.

◆

It's surprising how many people have never tasted homemade chocolate pudding and think of it only as a powdered mix in a little box. There's nothing quite like homemade, whether you eat it from a dish or use it as a filling for a pie or little tarts—creamy, soft and smooth, like satin on the tongue, with a rich, not too sweet chocolate flavor.

The recipe is prepared with the help of a food processor, which not only makes the job extra easy, but also guarantees a wonderfully smooth texture.

Chocolate Pudding

Preparation time: 10 minutes
Cooking time: 8 minutes (Microwave: 6½ minutes)
Yield: 4 to 6 servings

1¾ cups milk
¾ cup sugar (4¾ ounces)
¼ cup unsweetened cocoa powder (¾ ounce)
2 tablespoons cornstarch
1 large egg
2 large egg yolks
5 ounces bittersweet or semisweet chocolate
3 tablespoons unsalted butter
2 teaspoons pure vanilla extract

1. Bring 1½ cups milk and ¼ cup sugar to a boil.

2. Mix the remaining ½ cup sugar, cocoa and cornstarch in a food processor. Add the remaining ¼ cup of milk and mix to a smooth paste. With the processor running, add about 1 cup boiling milk. Return this mixture to the milk remaining in the pan.

3. Cook over medium-high heat, stirring often, until slightly thickened, about 2 minutes.

4. Mix the egg and yolks in a food processor, then pour about ½ cup of the hot chocolate mixture through the feed tube

while the processor is running. Whisk this mixture back into the rest of the chocolate mixture in the pan.

5. Cook over medium heat, stirring constantly, until thick enough to leave ridges, about 2 minutes longer. Set aside, off the heat.

6. Mince the chocolate in the processor until it is as fine as possible. Add the cooked mixture while it is still hot, add the butter and vanilla, and process until smooth, stopping as necessary to scrape down the sides of the work bowl with a rubber spatula.

7. Transfer to individual dishes and put a piece of plastic wrap directly on the surface of the pudding to keep a skin from forming. Refrigerate until well chilled, or up to 2 days. Serve with whipped cream if desired.

MICROWAVE: Put 1½ cups milk and ¼ cup sugar in a 4-cup glass measuring cup and cook on high power (100%) until hot, 2 minutes. Follow step 2. Cook on high until slightly thickened, about 1½ to 2 minutes. Follow step 4. Cook on high until thick, from 2 to 2½ minutes, stirring after 1 minute, then every 30 seconds. Finish as in steps 6 and 7.

Chocolate mousse has a seductive and sensual quality. If, as Maida Heatter says, chocolate is sexy, then this version from chef and owner Jean Louis Guerin of Jean Louis Restaurant in Greenwich, Connecticut, is the sexiest of all. You'd hardly expect to be served a plain mousse at such an extraordinary restaurant, so it's no surprise that it is served there with a pale gold, vanilla-scented custard sauce and a smattering of caramel sauce. A dollop of lightly sweetened whipped cream is a delicious alternative.

Bittersweet Chocolate Mousse Jean Louis

Preparation time: 20 minutes plus chilling time
Yield: 8 servings

1. Place the chocolate in the top of a double boiler over gently simmering water. Cook, stirring often, until melted. Or place in a glass dish and cook on medium power (50%) in a microwave oven, stirring several times, until fully melted, 3 to 4 minutes.
2. Beat the egg yolks and 1 teaspoon sugar with an electric mixer until they are thick and light-colored. Mix in the cream.
3. Whip the egg whites with the lemon juice and salt until foamy. Slowly add 2 tablespoons sugar and continue to beat just until the whites hold their shape, but are still creamy and moist. Fold in the remaining sugar with a large rubber spatula.
4. Thoroughly mix together the chocolate, the yolk mixture and half the egg whites; then gently fold in the remaining whites.
5. Transfer to a covered container. Refrigerate overnight or up to 2 days before serving.
6. To serve with the 2 sauces, spread 3 tablespoons Custard Sauce over bottom of dessert or salad plates. Carefully spoon a circle of Caramel Butter Sauce into a ring around the diameter of the plate, about ½ inch inside the edge of the custard sauce. Run a small, sharp knife through the Caramel Butter Sauce to make a design on the plate. Shape the mousse into ovals, using an oval ice cream scoop or 2 tablespoons, dipped in warm water. Arrange 3 ovals on each plate. Serve immediately.

8 ounces best-quality bittersweet chocolate, broken into pieces
3 large egg yolks
¼ cup sugar (1¾ ounces)
1½ tablespoons whipping cream
8 large egg whites
1 teaspoon fresh lemon juice
Pinch of salt
Custard Sauce (see page 321), optional
Caramel Butter Sauce (see page 315), optional

Desserts in bistros and brasseries tend to be simple and seasonal, often based on fruit. This recipe is typical of what you will find on such menus in the late fall and winter. Big, juicy pears are baked in a hot oven with a bit of butter and sugar so the juices caramelize. Served warm, they're set off with a dollop of cold *crème fraîche*. The contrast in both taste and temperature is sensational.

Caramel Baked Pears

2 large ripe Bartlett pears (1¼ pounds total)
2 tablespoons brandy
2 tablespoons sugar
1 tablespoon unsalted butter, melted
Crème fraîche or sour cream

Preparation time: 10 minutes
Baking time: 28 minutes (Microwave: 5 minutes plus 6 minutes broiling)
Yield: 4 servings

1. 15 minutes before baking, place the rack in the center of the oven and preheat to 450 degrees. Have a 9-inch pie plate ready.

2. Peel the pears, cut them in half lengthwise and remove the cores with a melon baller. Arrange pears in the pie plate with the tops pointing to the center.

3. Stir the brandy, sugar and butter together in a small dish. Brush over the pears.

4. Bake until the pears are just tender, about 22 minutes, brushing them once or twice with the syrup in the dish. Pears can be baked a day in advance, covered and refrigerated. Bring to room temperature before broiling.

5. Generously brush pears again with the syrup from the bottom of the dish, then broil, 6 inches from the heat, until glazed, 4 to 6 minutes. Serve hot or at room temperature with a dollop of crème fraîche or sour cream.

MICROWAVE: Follow steps 2 and 3 above, making sure to use a microwave-safe pie plate. Cook the pears, uncovered, on high power (100%) until tender, from 4 to 5 minutes, depending on how ripe they are. Finish the pears in a conventional oven, following the directions in step 5.

A delicate, fresh peach flavor and a diaphanously light texture make this a perfect conclusion to almost any summertime meal. The Caramel Peach Sauce is an exquisite complement.

Peach Mousse

Preparation time: 25 minutes (including thickening of the gelatin)
Cooking time: 6 minutes (Microwave: 2 minutes)
Chilling time: 3 hours
Yield: 6 servings

3 tablespoons fresh lemon juice
1¼ teaspoons unflavored gelatin
1 large, ripe peach (6 ounces)
3 large eggs, separated
⅓ cup sugar (2⅓ ounces)
½ teaspoon pure vanilla extract
¾ cup whipping cream
Caramel Peach Sauce (see page 318)

1. Put the lemon juice in a small dish and sprinkle the gelatin evenly over the surface. Let stand until the gelatin is moistened.

2. Peel the peach as follows: drop it into rapidly boiling water for 30 seconds to loosen the skin. Immediately transfer to cold water to stop the cooking. Slit the skin, peel, split and remove the pit. Purée the peach in a food processor or blender. You should have ½ cup purée. Mix with the egg yolks, sugar and vanilla in the processor or blender.

3. Transfer to the top of a double boiler over simmering water. Cook until the mixture is thick enough to coat the back of a wooden spoon, 4 to 6 minutes. Remove from the heat, add the gelatin mixture and stir until dissolved.

4. Refrigerate or freeze briefly, just until the mixture thickens but hasn't set, stirring several times. Watch carefully so the gelatin does not set.

5. Whip the egg whites with an electric mixer until they hold soft peaks. Whip the cream until it holds soft peaks. Whisk the peach mixture until it is smooth, then mix in ¼ the egg whites. Gently fold in the remaining whites, then the cream. Transfer to a 5-cup soufflé dish, cover and refrigerate until set, about 3 hours, or up to 1 day.

6. To serve, spread a pool of Caramel Peach Sauce over the bottom of individual serving plates. Rinse an oval ice cream scoop with warm water and scoop mousse onto the sauce. Serve immediately.

MICROWAVE: Follow steps 1 and 2. Place peach mixture in a 4-cup glass measuring cup and cook on high power (100%) for 2 minutes, stirring once halfway through. Remove from the oven, add the gelatin mixture and stir until dissolved. Finish steps 4, 5 and 6.

Baked soufflés are last-minute, to be sure, but they are so elegant that they're worth the extra effort. This one is puffy and lighter than air, delicately flavored with passion fruit juice. The center is very soft, almost like a sauce, while the edges bake to a soufflé-like texture. The last-minute work can be minimized by having everything all measured out and the dish prepared ahead of time.

Occasionally, fresh passion fruit shows up at the market, but expect to rely on canned. Some large supermarkets and specialty food stores stock pure passion fruit juice and it's often available through mail order. Just be sure you're not buying a sweetened blend. If you can't find passion fruit, try the lemon variation.

_____ Passion Fruit Soufflé _____

Preparation time: 15 minutes
Baking time: 13 minutes
Yield: 6 servings

5   tablespoons unsalted butter
9   tablespoons sugar (3¾ ounces)
7   tablespoons strained passion fruit juice or freshly squeezed lemon juice
4   large egg yolks
7   large egg whites
¼   teaspoon cream of tartar
1   tablespoon confectioners' sugar

1. 15 minutes before baking, place the rack in the center of the oven and preheat oven to 425 degrees. Use 1 tablespoon of the butter to butter a 6-cup soufflé dish, including the rim. Sprinkle the inside with 1 tablespoon of the sugar.

2. Bring the remaining butter and the passion fruit juice to a boil either on the stove top, in a non-aluminum pan or in the microwave oven.

3. Whisk 4 tablespoons sugar and the egg yolks in a large mixing bowl until light. Slowly whisk in the juice mixture.

4. Beat the egg whites with an electric mixer until they are foamy. Add the cream of tartar and continue beating them until they hold soft peaks. Add the remaining 4 tablespoons of sugar, one at a time, beating well after each addition, then continue to beat until whites are thick, glossy and moist.

5. Gently, but thoroughly, fold the whites into the yolk mixture. Transfer to the prepared dish and bake until golden brown, about 13 minutes. Sift confectioners' sugar over top and serve immediately. Make sure as you spoon them out that each portion includes some of the outer edge as well as the softer center.

A dreamy dessert that combines the comfort of a soft, old-fashioned custard with the warm taste of spiced pumpkin.

Indian Summer Pumpkin Flan

Preparation time: 15 minutes
Baking time: 35 minutes
Yield: 8 servings

1. 15 minutes before baking, place the rack in the center of the oven and preheat the oven to 350 degrees. Have ready a 6½-cup ring mold and a shallow baking pan large enough to hold it. Bring a large kettle of water to a boil.

2. Cook the granulated sugar and ⅛ teaspoon allspice in a small pan over high heat, stirring several times, until it is a rich, golden color and is completely smooth, 3 to 4 minutes. Immediately pour into the ring mold, turning the mold so the syrup coats the bottom. Set aside.

3. Whisk the pumpkin, brown sugar, eggs, remaining allspice, salt, and sour cream, until it is smooth. Add the cream, maple syrup and vanilla.

4. Pour into the ring mold. Place the ring mold in the larger baking pan and put on oven rack. Pour boiling water into outer pan to come halfway up sides of ring mold. Bake until the custard is set in the center but is not firm, about 35 minutes. It should still be soft when you take it from the oven as it will continue to cook. Remove from the water bath.

5. Cool to room temperature, then refrigerate at least 4 hours or up to 2 days before serving. Place a serving plate over ring mold, invert and place on the counter. Cover ring mold with a hot towel and let sit for 30 seconds before removing mold. The flan can be unmolded on a serving dish several hours before serving and held in the refrigerator.

Note: While many custards can be cooked in the microwave oven, this one did not produce consistently good results.

½ cup granulated sugar (3½ ounces)
1 teaspoon ground allspice
¾ cup canned solid-pack pumpkin
⅓ cup firmly packed light brown sugar (2⅔ ounces)
5 large eggs
½ teaspoon salt
½ cup sour cream
1 cup whipping cream
½ cup pure maple syrup
1 tablespoon pure vanilla extract

These are utterly charming little clusters of sliced phyllo dough, baked into lacy nests, topped with ice cream and a sauce that's reminiscent of baklava.

Baklava Sundaes

Preparation time: 15 minutes
Baking time: 9 minutes
Yield: 6 servings

PHYLLO NESTS:
- 6 *sheets phyllo dough, thawed, if frozen*
- 3 *tablespoons unsalted butter, melted*
- 2 *teaspoons sugar*
- ¼ *teaspoon cinnamon*
- 1 *pint coffee ice cream* Honey Walnut Sauce *(see page 313)*

1. 15 minutes before baking, place the rack in the center of the oven and preheat oven to 400 degrees. Have an ungreased jelly roll pan ready.

2. To make the phyllo nests, stack the 6 sheets of phyllo and fold them lengthwise into sixths. With a sharp knife, cut them into ⅛-inch ribbons. Fluff them with your hands to separate the strands. Divide into 6 clusters, spacing them evenly on the jelly roll pan, then shape into loose, 4-inch circles. Spoon the melted butter over them, then sprinkle with the sugar and cinnamon. Bake until golden, 8 to 9 minutes. Cool before using. Unless weather is very humid, the nests can be made a day in advance,

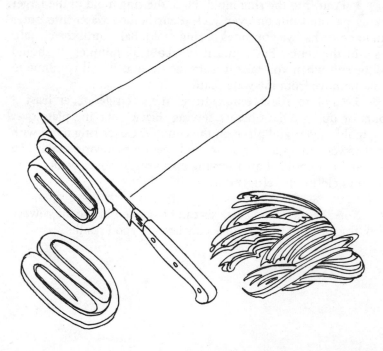

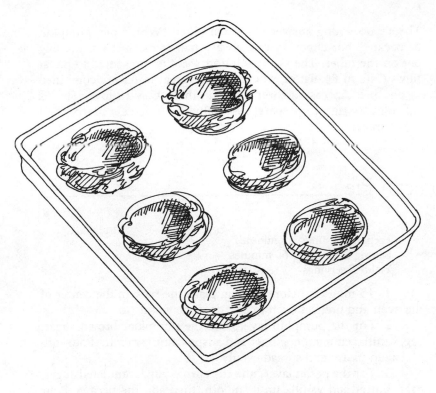

stacked between sheets of wax paper and stored at room temperature in an airtight container. They can also be frozen in an airtight container. If they are not crisp after storing, bake them again in a preheated 400-degree oven for 5 minutes a few hours before you assemble them.

3. To serve, place a phyllo nest on each of 6 plates. Top with a small scoop of ice cream and drizzle with hot Honey Walnut Sauce.

There's no wrong answer when I'm asked "Which pie, pumpkin or pecan?" but choosing one always makes me feel I'm missing out on the other. The sweet solution was first presented to me at Jilly's Cafe in Evanston, where the two great tastes are combined in one pie. An easy answer and one that's easy to love. This is ridiculously easy to prepare, especially if you have a pastry shell in the freezer.

————Pumpkin Pecan Pie————

Preparation time: 15 minutes
Baking time: 55 to 60 minutes
Yield: 8 servings

1 prebaked 9-inch Sweet Butter Pastry pie shell (see page 334)

PUMPKIN LAYER:
1 cup canned solid-pack pumpkin
¼ cup firmly packed light brown sugar (2 ounces)
1 large egg
2 teaspoons pure vanilla extract
1¾ teaspoons cinnamon
¼ teaspoon ground ginger
¼ teaspoon ground allspice

PECAN LAYER:
⅔ cup dark corn syrup
⅓ cup granulated sugar (2⅓ ounces)
2 large eggs
3 tablespoons unsalted butter, melted
1 tablespoon pure vanilla extract
1 cup coarsely chopped pecans (4 ounces)
Whipped cream or ice cream

1. 15 minutes before baking, place the rack in the center of the oven and preheat oven to 350 degrees.

2. For the pumpkin layer, mix the pumpkin, brown sugar, egg, vanilla, cinnamon, ginger and allspice until smooth. Pour into prebaked pastry and spread evenly.

3. For the pecan layer, mix the corn syrup, granulated sugar, eggs, butter and vanilla until smooth, then add the pecans. Pour over pumpkin layer.

4. Bake until the filling is softly set, 55 to 60 minutes. I prefer the pie served slightly warm on the day it is baked. It can be reheated in a preheated 350-degree oven for 10 minutes. Serve with whipped cream or ice cream.

Here the tang of a tart citrus filling is enhanced by a crown of fresh berries. The custard is soft and smooth, contrasting with a flaky butter crust and plump berries.

Lemon Custard Tart with Summer Berries

Preparation time: 10 minutes
Baking time: 15 minutes
Yield: 1 9-inch tart

1. 15 minutes before baking, place the rack in the center of the oven and preheat oven to 375 degrees.

2. Mince the zest with the sugar in a food processor or blender until the zest is as fine as the sugar. Add the eggs, butter and sour cream and run the machine for 1 minute. Add the lemon and orange juice and mix just enough to combine.

3. Pour the filling into the prebaked pastry shell. Place on a baking sheet and bake just until the center is softly set but not firm, about 12 minutes. Transfer to a wire rack and cool completely. The tart can be held at room temperature for several hours before serving.

4. Up to 2 hours before serving, cover with berries.

Zest of ½ lemon, removed with a zester or grater
⅔ cup sugar (4⅔ ounces)
2 large eggs
4 tablespoons unsalted butter, melted
2 tablespoons sour cream
¼ cup fresh lemon juice
2 tablespoons fresh orange juice
1 prebaked 9-inch Sweet Butter Pastry tart shell (see page 334)
2½ cups fresh blueberries, raspberries, blackberries or currants

This is one of my favorite uses for the food processor. Fresh fruit, at the peak of perfection, is frozen, then whipped into a fluffy sherbet bursting with flavor. It's low-calorie, high-impact, loaded with fresh fruit and endlessly variable, depending on what fruit is in season. Three cups of almost any fruit can be used solo or in combination. Bananas are sensational, especially with fresh pineapple or peaches; oranges and mangoes tropical and delicious, apples and raspberries a rare treat.

Liqueur is optional and helps define the flavor. Pick one that enhances the fruit you're using.

Strawberry Sherbet

Preparation time: 10 minutes plus freezing time
Yield: About 1 quart

3 cups strawberries
¼ to ½ cup sugar (1¾ to 3½ ounces)
1 large egg white or ⅓ cup plain yogurt or ⅓ cup whipping cream
1 tablespoon kirsch or framboise, optional

1. Hull the berries and cut them in half if they are large. Arrange them on a baking sheet lined with wax paper and freeze until solid. Once they are frozen, they can be used right away or double-wrapped in plastic bags and frozen for several months.

2. Put the frozen berries in a food processor with the sugar, adding according to taste as well as the sweetness of the fruit. Pulse the machine on and off several times to chop the fruit, then process continuously until the berries are minced into tiny frozen chips. You may have to stop several times to scrape down the sides of the bowl with a rubber spatula.

3. With the machine on, pour the egg white, yogurt or cream through the feed tube and process until the mixture is completely smooth and fluffy, up to 2 minutes. Add the liqueur, if using, and mix well. The sherbet can be served immediately or frozen. If it is frozen for more than 12 hours, let it soften just to the point where it can be spooned back into the work bowl. Process again, until smooth, to eliminate ice crystals.

Note: Any fruit you use should be cut into 1-inch pieces, then frozen, like the strawberries. Peaches, nectarines and apricots do not need to be peeled.

Bellinis, a cooling concoction of Italian sparkling wine and puréed peaches, were first mixed at Harry's Bar in Venice. Here I've taken the winning combination of flavors found in a bellini cocktail and churned them into a delightful icy version. Set afloat in a pool of champagne, this sherbet is both light and elegant.

Bellini Sherbet

Preparation time: 15 minutes plus freezing time
Yield: About 1 quart

½ cup sugar (3½ ounces)
½ cup water
1¼ pounds ripe peaches
1 tablespoon fresh lemon juice
1 cup champagne, chilled (see Note)
1 large egg white
Additional champagne for serving

1. Make a sugar syrup by cooking sugar and water in a small pan just until the sugar is dissolved.

2. Meanwhile, peel the peaches as follows: Add them to 4 quarts boiling water and cook just long enough to loosen the skins, 20 to 40 seconds. Immediately transfer them to a bowl of cold water to stop them from cooking. Slip the skins off the peaches, core them and cut into quarters.

3. Purée the peaches in a food processor or blender until smooth, stopping several times to scrape down the sides of the work bowl. You should have about 2 cups of purée. Add the hot sugar syrup and lemon juice and process for 5 seconds.

4. Refrigerate or freeze peach mixture until well chilled. Combine the chilled peach mixture and 1 cup of champagne in an ice cream maker and freeze according to the manufacturers' instructions. When mixture is slushy but not quite frozen, add the egg white and finish freezing. The sherbet can be served immediately or frozen. If it is frozen for more than 12 hours, let it soften just enough so it can be spooned into a food processor. Process until smooth, to eliminate ice crystals.

5. To serve, scoop into goblets and pour champagne over.

Note: Flat champagne is okay to use for making the sherbet, but the champagne that is poured over at serving time must be effervescent. If you are using leftover champagne to make the sherbet, and do not have any fresh champagne to pour over it, the sherbert can be served plain.

With so many ultra-rich, top-notch ice creams available, it's easy to forget how satisfying it is to make homemade. Yet there is something quite special about making ice cream at home. This is one of my favorites, not only because it tastes so good and creamy, but also because it is lighter than most—although it doesn't taste it—and is a combination I've yet to see anywhere else.

Banana Yogurt Ice Cream

Preparation time: 10 minutes plus freezing time
Yield: About 3½ cups

3 *large, ripe bananas (1½ pounds total)*
¾ *cup plain yogurt*
½ *cup sugar (3½ ounces)*
1 *tablespoon fresh lemon juice*
1 *teaspoon pure vanilla extract*
¾ *cup half-and-half*

1. Purée the bananas in a food processor or blender. You should have about 1⅓ cups of purée. Add the yogurt, sugar, lemon juice and vanilla and mix until smooth. Transfer to a bowl and stir in the half-and-half.

2. Freeze in an ice cream maker according to the manufacturer's instructions.

14·Sweet Sauces

There's more to the Sweet Sauces in this chapter than meets the eye. As it appears to be, this is a collection of some of my very favorite dessert sauces. In chapter 13, Desserts and Pies, I make several suggestions as to which sauce I especially love with a specific dessert, creating what is, to my taste, a marriage made in heaven. Beyond that, the sauces hint of a helpful and welcome shortcut to homemade desserts.

It is not at all uncommon to serve store-bought favorites for dessert. You may purchase something as simple as ice cream, pound cake or fresh berries and want to dress them up a bit, gilding them with a homemade finish. These sauces are the answer. No matter what dessert you choose to serve, it will go from good to better to best when further embellished with one of these homemade sauces.

As for easy, these sauces are that too. Some are so simple that making them hardly qualifies as cooking. Others take a bit of cooking, either on the stove or in the microwave oven, depending on which is easier for you. And not a single one of these delicious enhancements has to be made at the last minute.

You'll think of baklava when you taste this sauce. Use it on the Baklava Sundaes (see page 304) or over scoops of vanilla or coffee ice cream.

Honey Walnut Sauce

Preparation time: 5 minutes
Cooking time: 7 minutes (Microwave: 4 minutes)
Yield: About 1 cup

1. Put the honey in a heavy 1½-quart pan, bring to a boil, then cook over medium-high heat until it is a deeper brown, about 7 minutes.
2. Add the butter, lemon juice, cinnamon, cloves and salt, stirring until the butter is melted. Add the walnuts. Serve hot. The sauce can be made up to a week in advance and refrigerated. Reheat gently.

MICROWAVE: Put honey in a 4-cup microwave-safe measuring cup and cook on high power (100%) until it is browned and thickened, about 4 minutes. Add remaining ingredients as in step 2 above. To reheat, put in a microwave-safe dish and cook on high power until hot, 1½ to 2 minutes, stirring once after 1 minute.

½ cup honey
5 tablespoons unsalted butter
2 teaspoons fresh lemon juice
¼ teaspoon cinnamon
1/16 teaspoon ground cloves
Pinch of salt
1 cup walnut pieces (4½ ounces)

Try this delicious sauce over ice cream, pound cake or Bavarian cream on pancakes and waffles.

Cranberry Maple Sauce

Preparation time: 5 minutes
Cooking time: 12 minutes (Microwave: 3 minutes)
Yield: About 1¼ cups

⅓ cup pure maple syrup
2 tablespoons sugar
1½ cups cranberries (5½ ounces) (if frozen, do not thaw)
3 tablespoons unsalted butter
1½ tablespoons bourbon

1. Bring the maple syrup and sugar to a boil in a small non-aluminum pan, then cook for 3 minutes. Add the cranberries and cook until their skins burst and they begin to pop, 6 to 8 minutes, or slightly longer if they are frozen.

2. Cut the butter into 3 pieces. Remove the pan from the heat and whisk in the butter, 1 piece at a time, waiting until each is incorporated before adding another. Add the bourbon.

3. Sauce can be served immediately or refrigerated for up to 1 week. Reheat gently and thin with 2 to 3 tablespoons water before serving.

MICROWAVE: Combine the maple syrup and sugar in a 1½-quart microwave dish and cook on high power (100%) until sugar is dissolved, about 1 minute. Add the cranberries and cook until they begin to pop, about 2 minutes, or slightly longer if the cranberries are frozen. Finish as in steps 2 and 3.

This is as rich and delicious as a sauce can be, an exquisite amalgamation of cream, butter and sugar.

Caramel Butter Sauce

Preparation time: 5 minutes
Cooking time: 12 minutes (Microwave: 14 minutes)
Yield: 1⅔ cups

1. Combine the sugar, butter and ½ cup cream in a heavy 2-quart pan. Bring to a boil over high heat, then cook, stirring constantly, until mixture begins to color, about 4 minutes.

2. Reduce the heat to medium-high so that the mixture still bubbles, but not so vigorously. Cook, stirring often, until it is a uniform rich tan color, about 5 minutes longer. Remove from the heat and stir in the remaining cream. Return to medium-high heat and cook, stirring constantly, until the sauce is smooth and somewhat thickened, about 3 minutes. Add the pecans, if using. Serve hot. The sauce can be refrigerated for up to 3 weeks. Reheat gently before serving.

MICROWAVE: Cut the butter into 4 pieces and combine with the sugar and ½ cup cream in a 4-cup microwave-safe measuring cup. Stir so that the sugar is moistened, then cook, uncovered, on high power (100%) until mixture is a rich tan color, 10 to 12 minutes, stirring once after 5 minutes. Stir in the remaining cream and cook on high power until smooth and thickened somewhat, 2 minutes. Add pecans, if using. Reheat on high power.

1 *cup sugar (7 ounces)*
1 *stick unsalted butter*
1¼ *cups whipping cream*
1 *cup toasted pecans (4 ounces), if desired (see page 338)*

Imagine the pleasures of biting into the hard chocolate shell of an ice cream bar, baring the delights of smooth, rich ice cream beneath. That should give you some idea of what this sauce is all about, an intense chocolate sauce that hardens when it comes in contact with ice cream.

Chocolate Brick Ice Cream Topping

Preparation time: 5 minutes
Cooking time: 5 minutes (Microwave: 2 to 3 minutes)
Yield: 1½ cups

8 ounces bittersweet or semisweet chocolate, cut in small pieces
¾ cup pure coconut oil
½ cup unsweetened cocoa (1½ ounces)
½ cup confectioners' sugar (2 ounces)
4 tablespoons unsalted butter

1. Melt the chocolate with the coconut oil, cocoa, sugar and butter in the top of a double boiler over gently simmering water, stirring until smooth.

2. While the sauce is still hot, spoon over scoops of ice cream or sherbet. The sauce will harden in 15 to 20 seconds. The sauce can be refrigerated for up to 1 month before using. Reheat in the top of a double boiler over gently simmering water. Thin with 2 to 3 teaspoons coconut oil if it is too thick.

MICROWAVE: Combine the chocolate, oil, cocoa, sugar and butter in a 4-cup glass microwave-safe measuring cup. Cook, uncovered, on high power (100%) for 1 minute. Stir well, then cook on medium power (50%) until completely smooth, 1 to 2 minutes longer. Serve as in step 2. To reheat, cook on medium power, 2 to 3 minutes.

Note: Coconut oil is available in health food stores and some ethnic markets. Do not substitute any other oil.

I especially like this with fruit, either gilding a compote or served as a dipping sauce for fresh fruit. It's also devilishly good with the Winter Fruit Strudel. The recipe comes from Brad Ogden, the fabulous chef at Campton Place in San Francisco. Though he doesn't whip the cream before adding it to the sauce, I love the way it practically floats over your tongue when it is whipped. You can do it either way.

Sweet Vanilla Cream

Preparation time: 10 minutes
Yield: 1½ cups

1. Mix the cream cheese, sugar and vanilla in a food processor or blender until smooth.

2. Whip the cream until it holds soft peaks and gently fold into the cream cheese mixture. The sauce can be refrigerated for up to 2 days.

3 *ounces cream cheese, at room temperature*
3 *tablespoons sugar*
1½ *teaspoons pure vanilla extract*
⅔ *cup whipping cream*

The taste of caramelized sugar adds a beguiling note to fresh puréed peaches. Other fruits can also be used—plums, nectarines, strawberries and pineapple are all good.

Caramel Peach Sauce

Preparation time: 5 minutes
Cooking time: 7 minutes (Microwave: 7 minutes)
Yield: About 1½ cups

2 large, ripe peaches (12 ounces total), unpeeled (see Note)
¾ cup sugar (5¼ ounces)
5 tablespoons water
1 teaspoon pure vanilla extract

1. Remove the pits from the peaches and cut fruit into sixths. Purée in a food processor until smooth, stopping as necessary to scrape down the sides of the work bowl. You should have about 1 cup of purée. Leave in the work bowl.

2. Combine the sugar and water in a small pan and cook over high heat until it turns a rich brown, about 7 minutes.

3. Immediately turn on the processor and carefully add the hot syrup to the peach purée while the machine is running. Add the vanilla and mix for 5 seconds. Chill well before serving. If the sauce is too thick, thin with 1 to 2 tablespoons of water before using.

MICROWAVE: Follow step 1. Combine the sugar and water in a 2-cup glass microwave-safe measuring cup and cook on high power (100%) until mixture is a medium brown, 6 to 7 minutes. It will continue to darken after it is removed from the oven. Finish as in step 3.

Note: If the peaches are fuzzy, rub them with a towel to remove the fuzz.

Bittersweet Hot Fudge Sauce

Preparation time: 5 minutes
Cooking time: 5 minutes (Microwave: 3 minutes)
Yield: 1¾ cups

1. Cook the chocolate, butter, sugar and milk in the top of a double boiler over gently simmering water until smooth.

2. Off the heat, stir in the baking powder, then the vanilla. Serve hot. The sauce can be made in advance and refrigerated up to 1 week, or frozen. Reheat gently before using.

MICROWAVE: Combine the chocolate, butter, sugar and milk in a 1-quart microwave dish. Cook on high power (100%) for 1 minute. Stir well, then cook on high until smooth, 1 to 2 more minutes. Finish and serve as in step 2.

4 ounces unsweetened chocolate, broken into pieces
4 tablespoons unsalted butter
1¼ cups sugar (8¾ ounces)
½ cup milk
1 teaspoon baking powder
1 tablespoon pure vanilla extract

A cup of fresh strawberries can be puréed in with the raspberries or sliced into the purée just before serving.

_____Raspberry Sauce _____

Preparation time: 7 minutes
Yield: 1¼ cups

1 box (10 ounces) frozen
    raspberries, preferably in
    light syrup, thawed
¼ cup confectioners' sugar
    (1 ounce)
1 tablespoon kirsch or
    framboise

1. Purée the raspberries, their juice and the confectioners' sugar in a food processor or blender, letting the machine run for 2 minutes so mixture is as smooth as possible.

2. Press the sauce through a fine mesh strainer to remove the seeds, then add the liqueur. Chill well before serving. Can be refrigerated up to 4 days, or frozen.

Custard Sauce

Preparation time: 10 minutes
Cooking time: 5 minutes (Microwave: 8 minutes)
Yield: 2 cups

1. Scald the milk and ¼ cup sugar in a heavy 1½-quart pan. If you are using the vanilla bean, split it lengthwise and add it to the pan.

2. Whisk the egg yolks and remaining sugar until thick and lightly colored. Slowly stir in the scalded milk, then return mixture to the pan.

3. Cook over medium-low heat, stirring constantly, until the sauce is thick enough to coat the back of a wooden spoon. Remove from the heat as soon as the mixture begins to thicken. Do not let it come to a boil.

4. Strain into a small bowl, add vanilla extract, if using, and cool to room temperature. Cover and refrigerate until chilled or up to 2 days. Remove the vanilla bean just before serving.

MICROWAVE: Combine the milk and ¼ cup sugar in a 4-cup measuring cup. If you are using the vanilla bean, split it lengthwise and add it to the milk. Cook on high power (100%) until hot, about 2 minutes. Whisk egg yolks and remaining sugar in a 2-quart microwave bowl with a rounded bottom. Slowly whisk in the scalded milk. Continue to cook, uncovered, on medium power (50%) until sauce is thick enough to coat a wooden spoon, about 6 more minutes, whisking the sauce vigorously every minute. Finish as in step 4.

1⅔ cups milk
½ cup sugar (3½ ounces)
1 piece (3 inches) vanilla bean or 1 teaspoon pure vanilla extract
5 large egg yolks

This deep blue sauce is sensational on sponge and angel cake, vanilla or strawberry ice cream. I prefer berries that are a bit tart. If yours are very sweet, add a bit more lemon juice.

_____Down East Blueberry Sauce_____

Preparation time: 10 minutes
Cooking time: 7 minutes (Microwave: 3 minutes)
Yield: 1½ cups

2 cups blueberries
2 to 3 tablespoons sugar
1 tablespoon fresh lemon
juice
1 teaspoon tapioca
¼ teaspoon cinnamon
¼ teaspoon freshly grated
nutmeg
1 tablespoon unsalted butter

1. Put the berries in a small pan with the sugar, lemon juice, tapioca, cinnamon and nutmeg and let rest for 5 minutes.

2. Cook over medium-high heat, stirring often, until the berries begin to pop, about 7 minutes. Remove from the heat and stir in the butter. Serve hot. The sauce can be refrigerated up to 3 days. Reheat gently before serving.

MICROWAVE: Follow step 1, except put the ingredients in a 1-quart microwave casserole. Cook, uncovered, on high power (100%) until thick and bubbly, about 3 minutes, stirring once after 2 minutes. Stir in the butter.

Burnt Caramel Whipped Cream

Preparation time: 10 minutes
Chilling time: 4 hours
Yield: 1⅔ cups

1. Cook the sugar and water in a small pan over high heat until the sugar melts and turns a rich amber. Remove the pan from the heat and stir in the cream. Some of the cream will harden. Return the pan to high heat and cook, stirring several times, until it has melted.

2. Chill thoroughly—at least 4 hours. Whip with an electric mixer until the cream holds soft peaks. This can be used immediately or covered tightly and refrigerated for up to 3 days. However, once it has been refrigerated, it will not be as light.

⅓ cup sugar (2⅓ ounces)
1 tablespoon water
1 cup whipping cream

15 · Basics

Basic recipes are fundamentals, essentials and, in some cases, building blocks. They are important in my repertoire, recipes that I often turn to.

It concerns me that, because they are all grouped together at the tail end of the book, they may look like an afterthought. In truth, they are anything but. Each of the recipes is a useful preparation. At times, they will be used as is; at other times they will be added to other recipes. Each of these Basics is extremely versatile and has scores of applications.

All are complete do-aheads. With some exceptions, like the two Mayonnaise recipes, the Salsas and Roasted Red Peppers, they freeze well, too. Except for the stocks, most notably the Beef or Veal Stock, preparation time is minimal.

My own strategy is to make Basics when I have a bit of extra time to spend in the kitchen, and to keep them on hand in the refrigerator or freezer. Then, as the need for them arises, they are there, ready to be used in whatever manner is appropriate.

Different oils will change the flavor of this mayonnaise as will the addition of herbs, spices, nuts and/or citrus zest.

Basic Mayonnaise

Preparation time: 10 minutes
Yield: 1¾ cups

Process the egg, vinegar, mustard, salt, pepper and 3 tablespoons oil for 1 minute. With the machine running, slowly drizzle both the remaining oils through the feed tube in a thin, steady stream. The mayonnaise will thicken as the oil is added. Adjust the seasoning. Covered tightly, it can be refrigerated for up to 1 week.

LEMON MAYONNAISE: To ½ cup Basic Mayonnaise add 1 tablespoon fresh lemon juice and the minced zest of ½ a lemon.

MUSTARD MAYONNAISE: To ½ cup Basic Mayonnaise, add 1 more tablespoon Dijon mustard, or mustard of your choice.

PESTO MAYONNAISE: To ½ cup Basic Mayonnaise, add 3 tablespoons Pesto Sauce (see page 330).

TARTAR SAUCE: To ½ cup Basic Mayonnaise, add 1 tablespoon minced parsley, 1 tablespoon pickle relish, 1 more teaspoon Dijon mustard, 1 teaspoon minced shallot, ½ teaspoon fresh lemon juice and half a riced, hard-cooked egg *or* 1 whole riced, hard-cooked egg white.

1 large egg
1 teaspoon red wine vinegar
1 teaspoon Dijon mustard
½ teaspoon salt
Freshly ground black pepper
¾ cup extra virgin olive oil
¾ cup safflower oil

This is a thick, flavorful mayonnaise that can be used in all recipes calling for mayonnaise. Depending on which oil you use, it can be virtually free of cholesterol.

_____No Yolk Mayonnaise_____

Preparation time: 5 minutes
Yield: 1½ cups

2   *large egg whites*
2   *teaspoons Dijon mustard*
1   *teaspoon red wine*
    vinegar
    Salt
    Freshly ground pepper
1½ *cups oil—I use ¾ cup*
    each of safflower and
    extra virgin olive oil

Process the egg whites, mustard, vinegar, salt, pepper and 3 tablespoons oil in a food processor or blender for 1 minute. With the machine running, add the remaining oil in a thin, steady stream. The mixture will thicken as the oil is added. Covered tightly, the mayonnaise can be refrigerated for up to 3 weeks.

◆

This recipe, and the Red Pepper Marmalade (below), are recipes to build a reputation on. Each captures the essence of its ingredients in an intense and highly concentrated way. They cook down into thick, delicious, relish-like sauces that enhance many dishes. In September, I make several batches and tuck them in the freezer —they freeze amazingly well and bring summer pleasure to a winter table.

Try either on pasta, pizza, grilled or roasted meat and poultry, fish, omelets and vegetables, including baked potatoes.

Tomato Marmalade

Preparation time: 10 minutes
Cooking time: 60 minutes (Microwave: 33 minutes)
Yield: About 1¾ cups

1. Mince the garlic and onion in a food processor or by hand.

2. Melt 1 tablespoon butter or oil in a medium non-aluminum pan. Add the garlic and onion and cook gently, stirring often, until soft, about 10 minutes.

3. Meanwhile, core the tomatoes, cut in half horizontally and squeeze gently to remove the seeds. Chop in the processor in 2 batches or by hand.

4. Add the tomatoes and tomato paste to the pan along with the salt, sugar and pepper. Cook over medium heat until thick, about 50 minutes. Stir often during the last 10 minutes of cooking so the mixture does not stick. If there is any remaining liquid, increase the heat to high and boil it away. Stir in the remaining butter or oil. Serve hot or at room temperature. The marmalade can be refrigerated up to 4 days, or frozen. Adjust the seasoning, if necessary, before serving.

MICROWAVE: Follow step 1. Put 1 tablespoon butter or oil, the garlic and onion in a 2½-quart microwave casserole and cook on high power (100%) until soft, about 3 minutes. Follow step 3. Add tomatoes and tomato paste to the casserole and cook, uncovered, on high power until thick, about 30 minutes, stirring every 5 minutes. Stir in the remaining 1 tablespoon butter or oil, the salt, pepper and sugar. Serve hot or at room temperature. Can be refrigerated up to 4 days or frozen. Adjust the seasoning, if necessary, before serving.

1 large garlic clove, peeled
1 medium onion (4 ounces), peeled
2 tablespoons unsalted butter or light-tasting olive oil
6 medium tomatoes (2 pounds total)
2 tablespoons tomato paste
1 teaspoon salt
½ teaspoon sugar
Freshly ground pepper

Pesto is as versatile and as delicious as a sauce can be, putting it into the category of staples in my kitchen. Though the recipe is in two of my other books, it's too good to leave out here. It's most commonly used over pasta, but can go into scrambled eggs, breads, salad dressings, dips, mayonnaise and soup, on tarts and over potatoes.

There is no real substitute for fresh basil in Pesto Sauce, but in winter it can be made with 2 cups of fresh parsley and 2 table-spoons of dried basil.

Pesto Sauce

Preparation time: 15 minutes
Yield: About 2 cups

2 large garlic cloves, peeled
3 ounces Parmesan cheese, preferably imported
2 cups fresh basil leaves
1 teaspoon salt
¼ cup pine nuts or walnuts (1 ounce)
1 cup light-tasting olive oil, or equal parts olive and safflower oil

Combine the garlic, cheese, basil, salt and nuts in a food processor or blender and run the machine until the mixture is ground. With the processor or blender running, drizzle in the oil. Pesto can be refrigerated for a month.

Red Pepper Marmalade

Preparation time: 15 minutes
Cooking time: 35 minutes (Microwave: 20 minutes)
Yield: 2 cups

1. Mince the garlic and onion in a food processor or by hand. Peel the bell peppers with a swivel-bladed vegetable peeler, removing as much of the skin as possible. Don't worry if you can't remove all the skin from the folds of the peppers. Cut the peppers into ¼-inch strips with the all-purpose (4mm) slicer of a processor or by hand.

2. Put the garlic, onion, red peppers and basil in a 1½-quart pan. Cover and cook gently until the peppers are completely soft, about 30 minutes.

3. Add the tomato paste, pepper flakes, salt and black pepper and cook uncovered, stirring occasionally, until mixture has thickened and all the liquid has cooked away, about 5 minutes. Stir in the butter and remove from the heat. Can be refrigerated for 4 days or frozen. Serve hot or at room temperature.

MICROWAVE: Follow step 1 above. Combine the garlic, onion, bell peppers and basil in a 2½-quart microwave casserole. Cover and cook on high power (100%) for 15 minutes. Stir in the tomato paste and cook, uncovered, on high until the liquid has cooked away, about 5 minutes. Add the salt, pepper flakes and butter. Can be made in advance and refrigerated for 4 days, or frozen.

2 medium garlic cloves, peeled
1 medium onion (4 ounces), peeled
4 large red bell peppers (2 pounds total)
1 teaspoon dried basil
3 tablespoons tomato paste
⅛ to ¼ teaspoon crushed red pepper flakes
½ teaspoon salt, or to taste
Freshly ground black pepper
1 teaspoon unsalted butter

Though I prefer to use a hot red pepper in this salsa, to match the other vegetables, a green jalapeño or serrano may be more readily available. Either of these can also be used with good results.

Salsa Cruda

Preparation time: 15 minutes
Yield: About 2½ cups

8 small radishes (3 ounces total)
1 medium red onion (4 ounces), peeled
1 medium red bell pepper (6 ounces)
2 medium tomatoes (12 ounces total)
1 cup cilantro leaves
1 medium garlic clove, peeled
1 "finger hot" cayenne or other hot pepper
1½ tablespoons light-tasting olive oil
2 teaspoons fresh lime juice
½ teaspoon salt

1. Cut the radishes in half. Quarter the onion. Seed the red bell pepper and cut into 1-inch pieces. Core the tomatoes, halve horizontally and squeeze gently to remove the seeds.

2. Mince the cilantro, garlic and hot pepper in a food processor. Add the radishes and onion and pulse the machine on and off to chop roughly. Add the red pepper, tomatoes, oil, lime juice and salt and pulse just until the ingredients are coarsely and uniformly chopped—you'll still want to have some texture. Use immediately or refrigerate overnight. Drain any excess liquid and adjust the seasoning, if necessary, before serving.

Green Salsa

Preparation time: 15 minutes
Yield: 2 cups

1. Cut the poblano pepper, green onions and chayote or zucchini into 1-inch pieces. Cut the tomatillos in half.

2. Mince the cilantro, garlic, both peppers and the green onions in a food processor. Add the tomatillos, chayote or zucchini, oil, lime juice and salt and pulse the machine on and off until the vegetables are uniformly chopped but still have some texture. Use immediately or refrigerate overnight. Drain any excess liquid and adjust the seasoning, if necessary, before serving.

Note: Tomatillos resemble small green tomatoes encased in papery husks. Look for them in large supermarkets and Latin American grocery stores.

1 *medium poblano pepper*
6 *small green onions (2 ounces total)*
½ *a chayote squash or 2 small zucchini (use 5 ounces)*
4 *tomatillos (see Note)*
1 *cup cilantro leaves*
1 *large garlic clove, peeled*
1 *jalapeño or serrano pepper*
3 *tablespoons light-tasting olive oil*
1½ *teaspoons fresh lime juice*
½ *teaspoon salt*

◆

Garlic lovers take note. This adds a lusty touch to salads, pasta, breads, fish and vegetables.

Garlic Oil

Preparation time: 5 minutes
Yield: ½ cup

1. Mince the garlic in a food processor or by hand.

2. Heat the garlic and oil in a small pan just until the garlic becomes aromatic.

3. Strain into a jar, cover tightly and refrigerate up to 1 week.

4 *to 6 cloves garlic, peeled*
½ *cup light-tasting or extra virgin olive oil*

Crème Fraîche

Preparation time: 5 minutes
Standing and draining time: Up to 36 hours
Yield: 2 to 2½ cups

2 *cups whipping cream*
1 *cup sour cream*
2 *teaspoons fresh lemon
   juice, if necessary*

1. Whisk the whipping cream and sour cream together in a large bowl. Cover and let stand at room temperature until thickened, 12 to 24 hours.

2. Pour into a strainer lined with a paper coffee filter or fine-mesh cheesecloth. Place the strainer over a bowl, cover and refrigerate until it is the consistency of thick sour cream. Discard the liquid from the bowl.

3. Transfer the thickened cream mixture to a bowl and whisk in the lemon juice if a more tart flavor is desired. For desserts, I prefer it with little, if any, lemon juice.

◆

Butter Pastry

Preparation time: 20 minutes (including rolling and shaping) plus
   chilling time
Baking time: 24 minutes
Yield: 1 single-crust pastry, to fit up to an 11-inch round tart or
   pie pan

1 *stick unsalted butter,
   very chilled or frozen*
1 *large egg yolk*
5 *tablespoons ice water*
½ *teaspoon salt*
1½ *cups unbleached all-
   purpose flour (7½
   ounces)*

1. Cut the butter into tablespoon-size pieces. Put in a food processor and chop by pulsing the machine on and off about 6 times. Add the egg yolk, water and salt and process until the ingredients are mixed, about 5 seconds. The butter should still be in little pieces.

2. Add the flour and process just until the ingredients begin to clump together. Stop processing before a ball forms, or even begins to form.

3. Transfer the dough to a large plastic bag. Working through the bag, press the dough into a ball, then flatten into a disc, about 8 inches wide.

4. If you are using the dough right away, it must be chilled enough to firm it before rolling. Place it in the refrigerator or

freezer just until it is firm but not hard. The dough can also be refrigerated for up to 2 days or frozen. If so, let stand at room temperature until softened enough to roll without splitting.

5. 15 minutes before baking, place the rack in the center of the oven and preheat the oven to 400 degrees. Have ready the pie plate or tart pan you will be using.

6. Roll the dough on a floured board to a circle about ⅛- to ¹⁄₁₆-inch thick. Lift the dough several times and brush the board with flour to keep the dough from sticking. Lightly fold the dough in half, then in quarters. Lift to the pie plate or tart pan and position it with the point in the center. Unfold and ease it into the bottom and sides of the pan. Do not stretch the dough. Leave about ¾ inch of dough beyond the upper edge of the pan and trim the excess. Fold the overlap so there is a double thickness of dough around the sides. Crimp the edge to make a decorative border. Prick the dough with a fork at random, so steam can escape.

7. Refrigerate or freeze briefly, to firm the dough.

8. For a prebaked shell, line the pastry with aluminum foil and fill the foil with dried beans or rice to weight the pastry. Place on a baking sheet for easier handling.

9. Bake for 14 minutes. Remove the foil with the beans or rice. (The beans or rice can be used over again as weights.) Prick pastry again, and bake until it is lightly colored, 10 to 14 minutes longer. Cool on a wire rack before filling.

SWEET VARIATION: Add 2 tablespoons sugar to the work bowl with the butter. Decrease the salt to ¼ teaspoon.

Roasting softens and sweetens the flesh and lends a subtle, smoky taste to red, green or yellow bell peppers, poblanos, in fact all varieties of peppers. This method of broiling them in slabs is the fastest and easiest way to "roast" them as it isn't necessary to turn them.

Roasted Peppers

Preparation time: 15 minutes

1. Place the rack 6 inches from the heat and preheat the broiler. Line a jelly roll pan with aluminum foil.

2. Stand the peppers on a board and cut off the sides in 4 slices, following the natural contours. Arrange on the pan, skin side up. Broil until the skin is blackened.

3. Transfer peppers to a paper bag, seal it tightly and let stand at least 10 minutes. Slip off the skins. Roasted peppers can

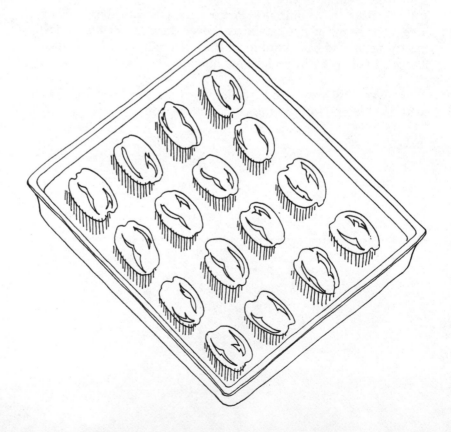

be refrigerated overnight before using, if desired. For longer refrigeration, arrange in a shallow container and cover with olive oil.

Almost any nut—from pecans to almonds, hazelnuts, walnuts and pine nuts—benefits from toasting. Its flavor becomes more distinct, its texture crisper.

_____Toasted Nuts_____

Preparation time: Up to 10 minutes

1. 15 minutes before baking, place the rack in the center of the oven and preheat oven to 350 degrees.

2. Spread nuts in a single layer on a baking sheet. Bake until their color deepens and they smell fragrant, 7 to 10 minutes. Watch carefully so they do not burn. Toasted nuts can be frozen for several months.

Note: Some cookbook authors recommend toasting nuts in the microwave oven. Baking them in the conventional oven is quicker and lends a deeper flavor.

Chicken Stock

Preparation time: 15 minutes
Cooking time: 1½ hours
Yield: 5 cups

1. Combine all the ingredients in a 6-quart pot and add water to cover. Bring to a boil, then reduce the heat and simmer gently, uncovered, for 1½ hours, skimming the top as necessary.

2. Remove and discard the large bones. Pour the stock through a large strainer lined with a double thickness of cheesecloth. Refrigerate the stock until the fat solidifies, then remove and discard fat. Transfer the stock to conveniently sized containers and refrigerate for 2 days, or freeze.

5 *pounds chicken bones and backs*
2 *medium onions (8 ounces total), peeled*
1 *large leek (8 ounces)*
1 *large carrot (4 ounces)*
2 *medium celery stalks (4 ounces total)*
8 *parsley sprigs*
1 *bay leaf*
2 *whole cloves*
1 *teaspoon dried thyme*

◆

Microwave Oven Chicken Stock

Preparation time: 10 minutes
Cooking time: 30 minutes
Yield: 4 cups

1. Cut the onion, carrot and celery into ½-inch slices. Place in a 4-quart microwave casserole and add the chicken bones and backs, water and parsley. Cover with plastic wrap and cook on high power (100%) for 30 minutes.

2. Remove from the microwave oven and pierce the plastic with a sharp knife to let the steam escape. Carefully remove the plastic. Remove and discard the large bones. Pour the stock through a large strainer lined with a double thickness of cheesecloth.

3. Refrigerate or freeze briefly until the fat solidifies on the top, then remove the fat. Or pour the strained stock through a gravy strainer to remove the fat. Refrigerate up to 2 days or freeze.

1 *small onion (2 ounces), peeled*
1 *medium carrot (3 ounces)*
1 *medium celery stalk (2 ounces)*
2 *pounds chicken bones and backs*
4 *cups water*
2 *sprigs parsley*

——Beef or Veal Stock——————————

Preparation time: 20 minutes
Cooking time: 10 to 11 hours
Yield: 2½ quarts

10 *pounds beef or veal bones, cut into 3- to 4-inch pieces (have your butcher do this)*
 4 *medium onions (about 1 pound total), peeled*
 3 *small carrots (8 ounces total), peeled*
 3 *medium celery stalks (8 ounces total)*
10 *parsley sprigs*

1. 15 minutes before baking, place the rack in the center of the oven and preheat oven to 425 degrees.

2. Place the bones in a single layer in 2 large roasting pans. Bake for 1 hour, turning them once after 30 minutes.

3. Quarter the onions and cut the carrots and celery into 1-inch pieces.

4. Add onions and carrots to the roasting pans and bake 30 minutes longer.

5. With a slotted spoon, transfer the bones, the onions and the carrots to an 8- to 10-quart stock pot. Discard the fat from the roasting pans, then add water to them and scrape up the browned bits from the bottom of the pan. Pour the water into the stock pot and add additional water to cover the bones.

6. Bring to a boil over high heat, then reduce heat and simmer gently, uncovered, for 1 hour, skimming the top as necessary. Add the celery and parsley and simmer gently for 10 hours. As the water evaporates, add more to maintain the original level.

7. Remove and discard the large bones. Pour the stock through a large strainer lined with a double thickness of cheesecloth. Return to the pot and boil until it is reduced to 10 cups.

8. Refrigerate stock until the fat has solidified. Remove the fat and pour the stock into conveniently sized containers. Refrigerate for several days, or freeze.

Fish Stock

Preparation time: 15 minutes
Cooking time: 50 minutes
Yield: 5 cups

1. Split the leek lengthwise and rinse under cold water, fanning the leaves open to remove all the grit. Cut into 1-inch pieces. Quarter the onions. Mince the shallots, 2 cloves of garlic, leek and onions in a food processor or by hand. Core the tomatoes, cut in half crosswise and squeeze gently to remove the seeds. Chop roughly in the processor or by hand.

2. Heat the oil in a 4-quart pan and add the shallots, garlic, leek, onion, tomatoes and wrapped fish heads and bones. Cover and cook gently for 15 minutes.

3. Add the water and wine and bring to a boil over high heat, skimming the surface as necessary.

4. Make a bouquet garni by wrapping the remaining 2 cloves of garlic, the parsley, bay leaves and thyme in cheesecloth, and seal with a twist tie. Add to the pan, reduce the heat and simmer, uncovered, for 30 minutes.

5. Discard the fish and the bouquet garni. Pour stock through a strainer lined with a double thickness of cheesecloth. Discard the vegetables. Refrigerate up to 2 days or freeze for 3 months.

1 *large leek (8 ounces)*
1 *medium onion (3 ounces)*
2 *medium shallots (1 ounce total), peeled*
4 *large garlic cloves, peeled*
3 *medium tomatoes (1 pound total)*
2 *tablespoons light-tasting olive oil*
2 *pounds heads and bones from non-oily fish, wrapped in cheesecloth*
4 *cups water*
1 *cup dry white wine or dry vermouth*
10 *sprigs parsley*
2 *bay leaves*
1 *teaspoon dried thyme,* or *1 sprig fresh*

Quick Fish Stock

Preparation time: 10 minutes
Cooking time: 25 minutes
Yield: 5 cups

1 large leek (8 ounces)
2 medium onions (8 ounces total)
3 cups clam juice
2 cups water
¼ cup dry white wine or dry vermouth
1 bay leaf
½ teaspoon dried thyme

1. Split the leek lengthwise and rinse it under cold water, fanning the leaves open to remove all the grit. Slice the leek and onions, either with the all-purpose (4mm) slicer of a food processor or by hand.

2. Transfer to a 3-quart pan and add the clam juice, water, wine, bay leaf and thyme. Bring to a boil, then reduce the heat and simmer, uncovered, for 20 minutes.

3. Pour through a strainer lined with a double thickness of cheesecloth. Discard the vegetables. Can be refrigerated up to 3 days or frozen.

Index

About the Author

Abby Mandel is the author of *Fast and Flavorful* and *Abby Mandel's Cuisinart Classroom*. Her weekly column, "Weekend Cook," is syndicated to newspapers across the country. She also writes a monthly column, "Shortcuts with Style," that has appeared in *Bon Appetit* magazine since 1977. She was also a contributing editor to *The Pleasures of Cooking*. She has made eight cooking videotapes.